Diamond Days

Charles H. Martin

Diamond Days:
An Oral History of The University of Texas at El Paso

Edited by
Charles H. Martin
and
Rebecca M. Craver

The University of Texas at El Paso

First Edition
Library of Congress Catalog Card No. 91-065177
ISBN 87404-245-3

The paper used in this book meets the minimum requirements of American National Standard for Information Sciences.

 Permanence of Paper for Printed Library Materials, ANSI Z.39.48-1984.

Book design by Rebecca Quinones

Table of Contents

Part III:

The University of Texas at El Paso
1967-1991

PREFACE

This composite portrait of the first seventy-five years of the life of The University of Texas at El Paso is the result of a collective effort by many individuals. In 1983, Haskell Monroe*, president of UTEP at the time, conceived the idea of the project. A history professor by training, Dr. Monroe envisioned an oral history of the University based on interviews with a wide variety of former students, professors, and administrators. He selected Vicki L. Ruiz, director of UTEP's Institute of Oral History, to head the undertaking. Rebecca M. Craver initially served as the chief interviewer and, after Dr. Ruiz accepted a position at the University of California at Davis, became the project's second director.

Unfortunately, the university's financial difficulties in the mid-1980s forced the Institute of Oral History to reduce its operations, causing the endeavor to be temporarily shelved. In the spring of 1989, Charles H. Martin, David A. Hackett, and Mimi R. Gladstein, director of UTEP's Diamond Jubilee Celebration, revived the project with the encouragement of UTEP President Diana Natalicio. Completed in December, 1990, under the supervision of Dr. Martin, this book is the final product of and a permanent legacy for the Diamond Jubilee.

The forty-four interviews herein are not intended to provide a complete institutional history of the University. Instead they offer a unique window through which to view the school's first seventy-five years, literally its "Diamond Days," focusing on both academic and social life. In the course of the project, approximately sixty interviews were conducted.

i

The transcripts of these and some twenty-five previously existent interviews constitute the History of the University Collection and are housed in both the Institute of Oral History's office and the Special Collections department of the University Library.

Selecting the specific individuals to be interviewed was not an easy task, so several priorities were established. First, the project's directors decided to aim for an equal chronological distribution of interviews, choosing subjects from each of the three major eras in the school's history. Secondly, the editors attempted to achieve a "balanced" perspective, deliberately seeking out the recollections of men and women from various ethnic and racial backgrounds, including both engineers and "Peedoggies,"* undergraduate and graduate students, and faculty as well as administrators. Our final priority was to interview as many individuals living outside of El Paso as possible, so that the narratives would not be exclusively based on recollections by local residents.

Due to obvious space limitations, not all of the interviews collected could be incorporated into this volume. The particular narratives included were selected because of their vivid descriptions of important incidents in the school's history, because of an individual's personal contribution to the college's development, and, most of all, because of their remarkable ability to recreate and preserve the spirit of campus and academic life from an earlier era. All of the transcripts have been edited for publication in order to enhance the narrative and eliminate repetitive or confusing sections. The words presented belong exclusively to the narrator, with the exception of the bracketed insertions, which the editors have added in order to clarify certain passages. Occasionally paragraphs have been rearranged so as to place them in a more logical order, and a few inadvertent errors in grammar have also been corrected. A glossary at the end of the book identifies prominent individuals in the university's history who frequently appear in the narratives. A name identified by an asterisk (*) in the text refers to a glossary entry.

Many individuals assisted with the project. Presidents Haskell Monroe and Diana Natalicio provided financial subsidies and faculty release time. Sarah John, Carole Barasch, and several students helped conduct many of the interviews. Anita Burdett, Georgina Rivas, and Agustin Ortega performed the time-consuming task of transcribing taped interviews into accurate transcripts. Angelica Gonzalez and Vicki Fisher provided crucial secretarial assistance. The Office of Alumni Affairs, especially Nina Stone, greatly aided our efforts by identifying potential candidates for interviews. Carl T. Jackson and Charles H. Ambler provided assistance from the UTEP Department of History. Nancy Hamilton shared her vast knowledge of the school's history with the editors and saved us from several potential errors. Her help is very much appreciated.

Finally, the editors would especially like to extend our deepest thanks to all of the individuals who so graciously consented to be interviewed and who gave so generously of their time and memories. Without their full cooperation this volume could not have been possible.

INTRODUCTION

He's a mining, mining, mining,
A mining engineer,
Like every honest fellow,
He takes his whiskey clear.

From the 1922 *Flowsheet*,
the first yearbook.

In the beginning it really was a "ripsnorting" mining school. Created by an act of the Texas Legislature in 1913, the State School of Mines and Metallurgy opened its doors to twenty-seven adventurous students on September 23, 1914, on the northeastern outskirts of El Paso in buildings that had previously housed the El Paso Military Institute. In order to reach their classes, students arriving by streetcar had to wind their way around tents and cavalry stables on adjacent Fort Bliss before entering the campus. Over the next two years the new institution's modest enrollment slowly grew to thirty-nine, but early one Sunday morning in October, 1916, a fast-spreading fire destroyed the Main Building and almost wrecked the school's future.

Despite this nearly fatal setback, college officials kept the school alive while searching for a more desirable and permanent location. Eventually they found a rugged but promising site on the west side of the Franklin Mountains just above the Sunset Heights neighborhood. Soon, in the midst of rock, cactus, and greasewood, the original four buildings of the present-day campus began to take shape. Their distinctive Bhutanese architecture, unique in this hemisphere, easily captured the attention of local residents and visitors alike. The idea for such a special architectural style originated with Kathleen L. Worrell, wife of Dean Stephen H. Worrell*, the first administrative head of the college, who was inspired by a 1914 photographic essay in *National Geographic* magazine.

Reputedly student life at the new campus was almost as rough as the terrain. Although female students began attending in September, 1916, the school had a predominantly male environment, and a rowdy one at that. Dynamite blasts and gun shots were heard on occasion, and many engineers indulged in tobacco-chewing and its inevitable unsanitary accompaniment.

Those early mining engineering students originated one of the school's oldest and longest-lasting traditions. Because St. Patrick was known as the patron saint of engineers, they adopted St. Patrick's Day as their special day of revelry, a day to cut classes and hold a grand picnic. By the mid-1920s virtually the entire student body would trek out to the desert near Oro Grande, New Mexico, where upperclassmen would initiate freshmen into the engineering society by herding them on their hands and knees through the dark tunnels of an abandoned mine, often prodding them along with paddles.

Although the school's original purpose was to train mining engineers, it gradually assumed an expanded educational role. In 1927 the El Paso Junior College merged into the Texas College of Mines and Metallurgy (the school's official name since 1920), adding many new courses in liberal arts and a sizable number of female students. Only 136 students had registered the previous year, but with the merger enrollment soared to a record high of 411. In 1931 the college became an accredited four-year school, headed by a president instead of a dean, and offering both Bachelor of Science and Bachelor of Arts degrees.

The Great Depression brought hard times to the campus. Several faculty and staff members had to be released, and the lucky ones who kept their jobs received a 25 percent salary cut. Many students struggled to scrape together enough funds to register and buy books, often paying on the installment plan or borrowing money from sympathetic faculty. Yet even during these lean years the campus continued to expand physically. With the completion of Kidd Field in 1933, the school's football team, the

Miners, at last had a football stadium of its own, and the addition of an adjacent field house, Holliday Hall*, provided students with a combination gymnasium, auditorium, and dance hall.

Though times were tough during the depression, students still found time for social activities. In order to support the athletic teams and boost school spirit, enthusiastic coeds formed a cheering squad called the Golddiggers. The number of women enrolling at "Mines," as the college had informally come to be called, grew steadily, so that by 1936 coeds comprised one-half of the student population. After Benedict Hall was completed that same year, the college could boast of its first women's dormitory. A growing number of Mexican mining students enrolled in the late 1920s and 1930s, adding an international dimension to the College of Mines. Many of these students returned home after graduation and subsequently played important roles in the development of their nation's mining industry.

The outbreak of the Second World War brought substantial changes to the campus. Almost immediately the male enrollment dropped sharply, as the war effort transformed students into servicemen. When wartime shortages eventually forced rationing of gasoline, many students turned to carpools or the city bus service for transportation to and from campus. The College of Mines also directly aided the war effort by serving as one of the nation's special training and education centers. Between 1942 and 1945 the school not only trained civilian pilots but also provided housing and instructional programs to hundreds of army cadets and navy personnel.

Shortly after the war ended, growing numbers of veterans descended upon the campus. Like schools across the nation, the College of Mines strained to meet the demands of this burgeoning student population. Enrollment tripled during the next two years, as the returning veterans took advantage of the GI Bill. Additional classes were scheduled, more faculty members were hired, several wooden military buildings were moved to the campus to serve as auxiliary classrooms, and a new landmark sprang up on the southwest corner of the campus. It was known as Vet Village, and it served as "home sweet home" for married veterans and their families. A cluster of trailers at first, the development assumed a more settled appearance after surplus army barracks were brought in and converted into apartments. Although planned as a "temporary" facility for World

War II veterans, Vet Village provided married student housing for seventeen years.

The returning veterans often added a more serious tone to campus life, but the postwar period also witnessed a revival of interest in campus politics as well as traditional social activities. The engineers sponsored their annual beard-growing contest and Hard Luck Dance to cap off St. Patrick's Day festivities, and students still gathered around the jukebox in Old Main's bookstore to socialize, drink Cokes, and listen to the sounds of the Big Band era. The college's curriculum added several new majors and a degree in business administration, expanding the educational choices available to students.

In fact, this growing diversity of majors and degrees aggravated a long-standing rivalry between the engineers and the liberal arts majors, whom the engineers had contemptuously dubbed "Peedoggies," a corruption of the word pedagogues. That rivalry intensified as enrollment in Arts and Sciences far surpassed that of the Mining and Engineering division. Increasingly non-engineers talked about giving the Texas College of Mines and Metallurgy a new name, one that would more accurately describe its expanded role and better suit its future direction. After much discussion, a new name was selected, and on June 1, 1949, the school officially became known as Texas Western College.

Most students and faculty welcomed the new name, but a few engineering students strongly disagreed and came up with a clever way to express their protest. In keeping with St. Patrick's favorite color, they painted a green line down the center of the campus, dividing the mining and engineering buildings on the west (labeled TCM) from the liberal arts section to the east (labeled TWC). In later years painting the green line became an annual prank associated with St. Patrick's Day, and even today it still symbolizes loyalty to the school's mining heritage.

Texas Western grew steadily during the 1950s. Professors had to learn how to lecture above construction noise as, one by one, buildings filled what had been rocky desert expanses downhill from Old Main. A science building, new dormitories, an administration building, and Magoffin Auditorium were all completed. In addition, a new Student Union Building afforded students expanded facilities where they could flirt with the opposite sex, play bridge, and stage various social functions.

Fraternities and sororities reigned supreme during the fifties, and campus life revolved around afternoon teas, homecoming floats, pep rallies, and formal dances. Contests abounded, and competition was keen for such coveted titles as Miss TWC, King of the Coed Ball, Flowsheet Beauty, Queen of the ROTC Military Ball, and Best-dressed Coed. Each fall new freshmen with their beanies atop their heads lugged sacks of lime and buckets of water up the slopes of Mount Franklin to give the Miner "M" a fresh coat of whitewash. Despite administrative disapproval, some students also participated in such unsanctioned activities as periodic "beer busts" by the river and an occasional panty raid at the women's dormitories. By far the best known prank of the era, perhaps the most famous ever at the school, came in 1952 when several students kidnaped a large alligator from the pond in downtown San Jacinto Plaza late one December night. The conspirators carried their unhappy victim up to the campus and sneaked him into the office of the chairman of the Geology Department, who received quite a shock the next morning upon reporting for work and opening his door.

Like other public educational institutions in the state, Texas Western historically had been racially segregated by law. After the federal courts declared such policies to be unconstitutional, many colleges in the state and in the South evaded or even defied the rulings. But Texas Western administrators chose to set a more progressive example. In September, 1955, twelve black students enrolled in the school without any controversy, reportedly making TWC the first four-year Texas public college to integrate its undergraduate studies. In contrast, The University of Texas at Austin deliberately waited until the following year before accepting black undergraduates, and Texas A&M College did not integrate until 1963. During the 1956-57 school year, Texas Western's athletic teams were successfully integrated, making the school a pathbreaker in this area as well. In 1966 another milestone was reached when Mrs. Marjorie Lawson joined the English Department, thereby becoming the first black faculty member at the college.

Academic development continued during the 1950s, despite occasional financial strain. The Schellenger Research Laboratories were established for electronic research and atmospheric testing, soon winning national recognition and millions of dollars in contracts. A college-wide Graduate School was created, and additional departments and degree plans received accreditation. Texas Western Press began printing books bearing the imprint of the college, and although no one was certain about the future of television, TWC added video production to its pioneering radio broadcasting department.

Growth, both in enrollment and in facilities, remained a major theme in the 1960s. In the summer of 1961 the college received a coveted honor when it was selected as the site of one of the first two Peace Corps training programs in the country. About fifty trainees spent six weeks on campus learning everything from language skills to road building in preparation for their tour of duty in Tanganyika. The graduates and several faculty members were even honored with a reception in Washington, D.C., at the White House, where they shook hands with President John F. Kennedy. The Liberal Arts Building soon reached completion, much to the delight of summer school students, since it was the first fully air-conditioned classroom building on campus. In 1963 an impressive new 30,000-seat, county-built Sun Bowl Stadium, carved out of the rugged hills on the northwest corner of the campus, went into service.

The sixties were the heyday of Miner athletics, and the new stadium served as the home field for several of the best football teams ever. On two occasions successful Miner squads were invited to the Sun Bowl holiday football classic. In 1965 Texas Western defeated Texas Christian University in the annual bowl game, and in 1967 the Miners again captured the Sun Bowl title with a victory over the University of Mississippi. Several gridiron stars, such as Fred Carr and Billy Stevens, went on to play professional football. Miner basketball teams also proved highly successful under a young, dynamic former high school coach named Don Haskins. Jim "Bad News" Barnes and Nate Archibald were just two of the outstanding players developed by Haskins. Probably the greatest moment in the school's sports history came in March, 1966, when the Miners captured the National Collegiate Athletic Association basketball title by defeating the University of Kentucky Wildcats by a score of 72-65.

Beginning in the mid-sixties, student concerns began to change. Peace symbols, frisbee throwing, miniskirts, tie-dyed shirts, and long hair styles for male students began to appear on campus. Like younger people all over the country, local students vigorously debated contemporary political, foreign policy, and minority issues, but their protests never reached the extremes of those at many other schools. Some students and faculty expressed their opposition to the Vietnam War by participating in marches in downtown El Paso, displeasing local supporters of American involvement.

More frequent campus protests came from Chicano students. In order to dramatize their demands for greater assistance for and sensitivity to the growing numbers of Mexican-Americans attending the college, a group of activists staged a sit-in demonstration at the Administration Building in December, 1971. When they refused to leave, university officials summoned the El Paso police, who removed and arrested thirty-seven protesters. As tempers gradually cooled, university administrators began addressing these issues, one result being the establishment of a Chicano Studies degree program in 1971.

Reflecting the more liberal rules of conduct becoming acceptable in American society, the previously strict regulation of student behavior was relaxed during the late 1960s and early 1970s. When new high-rise dormitories began to tower over the western edge of the campus, displacing Vet Village, their residents enjoyed unprecedented freedom. No longer were there rigid curfew hours for female students, and men and women gained expanded visiting privileges. In fact, both of the high-rise dormitories eventually went coed, though men and women were assigned to different floors. During the seventies a few students briefly adopted the national craze of "streaking," or dashing across campus in the nude. Shaken administrators expressed no regrets when this fad eventually disappeared. While the school's football teams fell on hard times, basketball continued its winning ways. And in track and field, the Miners became the dominant collegiate power of the decade, winning numerous NCAA cross country, indoor, and outdoor track and field team titles.

In 1967 the third and final major name change in the institution's history acknowledged the school's increasing importance to higher education. As the result of a decision by the state legislature, Texas Western College now officially became known as The University of Texas at El Paso. The prestige of the new name immediately won local acclaim and thus avoided the controversy of the 1949 name change. In 1973 its academic promise seemed to be confirmed when the university received approval for its first doctoral program. In light of the school's mining heritage, it seemed quite appropriate that this first doctoral degree would be offered in the field of geological science. The university further diversified its offerings in 1976 when it acquired a major new division, the College of Nursing and Allied Health.

Enrollment continued to grow in the 1960s and 1970s. This trend peaked in September, 1977, when a then record high of 15,836 students registered. To serve the seemingly ever-expanding student body, the university embarked upon a substantial building program, adding an engineering and science complex, a fine arts center, and an impressive Special Events Center which not only served the school's popular basketball team but also provided a much-needed multipurpose facility for the community.

The 1980s brought new challenges to the university. Enrollment growth unexpectedly came to a halt. The collapse of previously high oil prices, tight budget restraints, tuition increases, and Mexico's peso devaluations ushered in an era of retrenchment. Women increasingly assumed more prominent roles on campus, especially in student government. This trend was also noticeable in faculty hiring, as a growing number of female professors entered the classroom. And in 1988 the university received its first female president when regents selected Dr. Diana Natalicio to head the school.

The composition of the student body gradually became more diverse, as more "nontraditional" students enrolled. The number of Hispanic students attending the university continued to climb, and by 1990 they comprised 57 percent of the student population. Toward the end of the decade, total enrollment figures finally resumed their growth. In the fall semester of 1990 a new record of 16,526 students was achieved. The approval in 1989 of a second doctoral degree, a Ph.D. in electrical engineering, suggested that the school's academic future was bright. A six-story Bhutanese style library building, a striking symbol of the university's physical development and the largest building on campus, was completed in 1984. For the first time ever, the university possessed a building specifically designed and constructed to serve as a library. Other new buildings on campus adhered to the Bhutanese style, and a re-Bhutanization campaign provided facelifts for several older buildings in order to enhance architectural harmony.

During the 1989-90 school year the university celebrated its seventy-fifth anniversary. The Diamond Jubilee commemoration prompted much reflection on the school's past accomplishments and future aspirations. Much has changed over the years, but many things remain the same. Bells still signal the beginning and end of classes, professors still lecture in front of blackboards, students still pause in the Union to chat and flirt with each other, and proud parents attend commencement ceremonies to celebrate the awarding of diplomas to yet another graduating class. Over its seventy-five years the institution has evolved from a small frontier mining school to a large, multipurpose university with an international student body. Regardless of where future needs may lead, The University of Texas at El Paso will remain unique in its border setting and distinctive in its Bhutanese architecture, an educational jewel nestled in the rugged foothills of the Franklin Mountains.

Part I

Texas College of Mines and Metallurgy
1914-1949

*The event that really rocked the school was the fire
that . . . completely destroyed the Main Building.*

Fred W. Bailey
[1897-1989]
Student, 1915-1920

I was born in Coventry, England, on January 1, 1897, and came to
the United States in 1904. We lived in Philadelphia until 1909, when
my father accepted work at the Panama Canal Zone during the building
and construction of the Panama Canal. He worked on many phases of
the canal construction. I graduated from the Canal Zone High School
at Balboa in 1915. Incidentally, my senior year at high school coincided
with the first year of the opening of the Panama Canal to through traffic.

After conversations with my brother and after having seen many phases
of the excavation of the Panama Canal, I became convinced that mining
should be my field of endeavor. I was entranced and thrilled with the idea
of the extraction of minerals from the earth and with the apparent glam-
our and adventure that appeared to be closely associated with such an
occupation. I have never regretted the decision.

Another decision made at that time was the selection of the school I
would attend. A real estate salesman had been traveling all over the Canal
Zone, trying to sell to the Canal Zone employees an area that has become
a large residential section of Houston. My parents had purchased some
lots with the intention of settling in Texas when they left the Zone. It

was therefore almost a natural conclusion that I should go to The University of Texas at Austin. I applied for admission and was informed that instruction in mining was being discontinued, and I was directed to the State School of Mines and Metallurgy at El Paso. Admission was granted, and I started preparing for my first trip away from home. It was indeed a long one, from the Panama Canal Zone to El Paso.

My high school graduation present from my parents was a gold, seventeen-jewel Hamilton pocket watch and a trip from the Panama Canal Zone to Pennsylvania and Ohio to visit relatives, then continue to El Paso. The train stopped at Texarkana early one morning. At last I was in Texas and would soon be in El Paso. Although I had traveled long distances on the ocean by steamship and had passed through several states on this train trip, I apparently had no concept of geographical distances. I had heard many times and know now that Texas is big, but somehow that bigness was a new dimension I had not [fully] realized. I traveled over such a vast expanse of wide-open, apparently unoccupied and unused land that I could not help but wonder what I would find at the end of the journey. However, eventually I arrived.

El Paso in 1915 had a population of about 60,000. San Jacinto Plaza, with its alligator pond in the middle, was just about the center of the downtown section. After arriving in El Paso, I followed the transportation instructions as outlined in the school catalog. I took the electric streetcar marked "Fort Bliss" and told the conductor to let me off at the School of Mines. Fort Bliss was at the end of the line. [There were] a lot of residences on one side of an enormous parade ground and on the other side a long line of red brick two-story barracks buildings. The conductor told me to walk across the parade ground, pass beyond the barracks and the stables, and I would then see the school in the distance. So with a violin and a suitcase, I began the last leg of my journey from the Panama Canal Zone to the Texas School of Mines. It was only about five-eighths of a mile, but walking on a sandy desert road loaded with luggage was not easy.

I could see some people moving around, and when I arrived, three people met me. They were students doing some work for the college, preparatory to opening the fall term. They were Lloyd Nelson, Vere Leasure, and Clyde Ney, who comprised the first graduating class from the school. They greeted me enthusiastically and made me feel like I would really be a member of a mining student group. There were three buildings that

4

had previously been used by the El Paso Military Institute: the Main Building, the dormitory, and another small, one-story building that was used for assaying and ore milling instruction. The school had opened the previous year, the 1914-1915 academic year, with twenty-seven students and three members of the faculty. I enrolled for the second year of the school operation, the academic year of 1915-1916. There were forty-one students, five faculty members, and two advanced student assistants teaching chemistry and Spanish. We were few in number, but this enabled us to be a closely united group. Our instruction was direct and personal. I think our small number was an advantage to the students, and I think we were very well taught the basics of an engineering profession.

There was a lot of interest in football, baseball, and basketball; however, we were so few that it was necessary for almost the entire student body to participate. Financially we were not able to travel, and from an athletic point of view we were still unknown. Our main activity was football, and we played only local teams, El Paso High School and teams representing various units of the army. There were a great number of army teams, and we had all the competition we could handle. However, sometimes we had no substitutes, and our coach, Tom Dwyer*, quite often played with us when we played the big bruiser army teams. All our games were played at the Rio Grande Baseball Park, located at Wyoming and North Walnut streets, just four or five blocks east of Cotton Avenue.

Towards the end of the 1915-1916 school year, the School of Mines, along with other southwestern schools, received an invitation to send some students to a field day event to take place at the University of Arizona at Tucson. Tommy Dwyer, the coach, told us about the invitation and told us all to line up at one end of the football field. At a signal from him, we were to test our running ability by running the length of the field. I won that running event, and with no more practice than that, a few of us were selected to represent our school and were sent to Tucson. I was the only person from our team to win a medal. I came in third in the 100-yard dash.

The third academic year [1916-1917] was an eventful one in many respects. Earlier in 1916, during the unsettled political and revolutionary activities in Mexico, Pancho Villa had raided Columbus, New Mexico, and Brig. Gen. [John J.] Pershing, then commander at Fort Bliss, was sent into Mexico with several brigades of cavalry and a few battalions of field artillery to get Villa and his gang. Pancho Villa was not captured, but the large massing of troops here was perhaps the beginning of Fort Bliss' becoming a large training center in preparation for World War I. A city of tents adjoined Fort Bliss, through which the students and others had to pass going to and from the school. The school enrollment this year was thirty-nine, lower than the preceding year, but it included two girls, our first coeds. They were Ruth Brown and Grace Odell, who entered to take a two-year academic course with the privilege of taking the full mining course if so desired.

The event that really rocked the school was the fire that occurred early one Sunday morning in October, 1916, and completely destroyed the Main Building. I was awakened from sleep and saw the fire. Many of the soldiers were also awakened and came over to help put it out. They joined the students in forming a bucket brigade but could not save the building. However, the dormitory was saved, and the bucket brigade received credit for this. It was quite a shock and a terrible loss. The Main Building was really the school. Gone were the classrooms, all the laboratory equipment, the surveying instruments, the mineral collection, and all the school records. There was some demoralization among the students. Some left for home, some to look for work in the Arizona and New Mexico mines, but most of them remained. They were encouraged by the good intentions and statements of the faculty that we would be back on course within a few days. The fire could easily have become the swan song and death of the School of Mines. However, we survived.

After the fire, the first floor [of the dormitory] was turned into classrooms. A framed corrugated iron building was quickly built in front of the dormitory to be used as the chemistry laboratory. Classroom instruction had only a slight interruption, [since] the assay and mill building was not affected by the fire. The school activities were soon in full swing again, and the academic school year was completed on time.

While the fire was not the swan song of the school, it afforded the opportunity to look for a new location more strategically situated, so the academic year 1916-1917 was the last year the school operated east of Fort Bliss. The city of El Paso, the Chamber of Commerce, and the citizens had now become accustomed to having a college and once again showed plenty of interest. They offered help, land, and money. The present location became the new school site and the nucleus of the wonderful school we have today.

The building of the new school started in June, 1917. The buildings were not ready for occupancy for the fall semester of 1917-1918, so an arrangement was made to hold classes at Temple Mt. Sinai, located at Oregon and Montana streets. The Main Building and the Chemistry Building were ready a few weeks later, as was the Power House, but the dormitory was not ready until close to the end of the year. There were sixty-one students enrolled for the year 1917-1918. Probably about eight or ten of them were girls taking an academic course.

After we moved to the new school location, we started to enter into annual competition in all athletic events with the New Mexico Aggies, the University of New Mexico, Roswell [New Mexico] Military Institute, and the University of Arizona. We won a few football games, but I think we lost most of them. However, we were able to hold our own in baseball and basketball.

My recollections of the faculty are all pleasant. [S.H.] "Doc" Worrell*, with his trim goatee, was always immaculately dressed and very distinguished looking. He and his wife always tried to make the students feel like a united group and succeeded very well. The Seamons, F.H.* and W.H.*, had a lot of experience and were able to impart such practical knowledge to the students. Their homes were always open, and the students were made welcome on many occasions.

I consider [John W.] "Cap" Kidd* and Tommy Dwyer as builders of character [and] educators of men. I think they made the longest lasting and most favorable impressions on me. This was probably because I seem to have been with them a lot. While Dean Worrell was head of the school and naturally handled all the legal and financial matters, it was always Cap Kidd who appeared to be, at least physically, the "kingpin" in charge. It was Cap Kidd who took over the surveying, layout, and supervision of the building of the new school. It was Cap Kidd who had charge of the hundreds of activities around the school: operation and maintenance, heating and lighting, the building of pipelines, power lines, machinery installations, as well as being the general overseer of athletes. I worked with Cap earning extra money and learned plenty. Tommy Dwyer also remains bright in my memories, because in addition to being my college instructor, he was also the chief engineer of the company for which I worked on my first job after graduation. He was also best man at my wedding a few years later. I learned plenty from him.

The faculty joined with us in all our social events, which usually consisted of dances. At the old school before the fire, they were held in the large assembly room or auditorium of the Main Building. After we moved to the new school location, they were held at the University Club on the top floor of the Roberts-Banner Building at Stanton and Mills streets, or in the main ballroom of the Paso del Norte Hotel. Other gathering places in those days were the Sheldon Hotel dining room on the first floor and the ballroom on the mezzanine floor, the Modern Cafe in the basement of the Mills Building, and the Elite Confectionery at Mesa and Texas streets.

The United States entered World War I in April, 1917. Some students joined the military service before school opened, and when it did open, the war was one of the main topics of conversation. It seems that the students went through periods of military preference. Sometimes we all favored the navy, other times the army. It must have been navy month when the urge to go was too strong for me to resist. I joined the United States Navy in April, 1918. My father had also joined the navy, and I suppose he helped me in my decision.

I returned to El Paso for the opening of the 1919-1920 school year and with four other students graduated in May, 1920, with a degree of Mining Engineer. Just before graduation I was offered two jobs, one at the iron mines in Minnesota and the other in the silver and gold mines close to Parral, Chihuahua, Mexico. I did not have enough money to pay the transportation to Minnesota, where I really desired to go, so since transportation into Mexico was paid for me, I accepted the Mexico job.

As I have already mentioned, before coming to El Paso I lived in the Panama Canal Zone. The canal employees came from many parts of the United States and, in fact, from many parts of the world. I was accustomed to living with more than one culture. I found a similar state of affairs in El Paso, a new, fast-growing city with many peoples from different parts of our country and the world, with two prominent cultures, the Anglo and the Mexican, and a delightful blending of both of them. This resulted in what I considered a very friendly atmosphere, a mutual feeling of working and living together. I think this same atmosphere has continued to the present day. I like the people and the climate, even with the wind and sandstorms. [El Paso] would be hard to beat.

Interviewed by Robert H. Novak, January 24, 1974, El Paso.

The biggest objection most of the students had to the new location was the fumes from the smelter. They were pretty bad sometimes.

Ruth Brown McCluney

Student, 1916-1919

I was sixteen years old when I graduated from El Paso High School. At that time, of course, there was just one high school, and I was one of forty-nine graduates in 1916. That's how small El Paso was. My parents didn't want me to go away to school because I was so young. My father read in the paper along in the summer that the Texas Legislature had decided that this school would be open to women. He contacted Dean [S.H.] Worrell* at the College of Mines, and he said as far as he knew there was no objection to girls going. There was another girl [Grace Odell] in my high school graduating class who didn't have any way to go away to school, and so she decided she'd go, too. We enrolled the first of September. But she didn't like it, and I think she dropped out at the end of the first semester.

The way I got to school was by streetcar. We lived in Alta Vista, on Hueco Street, and the streetcar went to Fort Bliss. That's where it ended, so I had to walk. It was over half a mile, past all the stables! It was a cavalry post, 7th Cavalry. Very odoriferous. Someone asked me if I was ever in trouble going through the military post, because I walked the whole distance. A lot of the time there were other students on the streetcar

9

who went with me. And you may know Fred Bailey; he's one of the Exes. Well, he was a good friend of ours and went to the same church. We were all in a bunch together. My mother took him aside and told him that her daughter was too young and would he look after her out there when I started to go to school, because I wouldn't have other girls around. I guess Fred did a good job, because nothing ever happened to me.

At any rate, my first semester out there on the campus, which was just east of Fort Bliss, was pretty difficult because they enrolled me in all of these engineering subjects. They did have an English teacher. They hadn't had one until that year, so I did take English from a man who was not an engineer. But I had physics from [John W.] "Cap" Kidd*, who is a legend in this school. Since I had not had it in high school, I had a rough time.

Cap Kidd was an institution around here. He was a fine engineer — that was his profession, a civil engineer. I don't think he disliked me, but I had the feeling all the time that he probably wished I wasn't there because I was a girl! And I would've just died before I would've asked him to explain anything to me, because I was really afraid of him. And I passed the physics course, and then the next year I took advanced math from him. His personality was so unusual, and I couldn't imagine anybody ever opposing him on anything. And yet he loved those boys; he loved the school; he'd do anything to promote the school!

But along the first of April war was declared in Europe, and we lost some of our students. They just couldn't wait to go down and enlist. Now, Tom Clements was one of the students that enlisted in the navy. I knew him in high school, and I'll never forget a date I had with him. He wanted to go see one of the D.W. Griffith films downtown; I think it was "Birth of a Nation." Anyway, when he came to get me and we got on a streetcar to ride to town, he brought a box of candy. We sat there and ate almost all that box of candy that afternoon. Then they brought a whole lot of recruits in for the war, to train them at Fort Bliss. I found me a soldier, so I wasn't interested in any of the college boys anymore. He was a preacher's son from Illinois and was lonesome. And my mother took everybody under her wing. I went with him quite a while, but finally we went different paths.

[There was a fire at the school that year, but] I don't think they discovered who set it. As I remember it happened on a weekend. When we came back to school on Monday morning, there was nothing left except a lot of rocks and pillars of the Main Building. Well, they patched up the building that they were using for a boys' dormitory. Of course, they didn't have any girls, so they didn't need anything else. They had it switched around and put classrooms in some of the rooms. And our chemistry lab was in a temporary building that they erected; it was just mostly sheet iron. We continued there the rest of the year under those conditions, which were rough. But I was so involved in my classes that it didn't bother me.

There were more girl students in the second year I was at school. [That's when] they were building the new campus. There were three buildings. They hurt my feelings [now] by saying "Old" Main. It was the Main Building! They would finish up one floor of a building, and then they'd let you come out for the classes in that building. Otherwise during my second year, we met in an old Jewish synagogue. It was the rabbi who instigated this college idea, community college I think they called it. And then's when the girls came in. What he wanted and what Mr. [A.H.] Hughey*, who had been my high school principal wanted, was to make a teachers' college out of this whole business. There was quite a hassle over that, I think. But at any rate, they opened up this section for education courses. In fact, I got my certificate while it was still the School of Mines. Everything aimed toward the new campus, toward getting some buildings, getting things started. And then of course, when all these people came in for the combination junior college and the School of Mines, then's when they hired the women teachers, and more men teachers, too.

The reason I stayed a third year was because Mr. Frank Seamon* wanted me to take a job as the freshman lab instructor and lab assistant. He had more work than he could do, so they offered me thirty dollars a month, and that was too good to pass up. I ended up taking a harum-scarum course [load] of most everything that I could find, in order to get more hours. I took assaying as a chemistry course. I took a lot of geology courses because it was allied with the science field, and my professor was Mr. [H.D.] Pallister*. Another university sent bushels of fossils, unclassified. Mr. Pallister told me that if I would classify those fossils, he'd give me an hour's credit. And you talk about getting into work! I practically lived in that place, because every fossil had to be checked according to pictures and descriptions. I didn't know there were so many kinds of gastropods in the world!

The biggest objection most of the students had to the new location was the fumes from the smelter. They were pretty bad sometimes; I don't think they've conquered that yet. And at that time they were doing a land office business. Mr. Seamon always went to the smelter and got samples that their chemists had tested. We had to run the tests and get the same results, or we didn't pass the work. That was good training, but it was hard.

[I would ride the streetcar] up Mesa Avenue. I still had about the same distance to walk as I did at Fort Bliss. It was very rocky, and I remember I'd get so tired climbing the hill up to the streetcar in the afternoons. It was a long pull! I'd watch and see if Cap Kidd was ready to leave. He had an old Hupmobile, and he'd always pick up anybody who was walking and take them up to the streetcar. Of course, I had to transfer when I got downtown. But everybody did it; you didn't think too much about it.

I wore middies and pleated skirts. And every Sunday I had to iron those pleated skirts, starch them, and then wet them real wet and pin them to the ironing board with pins to hold the pleats down and iron those pleats until they got dry. That's a job! But that was the uniform, and if you were really stylish you got them tailor-made.

I think I had a little something I carried my lunch in, like a thermos kit or something. We didn't brown-bag it like we do now. They served food to the boys in the dorms, but not one time did they ever ask me to eat over there. I think that was their territory. And I didn't mind. Miss Ruth Augur was the registrar, and she was sweet to me, so we used to stay together. We ate together.

I remember I went to school every day, especially in [my] third year. I worked all afternoon. Of course, I had all that lab work to do in both geology and chemistry, and I had no free time in the morning. A lot of my classes were getting pretty hard. But all of my classmates were serious about getting an education. They didn't fool around.

I made all A's in those three math courses my freshman year. That helped my feelings, and I think I must have done pretty well in chemistry, or Mr. Seamon wouldn't have put up with me. He had the reputation of being very strict and very hard, but it was a blessing. Unless you learn it right and do it right, it's no good. When I look back on it, I think Mr. Seamon's influence on me was the thing. In fact, twenty years later when

World War II started, I went to work at General Dynamics at Fort Worth in the chemistry lab, using the techniques that Mr. Seamon had taught me.

Interviewed by Rebecca Craver and Vicki L. Ruiz, October 21, 1983, El Paso.

No freshman was allowed to sit on that bench. That was the holy of holies.

Fay Wynn Nelson

Student, 1929-1935; 1954-1956

We were connected with [the University] so long and for so many years and saw it [grow] from such a little school to what it is now. It's very dear to my heart. Of course, [my husband] Lloyd* was there forty-four years. Isn't that something? Lloyd, Vere Leasure, and Clyde Ney had been to the New Mexico School of Mines, which was in Socorro, New Mexico. They had been there two years. When this school opened in 1914, they came here. They are the first three graduates. They called it the Texas School of Mines, and then later it became Texas School of Mines and Metallurgy. It was put here because there were so many boys from Mexico in this area who wanted to come to a mining school. At that time mining was very important.

The first administrator was Dean [S.H.] Worrell*. He was a very distinguished looking man with a goatee and was perfectly groomed, never a hair out of place. The boys liked him very much. Mrs. Worrell was very nice. She did a lot of traveling. It was through her travels and her desire, when they started the School of Mines over here on this side [of the mountain], to make the buildings in the Bhutanese [style]. After that, John W. Kidd* came here, and of course he was instrumental in really making

15

the school. He was *very* popular with the boys. He was a short, fat man with a tummy. And Nina Kidd was a great person.

Dean Kidd asked Lloyd if he would fill a two months' position, and he did. Then Lloyd had an opportunity to go to Santa Rita, [New Mexico], to the Kennecott [Copper Company] and to work in the office. So we were there for ten months, I think. Then one night he came home from the office, and he said, "Honey, I had a call from Dean Kidd today. He asked me if I'd like to come and take a place in the Engineering Department. I'd like to try it." And we were there forty-four years. He came to stay just a little while and stayed forty-four years.

The school was placed on this side [in its current location]. They had [several] buildings, but they didn't have a bookstore. They'd have to get their books at a bookstore downtown. But they had a little room down on the first floor [of Old Main]. The students I guess were running it, and they'd just have books once in a while. Somebody came to Lloyd and said, "Prof, how about buying the bookstore?" Well, it was debts, that's what it was. Anyway, Lloyd and Gideon Fisher, an older student, decided they'd buy the Co-op. They put in books which were necessary for the students, and they only opened it between classes. Well, then it outgrew that little room, so they decided to put the Co-op in a [larger] room on the left-hand side of Old Main on the first floor.

By that time it was progressing to where it was open all the time. Not only did they have books, they had Cokes and sodas. The students had no Student Union, no place to meet. So along this side, I can see that old bench. My brother A.O. Wynn, the manager of the Co-op for several years, [can't recall] where that old bench came from. It was just an old wooden bench, splintery and everything. And it was all the length of that south wall. And I want you to know that was the meeting place between classes for all the school. If there was an election going on, that's where the candidates met. Many love affairs [began there]. They'd sit and giggle at each other. No freshman was allowed to sit on that bench. That was the holy of holies.

The first faculty were all good friends of the boys. They had a Professor [H.D.] Pallister* that the boys were very fond of, and then they had two Seamons. W.H. Seamon*, the elder man, and his wife were very popular with the student body. Every Sunday evening they had open house for the boys and the faculty. Of course, the faculty wasn't very big. And the boys could come and bring their girl friends, and they had something to eat and music and dance. They had that great big veranda. Then there was a [relative], and his name was Frank Seamon*. He was in the Science Department, and he was popular, too.

Howard Quinn* came two years after Lloyd. He and Lloyd had the Geology Department for many years, and they shared the same office. Mary Quinn and I used to have a tradition that every time a new faculty member came she and I would take the wife — sometimes we'd include the men, but not often — and we'd go to lunch at El Minuto, which was a Mexican restaurant down on Second Street. It was considered the best place in town to get Mexican food. That was their initiation into the faculty.

Lloyd was the sponsor of the APOs [Alpha Phi Omega*], which is the engineering fraternity. And in those days they had St. Pat's Day. Of course St. Pat is the patron saint [of engineers]. And Lloyd and I were always asked to chaperone the picnic. We always looked forward to it on the seventeenth of March. I often think of the fun we used to have. Dean and Mrs. Kidd were usually there with us. They would go out to the tin mine up near Oro Grande. They would take those freshmen, and they'd line them up just like a herd [and] blindfold them. They'd make them crawl on their hands and knees through that tunnel. St. Pat was inside the tunnel. When they got there, some person would take a stick that had cotton on the end of it, and they'd jab it in their mouths. [On the stick] was the vilest [mixture]. I'm sure it must have been horrible from the expressions on these boys' faces! Then, they would take the blindfold off, and they met St. Pat. They were initiated then. After all the boys had gone through, then they'd have a big picnic. They'd have barbecue, beans, potato salad, and lots of things to drink. I don't mean hard liquor, but probably beer. Anyway, they had lots of fun.

I got my B.A. in Education in '35. I taught here in the city schools for many years, and I got my master's in 1956. When I was getting my master's I would take courses after school or at night or in the summer. They didn't have the quick registration by machine. We lined up and went through. I remember Dr. [Anton] Berkman*. He was a real good friend of ours. Tony was always on the registration line, and he'd say, "Oh, no, not [you] again!" I had the responsibilities of my home and my two children and husband, but I had the encouragement. Lloyd encouraged me and helped me out so much.

17

I took a course in trigonometry from Lloyd one summer. During class he wouldn't say "Mrs. Nelson" or "Fay." He'd say, "You." I never worked as hard in my life as I did on that course, and I made a B. One of the other professors said to me, "Fay, do you mean to tell me you let him get away with that, that he only gave you a B?" And I said, "My goodness, I was so grateful to get it." So they were talking to Lloyd, and Lloyd said, "Oh, my! That was some summer. I had trigonometry for breakfast, I had it for lunch, and I had it for supper, and then after I went to bed!"

Lloyd loved the school. He and the boys were very close, and there was a feeling amongst them that was very fraternal. He was very popular with the Mexican engineers because he spoke their language. He was born in Santa Rita, New Mexico, in a mining town, and he spoke Spanish, but it was down to earth, what the kids talked. Where you would say, *"Como está Ud.?"* he'd say, *"Qué tal?"* out of the corner of his mouth. Well, that of course used to sway them. And then he'd say something to them in Spanish which sometimes I don't think was too [proper]!

I was greatly touched by the chair that they [established] in honor of Lloyd. [The development office] always sends me notice whenever anybody has donated to the Lloyd A. Nelson Chair, and I always sit down and write a note to these boys. And I am really amazed, because these men are successful businessmen. Some of them live in New York; some of them live in Mexico; they live all over. And it wrings your heart to think that they remember. They loved Lloyd, and Lloyd loved them.

Interviewed by Rebecca Craver, January 16, 1984, El Paso.

My, it was fun! We had an awfully good time. . . .
I was always a little afraid my paycheck would come
with an amusement tax on it.

Mary Kelly Quinn
[1900-1989]
Faculty, 1925-1945; 1947-1965

I never went to the College as a student, but my sisters, Anne and Charlee, were students out there in the days when it was a ripsnorting mining school. Anne was there in 1921 and 1922, I guess, and Charlee must have been there in '22. I graduated from Wellesley, and then I came in '25. When I [started] teaching, there were something like seventy-eight students. Howard [Quinn*] was at the College a year before I was.

Well, I tell you, you've heard about these people in the colleges that have a chair? Well, I had a sofa. Originally what I had intended to teach was English, but Mr. [E.A.] Drake* wanted to teach English. So he taught English, and I taught history. I taught American history, I taught ancient history, I taught psychology, and when the school got big enough, then I taught sociology. Let's put it this way: I don't know what I taught, but those were the classes I held. Sociology [became] a separate department only one year before I retired. Originally it was history, government, and sociology all in one group.

There are two courses I taught out there that I loved better than any. One of them was "Comparative Cultures, The United States and Mexico."

19

Now are the days when there are people starving for Mexican courses; I think of the days when I used to have to go around and invite them in. I thought it was a disgrace for people to grow up on the border and not know the two countries. The other thing was: I thought it was a disgrace that a number of Americans of Mexican descent had no pride in their background. I don't mean get out there and demonstrate; that's not my idea of pride. But they didn't know their background. And so I just adored that course. That was my love.

The other one was a course in marriage and family living. It was open originally to sophomores without any prerequisite, but it was not the juicy course that you think. It was intended to teach people to act like human beings in a marriage. I enjoyed it, and the students found it very practical. I always think of two boys that came up at the end of the first semester I taught it, and they said, "We enjoyed your course." I always distrust people who tell me that. And I said, "You did?" One of them said, "Mrs. Quinn, I think we ought to tell you the truth. We took that course because we found a woman teaching a course in marriage and family living, and we thought we could give you a hard time. It wasn't that kind of course at all; it was a practical course."

Before we were married, Howard and I were both on the staff. We had permission in writing from the Regents to continue to teach after the marriage. But the Texas Legislature, many years later, when I was a much better teacher and had better training, passed a [Texas Employment] law* that a man and his wife could not both draw pay from the state [if they taught at the same institution]. The law was aimed at a man at [Texas] A&M. It was slipped through when the legislature was away one weekend, and then when the bill came out, here this was, that a man and his wife couldn't both work. Dr. [D.M.] Wiggins* was president at the time, and I always thought he didn't play quite fair there. He didn't say, "Are you or Howard going to stay?" He made it very plain he was keeping Howard, and I could do anything I pleased. Well, I decided I didn't want to teach in the city schools; they wouldn't pay me enough. So I sold life insurance.

I think there's a person who should be mentioned in any history of the College, and that is Mrs. W.H. Seamon. Mrs. Seamon was a Campbell from Virginia. They traced her line down from George Washington and Martha Washington. She was the most perfect lady I have ever known, in a sweet, gentle way. Her father was killed during the War Between the States, when she was about three years old. She told me one time that she remembered the sadness of the time. Anyhow, she married W.H. Seamon*. With the background of all the Virginia gentility that could possibly be, Mrs. Seamon came down here with him, and she camped all over Mexico. At one time her husband was Villa's chief geologist and engineer in Mexico, when Villa was in charge of northern Mexico.

W.H. Seamon became head of the Geology Department. We had no recreation rooms or anything of that kind up there, so Mrs. Seamon opened her home every Sunday night to every student of the College and his girl or her date. She had a buffet for us. As Mickey McGee Goodwin said, "If you didn't get taken to Mrs. Seamon's on Sunday night, you weren't anybody." For years she had that Sunday night open house. She asked all the students, and she was perfectly charming to them. She taught a lot of us the first manners that we had ever been exposed to. She was just perfectly adorable to everybody.

We had no medical facilities at the College at all. You have no idea of the bare bones of the College. Well, Dr. Dale was one of the students, and he had the flu. She took him to her house, and he stayed there, and she nursed him until he was well. Seamon Hall is named for W.H. Seamon, but I don't think any history of the College should ever be written without including Mrs. Seamon.

Ruth Augur* was the registrar, and she was one of the most colorful mortals we ever had. She was quite a character. I can still remember there was a phone in her office, and Cap — that's Dean [John W.] Kidd* — Cap's office was down here on the other side of the stairwell, in the Main Building. Ruth Augur would step out here and scream, "Cap, Cap, someone wants you on the phone!" Cap would take down his extension and talk on the phone. It apparently never occurred to anybody to invest the money to have a buzzer from place to place, or two phones.

The other thing I remember about Ruth was when I was in her office one day, and this boy came in and put down ten dollars. She said, "Now just a minute," and she got out a little index card and marked it off. He was paying his tuition, piecemeal, as the semester went along. The school was small enough, and she knew at the end of the year his tuition would be paid.

It's a different age. My, it was fun! We had an awfully good time. At least I did. You know, I was always a little afraid my paycheck would come with an amusement tax on it. It never did, but I always thought someday it might.

Interviewed by David Salazar and Mildred Torok, March 8 and 15, 1973, El Paso.

You'd tackle someone, and your hands would slide on the ground, and you'd pick up the gravel. . . . I played center, so when I'd get over the ball, why there was always blood on the ball!

Thad A. Steele
[1907-1990]
Student, 1928-1932

I came [to the College of Mines] from a junior college up in Oklahoma, looking for a place to finish school. And being an athlete, why, I was naturally looking for a place where I could go and play. I could come to the College of Mines and be eligible immediately, so I came out here on an athletic scholarship.

We had a group of people in El Paso that were trying to build up the athletic part of the school, so [they provided jobs to athletes] all over town, like in the courthouse, where there'd be one in the tax collector's office and one in the Sheriff's Department, several people in the fire stations, some at the smelter, some at the cement company. All over town you had a job, and you had to work. You worked, and you got room and board [and] fifty dollars a month.

The first year I worked at the tax collector's office and in the [city] engineer's office. The last two years I worked for El Paso Natural Gas Company. The first year I lived in a home, with a family, and they provided just a place to sleep. After that, we had a dormitory, and I lived there.

23

The coach when I came here was a fellow named B.J. "Doc" Stewart. He had coached at The University of Texas, and he brought out his captain of the football team, a fellow named Mack Saxon, as his assistant. So the first year that I was here, it was Doc Stewart and Saxon, and then the rest of the time it was Mack Saxon and Harry Phillips. We had two coaches in those days. Big staff!

We had a practice field right back of the dormitory, and there was very little grass on it. It was mostly gravel and just a few little concrete steps out where people could sit. But you couldn't play a football game there. We played our games at the El Paso High School stadium. They had very little grass there, I can assure you. You'd tackle someone, and your hands would slide on the ground, and you'd pick up the gravel. The fact is, I still have scars on my hands. I played center, so when I'd get over the ball, why there was always blood on the ball!

We played Arizona, the New Mexico Military Institute, Hardin-Simmons University, New Mexico School of Mines, Arizona State, and The University of Texas. The last three years that I played football, we only lost one game a year, which was a whale of a record in those days. I'd have to get my schedule so I'd have the afternoon to practice football and basketball and baseball, whatever sport I was involved in. I played all of them. I was the "Outstanding Athlete" two years in a row.

The freshmen in those days had to wear green beanies. Usually right at the beginning of school [in the fall] they had what they called "M" Day. You would enlist the freshmen to do all the hard work. They had a lot of overseers. The "M" was up on the side of the mountain [above Scenic Drive]. They'd carry the lime up there and the water, and they'd mix it and paint the "M." It was a big day. The kids would be just covered with that lime. At Homecoming they'd light the "M" at night. They'd go up there with some kind of an oil, and they would outline the "M" with fire. They'd keep it burning all night.

We did some of the meanest pranks. We had a fellow that we all liked, and somebody told him that his feet smelled. They took some Limburger cheese, and they smeared it in his shoes. He had a little throw rug in his dormitory room, so they lifted up the throw rug and rubbed this Limburger cheese [there]. He didn't have a car, but we put some on the exhaust pipe of another car. And this guy that had the car told him, "I don't want you riding in my car anymore. You smelled up my car!" So everybody

24

was complaining about his feet smelling. He would wash them; he would douse them with talcum powder; he would do all of that.

We didn't have many cars in those days. There were only four people in the dormitory with cars most of the time that I was going to school there. They had touring cars, and you could get six, seven, eight [in them]. We belonged to the nickel beer group, and they'd come through the dorm and holler out, "Today is nickel beer day!" Boy, we'd load up that car, and we'd all go to Juarez. For a nickel you could get a beer and a free lunch — a taco or a bowl of chili. You could go to four bars, and for twenty cents you would have all of this.

You could go to Juarez and buy a keg of beer and take it to "the Rocks" down on the river and have your beer bust down there. "The Rocks" were below the Hacienda [Restaurant] going around the curve down there off to the right. What happened was that the [Rio Grande] made a curve, and washed-out rocks were exposed on a high rise. That was what we called "the Rocks."

I used to promote dances. J.B. Andrews was my very good friend, and he conceived the idea that we ought to promote dances. So we went into partnership. They'd be at the Woman's Club or maybe at one of the hotels or at the Toltec Club, which used to be the Elks Club. The Lillian Jackson Band would always play. Sometimes we'd make more money off selling the soft drinks than we'd make off the entry fee to get in.

They always had the Hard Luck Dance. What I did once, I'll explain. I put on a pair of blue jeans and wrapped them around, and I put strings around them so they would fit tight, and I used a shirt and a sweat shirt. Then I had a big pair of long john underwear, [which] had the trap door on the back. When the dance was going on real fine, and everybody was out on the dance floor, I went in. I had on a hat and a long overcoat. I just walked in and shot my hat off and took the coat off. I stepped out on the dance floor and tagged a girl. I'll tell you, when they saw me in my underwear, why, the dance stopped! Everyone just backed off, and they left the two of us on the floor. Then finally whoever the [chaperone was] told us, "Thad, I think your joke has gone far enough. You'd better get decent." Then I just started undressing. I peeled it off right there in front of them. We had fun in those days.

I was in Dr. [Howard] Quinn's* geology class [where] you have to identify rocks and all of that. Well, it was a tough course, and I was barely getting

25

by. I came back home from Christmas vacation with chicken pox, and they quarantined me in my room. I was living in a room downtown in a rooming house. And since I had chicken pox I couldn't take my exams, so they postponed them to the next term. I was going to take this make-up test. Dr. Quinn told me there wasn't any use in me taking it, that I wouldn't pass. I said, "Well, I need that credit," And he said, "Well, no use for me to give you a test, because you're going to flunk it."

I went to Dr. [Lloyd A.] Speedy Nelson*, and I told him my problem. He said, "Well, I'll help you pass that course." So he got the last six exams that had been given by Dr. Quinn, and he told me if I would study those six quizzes, he thought I could pass the course. And by golly I studied on it for about six weeks. Then I told Dr. Quinn I wanted to take the test, and he reluctantly scheduled it for me. I'm sure he just went through the test papers and pulled out one and said, "Here's your test." I know that I must have made a 90 or above on the test, but he told me that I got a D double minus, D being passing. I told him I wanted to review that with him. I said, "Dr Quinn, I thought I had prepared myself real well for this test, and I'd like to have you go over that paper once more." He didn't volunteer that he would do it, but I got it changed to a D. He erased the double minuses!

I'll tell you another story about that Speedy Nelson. We were going on a geology [field] trip, and Speedy and Berte Haigh* were heads of the trip. There were sixteen of us in the group, and we went maybe 100 miles east of here up in the mountains. We plotted and surveyed the levels, the grades, and we got samples of rocks and fossils. We classified everything. We were there two months. They had several big tents, and we had our cots.

Anyhow, the first night we were there, we got in a poker game, and I won about twenty-five dollars. I gave Speedy Nelson twenty dollars the next morning, and I said, "Now, I want you to keep this until the camp is over, and I'll get it back in El Paso." About three nights later we were in a poker game, and I went broke. I went to Speedy for some money. And Speedy said, "No. I keep my promise. You asked me if I would keep this for you until you got back to El Paso. So I'm keeping my promise. I will give it to you in El Paso." I didn't get my twenty dollars until I got back home. But I thought that was a good lesson he was trying to teach me. He was quite a guy.

I was trying to major in geology. The last two years that I was in school, it was during the depression, and people were out of jobs. Even people with degrees that had been working for a mining company were back home without a job and taking a refresher course. So I changed my major the last year, and I qualified for teaching and coaching. After coaching for four years, I looked at all the businesses around here that I thought I would like to work for, because I couldn't see any future in high school coaching as a lifetime job. I started working for Southwestern Portland Cement Company, and I was with them thirty-nine years.

Interviewed by Rebecca Craver, December 6, 1983, El Paso.

Those people down there ... could never think of us as anything but a little cow college out in the sticks, where we probably went barefoot across the campus on cowtrails.

C.L. Sonnichsen
[1901-1991]

Faculty, 1930-1972

I belonged to the Harvard Glee Club, and I went out on the spring trip in 1927. That was the year I took my master's degree. When the spring trip was over I came back, and all the good university jobs had been picked over. The best thing I could get was a job at Carnegie Tech, where I stayed for two years. Then I went back to Harvard and finished my doctorate. Naturally I was pretty nearly out of money.

I needed a summer job, and one came up at the Texas School of Mines. It hadn't become really a college yet. It wasn't a four-year college until the fall after I got there. There were eight applicants, and I got the job. I am perfectly sure that I got it because I'd had experience in a technical school teaching English. That means that since I had to go to a technical school because I got back late after being out with the Harvard Glee Club, my tonsils are responsible for the whole thing.

I came in the summer [of 1930]. Summer school was just getting started. It was a very bleak and barren place. You know what it must have looked like up there on the hill with hardly anything. Those junipers in front of Old Main had just been planted by a janitor named Gabriel. But that was about the only greenery we had around there. We had tennis courts down where the [Psychology Building] is now, and the engineers used to play tennis in their high boots. It was really a wretched place.

I didn't want to stay. In fact, I thought that I would go home as soon as this summer was over. I wanted to go back to the green East, but that was the year that the bottom dropped out. The depression was on, and there were no jobs back in the East. So I thought, "Well, maybe I better stay here. I will stay if they ask me." They didn't ask me, though. It got halfway through the summer, and I had no job for the fall, so I had to do something. Our first president had been appointed. His name was John G. Barry*. He was a consulting geologist and had an office in the Mills Building. I thought, "Well, I'll go see him. It can't hurt." I went down to see Barry, and there was a barrier — his wife [Alice]. She was his secretary, and one had to go through her. I thought, "Well, I'll do the best I can." I told her who I was and what I needed, and then I found out that she had been Miss Pierce of Boston, who had run Miss Pierce's School for Girls. She knew all the places where I hung out in Cambridge and Boston. We had the best time, and I was hired without a bit of trouble.

I caused a good deal of discontent. You see, I [was one of] four Ph.D.'s brought in that fall for the beginning of the school as a four-year college. The faculty who were there already resented us very badly. They had M.A.'s, but there were no Ph.D.'s on the faculty. So they went down to see Barry to try to tell him that they thought the present staff was adequate and they didn't need all these people with advanced degrees.

The dormitory was right next door to old Keno Hall*. That was where all the boys lived, and that's where I stayed the first summer I was there. They had their all-night poker games; they had all kinds of goings-on over there. They'd just pop over [to class] without bothering to put on a shirt and tie. They'd sit there and listen to their lectures, and the profs didn't seem to mind. It was a disorderly, male environment. When the women came in, I think they were a little bit resentful because they had to spruce up.

There were lots of pranks in the dorm. It was a prankish place. We had a club [the Purity Squad] — I wasn't a member — that was devoted to the observations of life in what you might call the raw. There was a little hill over where the old stadium is now. It was a favorite place for people to park for romantic reasons. So the members of this club used to climb up on top of that little hill where nobody could see them, or they thought nobody could see them, and see what went on. You know, they say you can learn more about life outside the classroom than in, and they were putting that to the test. I can remember when the club broke up. We had a boy from Buffalo named Rudolph Koukal, who was an enthusiastic member. Somebody saw him up there. They were carrying a shotgun, and they took a shot at him! I saw him come over the hill with his shirttail flying out behind him and his face as white as a sheet. That was the breakup of the observers' club.

At the beginning, of course, it was an engineering school, and the engineers thought that it was something that was reserved for them. They didn't like the academic side. They realized that you had to have some academic courses, but they didn't like very much to have the tail wag the dog. I remember the first sign of that came when we had our first graduation class. We had had graduations in which the kids didn't get degrees [but instead received] certificates for mining specialist. But now we're going to have degrees, and the graduating seniors wanted caps and gowns and all the academic regalia. It came up at a big faculty meeting. Dean [John W.] Kidd*, the engineering dean, said he was not in favor of it, that it did not fit in with the purposes of this school. He said he voted for democratic dress. But they outvoted him. I think [the ceremony] that we have now is a result of that. I think old Cap Kidd probably turns over in his grave when the mace bearer comes in and the banners follow [with] all those medieval trappings. I don't think he likes that a bit.

The term "Peedoggie"* originated with Dean Kidd. It comes as a corruption of pedagogues. Of course, we had education majors, which would be the opposite, the complete antithesis, of the ideal of the engineer. So Dean Kidd called them Peedoggies with great contempt. He and his students would prove their manhood by sitting on the steps of Old Main chewing tobacco and seeing who could spit the farthest. That was supposed to put the Peedoggies in their place, I guess.

The real fireworks came when we changed our name and became Texas Western College [in] '49. That's when they painted the green line. I was out of town when they painted it, and I didn't know about all this. I'd spent the summer on a research trip, so when I came in I stopped to telephone my wife from a bar out near the airport. Dean [Eugene M.]

Thomas* was there with a bunch of faculty members and students with their heads all over the table, obviously making medicine. They were going to do something about this name change.

They did. They drew the green line. It was just to the northwest of the Main Building, and they drew it across to the other side of the campus. On one side it said TCM, and on the other side it said TWC. There was an unspoken rule that TWC was not supposed to cross the line. The idea was: Let's keep this thing separate. The feeling got so spiteful that the president had to call Dean Thomas in and tell him to get that [line] off of there and stop this foolishness, which he did.

Mexican students were with us from the beginning. They tell me a fourth of the mining engineers in Mexico were trained at our university, so we had particularly strong representation from good Mexican boys who came up and took our courses. There was one named Trespalacios that I remember, and Emilio Peinado, who became a builder. There was a problem about social life. For instance, for a while they didn't get into sororities. Then several people who were of mixed blood got in. I was the sponsor of the first Mexican social group. We had considerable debate about what to call it, so we called it Mu Epsilon Chi — MEX. Eventually they got rid of the name because they felt that there was an implication of condescension. I was out of it by then, but they just naturally disappeared after a while. But I was happy that I could do what I could to further the cause with respect to the first Latin American fraternity, and it makes me happy that things are better now.

I felt that the University's main reason for being was that we had a chance to work with these two cultures and that our situation demanded it. I think they have done it more and more, and that's what they ought to do. We don't take advantage of that opportunity. If we try to be "Harvard on the Border," if we try to be a medieval university with chains of office and so on, we are far astray.

I've served under a lot of different administrations, from the beginning as a four-year college right up to 1972, when I retired. The first president, Barry, was a shift boss. He was a mining engineer, and he commanded the faculty; that's what he did. He didn't make [quite] all the decisions himself. He called faculty meetings whenever he was in doubt, so we had innumerable meetings on the top floor of Old Main. I can remember Mr. [E.A.] Drake* and me going up the stairs together to another one. Mr. Drake would stomp on the stairs and say, "Damn, (stomp), damn, (stomp), damn, (stomp)," like that, because he didn't like them.

Dr. [Dossie M.] Wiggins* came in as president [in 1935]. He was a businessman; he stood in very well with the people downtown. He didn't have the same ideas that most academically trained presidents have. He was a specialist in education from Hardin-Simmons. He was the one who called a faculty meeting one time and said that there was some dissatisfaction about the way the faculty was being treated. He said he wanted us to know that he took the same attitude towards the faculty that he would have if he was buying mules. [He] said it was his business to get as much mule for his money as he could.

What was bringing this on was that there was beginning to be a demand for research, and he didn't think that we could ever be a research institution. He said we were a teaching institution. "If you want to do research, you can do it on your own time," he said. "And if that isn't the way you like it, I will be glad to write you a recommendation for any school you want to go to." That was when Dr. [Frederick W.] Bachmann* invited us to his home to see a new faculty picture be unveiled, a picture of the twenty-mule borax team. After that he always called us "Dossie's mules." So we had our growing up to do about relations between the faculty and the administration. It was a long time before we had faculty representation [on] any kind of body which could at least recommend a course of action to the administration, but finally that happened.

I remember we did waste a lot of time. When Dr. [Joseph R.] Smiley* was elected for his second administration [1969-1972], we had a selection committee the way we always do. We were told by these people in Austin that Smiley was not to be considered as a candidate, so we considered everybody else. We brought them in from as far away as Indonesia and wined them and dined them. Then we got a message [from the chancellor of The University of Texas System] that Dr. Smiley was the preferred candidate. I do not know what machinations went on backstage. Of course, Smiley had been at the University [of Texas in Austin] and did a good job down there, so after all our deliberations we were practically instructed which man to choose. Since we all liked Smiley, we were glad to do it, but you have to till the soil and plant the seeds before the faculty is regarded as anything more than hired help. After a while we became professors that had some dignity, but it took a little while.

My Southwest Literature class was the course that I was the most enthusiastic about. I think it was good for these kids to learn about their own background. I went at it pretty hard, and we had fun in the class. We talked about a lot things that were not strictly academic. I remember I used to always have a folk song session. I'd bring the guitar, and sometimes I brought some other musicians. I had this old folk song sheet, and we would sing folk songs. I can remember that Dr. Wiggins saw me going across the campus one time with my guitar, and he says, "Where you going with that?" I said, "I'm going to teach my class." And he said, "You be careful."

When I was dean of the Graduate School, I kept two courses. I taught half-time while I was a full-time dean. That was a good idea, because if you give up those classes you don't get them back; they get somebody else in to teach them. I taught two classes and was able to rotate them, and I kept pretty nearly my full repertory of courses. When I had to go back to full-time teaching, then I had something to teach.

It was awfully hard for us to justify graduate work. The big hassle came when we set up a system-wide graduate school. That was while I was dean, in the early 1960s. I made innumerable trips to Austin to the graduate school meeting. All the deans from all the graduate schools came in, and we hoped that maybe we would have an interchange of courses. That was where we went aground with The University of Texas. They were not about to admit that the graduate courses we taught were on a par with theirs. So when we tried to get that implemented, the whole thing just collapsed.

But you see, the big trouble was [that] all those people down there, many of them from the East, could never think of us as anything but a little cow college out in the sticks where we probably went barefoot across the campus on cow trails. They still have that image. So when Dr. [Joseph M.] Ray* was president, he got around to changing that image. He made sure that they saw what we had. He would ask for a departmental evaluation, and he'd have somebody from Austin come out and look us over. They always went back with a much better impression that they'd had before, because they had never seen us. They didn't know anything about us, and you always feel that anything you don't know about must be inferior. That's human nature. He managed to change that image a good deal by just bringing them out there and letting them look.

I got a lift out of teaching, and I always felt better after I had been in class. I loved to teach these kids. The funny thing was that when it was time for me to stop teaching, I left my last class without any great regret — no ceremony or tears or anything. I just taught it, and that was the end. I had been approached by the Arizona Historical Society about a job. They needed an editor. I thought I could do it, so I accepted. That was probably healthy for me. At seventy you don't always have a new life. I had a new one, and it was a pretty good one. I don't understand anybody who retires and finds himself bored to death. It seems to me that you should prepare for your retirement just as you've prepared for life.

Interviewed by Rebecca Craver and Vicki L. Ruiz, January 13, 1984, Tucson, Arizona.

He wasn't too patient with the Peedoggies*. . . . He enjoyed setting off dynamite where they were because it made them nervous!

Berte R. Haigh
[1890-1986]
Student, 1921-1925
Faculty, 1928-1934

Frankly, when I first entered here, I wasn't exactly sure what geology was. I wanted to be a mining engineer. I was sent here by the Veterans' Division of the Public Health Service as a World War I veteran. I came here for disability rehabilitation [in] October, 1921. The College was already here on the mesa, and there were five buildings: Old Main, the Power Building, Seamon Hall, two dormitories, and [John W.] Cap Kidd's* residence. At the time I came here, it was not Cap Kidd's [home]; it was S.H. Worrell's*, who was the dean. He called me in for an interview to find out why I was here. We got along all right, but he was rather aloof.

The first class I walked into after I got through registering was a class in algebra. [Lloyd A.] Speedy Nelson* was the teacher. I had W.H. Seamon* in geology, F.A. Seamon* in chemistry, Cap Kidd in mathematics, Arthur Pearson in physics. E.A. Drake* was one of my professors, and [so was] Mary Quinn, who was Mary Kelly then. I took a course in history under her my senior year. She was the only woman on the faculty

37

at that time. My modern language teacher was Manuel Enriquez. We called him Henry. I think he left about '27, because he wasn't here when I came back in '28. It was a small staff, but very, very efficient. We had five girls when I was here. None of them completed the course. They went off to somewhere or another, and of course the other degrees were not available at that time.

Cap Kidd got along with his students very well. There were a few of then that took quite a while to understand him, but Cap was very helpful. He wasn't too patient with the Peedoggies*. No, he was not, there's no question. He enjoyed setting off dynamite where they were because it made them nervous! I think he was little rougher on them than he was on the engineers.

He could be awful rough if you went contrary to him, and he was a master of sarcasm. He could flay you unmercifully, but there was always something behind it. He didn't use sarcasm just for the sake of showing that he was the prof. There was a meaning behind it. He taught me a lesson one day in a class in calculus. When Cap was teaching lecture classes, he would always start off and give us a thirty-minute dissertation on the politics of the subject at hand. This particular time he had assigned five problems, and for some unknown reason I had actually tried to work them. I got stuck on one. I worked that thing back and forth, went through it three or four times, and I got stuck in that same mud hole every time. I finally gave up and went to bed. After about four hours' sleep, I walked out here. I was living at the American Legion. We all had to walk to school then; [we] didn't have buses and cars. I got in calculus class, and Cap gave his usual dissertation. Then he said, "Well, gentlemen, I think it probably would be presumptuous on my part to assume that anybody worked these problems that I assigned, but in the event that some of you did and had a little trouble, tell us about it."

Well, I popped off and told him about my trouble. He said, "All right, come up here and put it on the board." I guess I worked from memory, and I went up there. I put that thing back and forth across the board, and I got down to that same mud hole. I say, "Well, here we are, Cap, wheels are spinning." That may sound a little familiar, but we called him Cap. He liked it. Cap was sitting on the front row with a yardstick in his hand, rocking it back and forth across his knees, and I could see his eyes going back and forth across the blackboard. Finally he said, "Haigh, I've been waitin' for this a long time. Sit down, and I'll show you how big a damn fool you are." He walked over to the blackboard and picked up the eraser and made one swap. I had an $(a+b)$ and an $(a-b)$ and forgot to cancel them out. But he taught me right then to triple check. That's the way Cap was.

Cap knew all the mining men here in town. He was a very active member of the AIME [American Institute of Mining and Metallurgical Engineers], and I think he was a charter member of the El Paso engineers' association. He had a very wide acquaintance. Everybody that knew him, knew his efficiency. They also knew that he was absolutely honest and wouldn't recommend a man that he didn't think could do the job. He sent boys to Mexico; he sent boys to South America. We had a large group of graduates working in Bolivia in the tin mines, and there was a great number of graduates who went to the Philippines to work in mines over there.

I arrived here when I was thirty-one years old. That made me about ten years older than anybody else in class. The sophomores were carrying on their regular exercises with the freshmen, and they didn't know what to do with that old man. Finally somebody developed the idea that they might take the old man on a snipe hunt. They approached me on the subject, and I was agreeable. I was a little bit familiar with the southern end of the Franklin Mountains and knew a couple of trails over there, and I also knew about where the location of the snipe was going to be. In fact, I had been on a snipe hunt long before I ever came here. But I went with the boys.

The night I was going to the snipe hunt, I borrowed a car down at the American Legion, an old Model T Ford. I parked it down there by the foot of Mt. Franklin on this side, down below where that beacon light was. The boys took me over to just about the same place, a large flat rock, parked me on that rock with a big gunny sack and a Coleman lantern, and then they took off down the hill. The instant that I could not hear the habrails on the rocks anymore, I took off. I had my trail picked. I came over this way on the mountain, right down to my car. I knew where they were going. And when they walked into the Big Kid Bar in Juarez, I was standing there with my foot on the rail and a schooner of beer. That was the last hazing that happened to me.

I believe this happened in Kelly Hall. It was at that time a dormitory, and some of the boys came back from Juarez one Saturday night and proceeded to set up garbage cans down at the end of the hall and have target practice. Cap was living right there in his residence, and he was up there right quick. I can't remember all the details, but it was quite a commotion. I do remember those boys had to replace the garbage cans, and they had to hire a contractor to patch the holes in the wall.

I graduated in 1925. They only had seven of us that graduated, all in mining engineering. I reported to San Angelo for the Dixie Oil Company, which became the Pan American, and I stayed with them until 1928, when Cap Kidd invited me to come over there and join the faculty to pinch hit for one year for Speedy Nelson, who was going to Colorado to get his master's degree. And then as soon as he returned, Howard Quinn* was going to Harvard to get his doctor's degree. I came here on a three-year leave of absence from the Dixie Oil Company, and all I was teaching was geology.

At the end of three years, Cap Kidd called me down to his office. [He] told me to get on the telephone and call the people in San Angelo and tell them that I wasn't coming back. And I was then assigned to part-time engineering and part-time geology. I stayed three more years, until '34, at which time they transferred me over to [the University of Texas land management system]. I enjoyed every bit of [my years at Mines]. Probably extracurricular activities were more enjoyable than the teaching was, because I never was cut out for a teacher.

When I graduated in '25, the total enrollment was 127, and when I came back it was 750, because in the meantime, in 1927, they had absorbed the El Paso Junior College. There was quite a division between the Peedoggies, as they called them, and the engineering group. And the engineers I think dressed a little off just on purpose to accentuate their independence. They chewed a little tobacco, but I don't think we had a snuff user in the whole group.

When I came [back to teach] they certainly needed more space, but the acquisition of the space was pretty slow. It was like they just couldn't realize in Austin what was going on out here. I don't think there's any question but that for a good many years we were treated pretty much as a stepchild. There were times that I was convinced that if it hadn't been for friends in the legislature, they would have gotten rid of us.

40

Of course you've heard the story about how Holliday Hall* was built. Bob Holliday* was a member of the Board of Regents, and Bob Holliday was the strongest supporter among the Board of Regents that the College of Mines ever had. He also had something to do with the local Public Works Administration [in the 1930s]. They were building Scenic Drive, and a great deal of the material that was placed up on Scenic Drive would mysteriously get transferred over here to the campus and was used in the building of that field house. So for a long time — well, all the time I was out here — it was spelled Hauliday, h-a-u-l.

Interviewed by C.L. Sonnichsen, Bud Newman, and Leon Metz, June 3, 1969, El Paso.

We always had to wear old shoes on campus
because every place you went, there were rocks.

Lurline Hughes Coltharp

Student, 1929-1931
Faculty, 1954-1981

In 1929 I came out to the Texas College of Mines. When I graduated from high school at fifteen, my parents thought I was too young to go away to school to the big, wicked University [of Texas in Austin]. They kept me at home, and I came out here. I remember that I was allowed to have a car to come up here, but I think it was the family car, and my family had to do without it when I had classes.

The best parking place was the one right in front of what is now known as Old Main. It was just known as Main Building then, and we parked right there. The reason we liked that location is because there were steps there, and you didn't have to get your shoes so scuffed up on the rocks. We always had to wear old shoes on the campus because every place you went, there were rocks. The gathering place was the bookstore. You went inside Old Main and the first room to the right was the bookstore, and we had a lot of fun going in there. There were not only books, but you could buy Cokes, and you could stand around and visit with the boys.

It was the fall or spring of my first year that I took geology. This was lots of fun because I was the only girl in the class. Dr. [Berte] Haigh*

43

had an extra class meeting which I was not told about, and he gathered all the boys together and laid down the rules of conduct. One day we were doing plane table work out in back of Kelly Hall. Between Kelly Hall and Old Main was all just rocky terrain then. We had the plane table, and we got it all set up, got it all leveled, and everything was fine. But, I went around to do something and kicked the plane table leg and unleveled it. And I said, "Oh damn!" The boys just shrieked! They said, "Dr. Haigh told us that he would skin us alive if we said one cuss word in front of you, and here you're the one who said damn."

In the spring the engineers had their initiation up in Oro Grande, and that was jillions of fun, because the boys smeared the initiates with paint and goo and catsup and made them crawl through one of the old mines. You left the highway at Oro Grande and went around some of those mountains to where there were abandoned mine shafts. We thought it was exciting. I think the boy I had a date with had a Model T, and we went up to Oro Grande, spent the whole day, and came back.

I'm just remembering some of the real fun things that happened. In 1930 I was going with one of the football players. That year we had brought in a bunch of ringers. They had played for other colleges, and they were way beyond the age of college people and big and strong. We brought them all in, and we won every game that year. I thought, "Oh, look how manly, look how wonderful." I was enchanted with one of these professional football players who was supposed to be a college student.

One morning I got there a little early and parked my car in front of Old Main and had the perfect parking place. I remember that he came up to the window to speak to me, and I said, "Oh, how are you?" I was so thrilled to be talking to him that I was leaning out of the car visiting with him. In a little while he had to say, "Excuse me, I gotta go." The next day I learned that he had been chewing tobacco when he'd come up and seen me, and he didn't want me to know that he chewed tobacco, so he couldn't spit. He had swallowed [it] instead. And this great big, husky football player was laid out for twenty-four hours up in the dormitory. He was laid out for twenty-four hours because he wouldn't spit in front of Lurline.

That fall, the fall of 1930, a bunch of us said, "There's not enough pep for all these football games." We thought we were so lucky to have all these fine football players. Of course, it was only later that I found out that they had all been purchased. But anyway, we said, "We've got to have more P-E-P," so a group of us got up a little pep squad. My mother, Mrs. Frank A. Hughes, dreamed up the name "Golddiggers." We thought this was very funny, because we would never dream of being a golddigger. We were the kind of little girls that when a boy took us on a date, and we stopped at a drive-in for a drink, and he said, "What will you have?" we'd say, "I'll take a small Coke, please," because we weren't going to spend more than five cents of the boy's money. Money was too scarce a commodity. So we thought the name "Golddiggers" was funny.

I remember that we all wore orange tops and white skirts. We marched in the Homecoming parade. To this day I can still see us marching past the Cortez (it was the Orndorff then), lined up about three or four abreast. The Homecoming parade went through [downtown] El Paso in those days. We all sat together at football games and yelled extra hard because we were the Golddiggers.

My sophomore year — I just can't tell you how many good things happened that year. I just remember my sophomore year as having stars all around it, because it was fun every day. You know, the world was your oyster. I was elected president of my sorority, and I was elected one of the three school beauties both years I was here. Oh, it was heaven!

When the boys had their initiation at Oro Grande that spring, we got together and said, "We are going to initiate the new girls." We took them over in back of where the English Department is. It was a canyon, and we made everybody walk down this little path. We initiated all the new girls. I was St. Patricia. I had long, flowing hair and a long, green robe. All the girls had to come up and kiss the Blarney Stone. And I think we daubed them with something for initiation. I think we put a little "x" on them, but we didn't treat them badly.

I was thrilled to death to be coming to Mines, because I wanted to be an engineer. My father was an engineer, and I wanted to be an engineer. That's why I was taking geology. So I was talking about being an engineer, and [John W.] Cap Kidd* took me aside. He said, "Lurline, in order to be an engineer you have to have calculus. I am the only one on the faculty who teaches calculus, and I do not want you to be an engineer. I do not want a woman bothering my Engineering Department." He said, "I don't care if every paper you turn in to me in calculus is 100 percent, I'll still give you an F, and I will fail you in calculus, so that you can never be an engineer." And he meant it. So I became a history major. Then my parents said, "Look, you've got to have something besides history." So I took an extra major in education; I had two majors when I graduated. But in my junior year I went down to the big, wicked university at Austin!

Interviewed by Rebecca Craver, January 27, 1984, El Paso.

The boys had been allowed to smoke and chew tobacco in class and spit out the window.

Bulah Liles Patterson
[1890-1986]
Faculty, 1927-1967

I had graduated from the University of Chicago and had started teaching in a Dallas high school in the fall of 1927. I had a call saying that the College of Mines and Metallurgy needed a math teacher. The College had grown suddenly due to the fact that El Paso Junior College, which was located on the fourth floor of El Paso High School, had not opened due to lack of funds. I had wanted a college teaching position in Texas, so I said, "Yes." I got ready right quick and took a train out there.

My mother was very much disturbed when she found out that I was coming to El Paso. A bunch of Mexicans and drunken cowboys — that was her idea of El Paso! Well, I wasn't really too surprised at the campus. There wasn't a paved street out there on that hill. It was all rock. I didn't have a car. I walked across from North Mesa, and there was just a little trail about two feet wide, uphill and downhill and across the mountains. Well, the buildings were a surprise — that [Bhutanese] architecture! There were only four buildings and a little mill that had to do with metallurgy.

I started the Monday after Thanksgiving in 1927. And at that time there were only two women teachers out there — Mary Kelly Quinn and Anita Lorenz. I was assigned five three-hour classes a week, which every faculty member had at that time. I walked into those classes, and the vast majority of the students were boys, or men. Now, I had a few girls because they had come over from the junior college, but not very many. When I first came out there, I taught algebra, trigonometry, and analytical geometry. They didn't have the academic and the engineering math courses separated at all. Later on, when there were so many academic students and they required six hours of math, they separated it and gave the academic students a general survey of the math. It wasn't the intensive course in mathematics that the engineers had.

The dean of engineering was Dean John W. Kidd*. He was a very outstanding character and objected to me — 'I'm not going to have women teaching my engineers!" But I wasn't there very long until he was very glad to get my students, because I soon had a reputation of being rather "hard-boiled," because I worked very hard myself, and I expected my students to do likewise. I graded homework papers, and it was really quite a job. You think about how many students you have turning in a paper. I had three classes a day, [so] that was 120 papers a day. I worked almost day and night to keep up with them, because I didn't know how else to teach. Of course, I was accused sometimes of teaching just like high school, but it was the only way that I could put my subject across.

I had a routine like this: We'd go into class, and I would take up their homework papers. Then I would say, "Are there any particular problems or questions you want to ask?" There would always be some. We would go over those. Then, I would take up the new work. Now, some teachers never did take up the new work. But I did. I took up the new work, and I went over it. Then I sent them to the board, and we practiced on that. I always sent my students to the board. They said that was high-schoolish. I didn't care whether it was high school or not, I was interested in them learning. It irritated me no end to get a classroom with one little ole board, because I wanted to see my students working, and I sent them to the board.

In the early years, the graduation ceremonies were held on the tennis courts. And every once in a while there'd be a sandstorm or a shower. More likely a sandstorm would come up and ruin the graduation, but on the whole we were pretty lucky. There weren't too many of them that were ruined like that. All the faculty members were expected to go to the graduation. But you realize then the faculty was small, and they wanted to make a big showing. In fact, I had bought my cap and gown at the

University of Chicago when I graduated. It was a good thing, because a lot of the faculty members would have to rent them every year, and that was a nuisance.

Faculty members also had to chaperone the dances that the students had. They were *chaperoned*, too; it wasn't just in name only. Their dances were held in the gymnasium [Holliday Hall*], close to Kidd Field. They usually had a local band. It wasn't many years after that until the Miners had a band, and they would play for the dances, too. I remember [at] one dance they had a little disturbance. One of the boys took a swing at a faculty member, because the faculty member was half drunk; [he] knocked him down. He was dancing with this boy's date, and he put his hand down the back of her dress. The faculty member didn't retaliate; I think it sobered him up. I was one of the chaperones, and I went to see, and by that time the faculty member had gone [out the door].

I'll have to tell you one story, just to let you know what a hard-boiled teacher I was. One president came in with an idea: to build up the enrollment of the college regardless of who we got. Before he came here, we would have a whole bunch of failures each semester because our standards were high. If they didn't pass, they didn't stay in college. When this president came, he didn't want any teacher to fail anyone. I remember the president saying one time in a faculty meeting that he was not concerned about teachers. He said, "I hire teachers just like I'd buy mules, as cheap as I can get them, and I'll watch their records to see how many failures they have." It wasn't very long before he found out that I didn't pass a student who didn't make the grade, though I was willing to give a student any help I could.

The previous president had put Gladys Gregory* and me on the athletics committee. We and a few others on the committee lived up to the rules, and unless a student earned sufficient grade points, he was bumped off the team. A football player had failed his math course. A D would give him enough points to stay on the team. He went to the president, asking him to get me to change his grade from F to D. The president called me in and said the boy said he had learned more math in my course than he'd ever learned in any math course — "and she still failed me." The president asked if I'd change his grade. I said, "No, that was what he made. If you want it changed, go to the registrar's office and put your initial on the change." [That] was the procedure to change a grade after it was recorded. I never followed up to see what happened. Needless to say, I was not a favorite with that president, and Gladys and I were soon off the athletics committee.

I was strict! I didn't put up with much. When I first went out there, the boys had been allowed to smoke and chew tobacco in class and spit out the window. And I said, "No more smoking!" There was a guy named Pennington. He came in one day smoking a cigarette and went and took his seat. I kept waiting and gave him a hard look, but he didn't pay any attention. He just kept on smoking the cigarette. So, I said, "Pennington, throw out your cigarette." He said, "I will, when I finish this." I said, "Well, you just go out now and finish it and [don't] come back to this class until you do." When the teacher did anything like that, the deans would stand behind us then. Boy, Dean Kidd or Dean [Eugene] Thomas* and Dean [C.A.] Puckett* all stood back of the teachers. So Pennington came back to class and never did smoke again.

The last year I was up there — it was in the mid-sixties — some students had begun to go just as far as they could. One guy came to a class one day with sandals on and no socks. I didn't say anything much. I just said, "I think you better wear socks." The next class, he came barefooted. I sent him out of class. I called Dean Thomas, who told the student, "Well, you can go to that class properly dressed, or I'm dropping you right now. You can take your choice." The student dropped out. Times were changing. He was one of those "hippies."

One student told me one time, "You know, Mrs. Patterson, freshmen hated you with a vengeance. When they get up in calculus, they begin to say, well, maybe she was right about that. And they begin to like you a little better. When they get on up into junior and senior math courses and their engineering courses, they love you." Because they found out I was demanding, they appreciated me.

I really like teaching. I don't admit at all to being a soft teacher; you can't be soft in a course like mathematics. To my way of thinking, in mathematics people need a teacher. Now, in history, and maybe in English literature, they can read it and get it themselves if they want to. But that's not true with mathematics. When people tell you, "Well, I never had to study mathematics," they're lying.

Do you remember the Russian Sputnik? It was the year of the Sputnik, and they got all stirred up, and math courses were very popular. One day, I had sent them to the board, and they were kind of dragging that day. I said, "Now let me tell you, if you guys don't get busy and get to doing something in here, the Sputnik will sure get us." One of the boys said, "If it does, Mrs. Patterson, it sure won't be your fault."

Interviewed by Rebecca Craver, October 6, 1983, El Paso.

The legislature got a bill introduced to kill the College of Mines, just abandon it. Vamoose.

Leon Denny Moses
[1897-1979]
Faculty, 1927-1962

I came west to grow up with the College of Mines. It had been a mining school which admitted a few women and others who wanted to take just a course or two of academic work, and the rest of it was engineering, especially mining engineering, under the direction of Dean John W. Kidd*. There was a junior college on the top floor of El Paso High School. The city fathers of El Paso decided that they didn't want to keep up that extra expense, so they decided to dump it. The state very graciously offered to let the College of Mines expand the academic department and give two years of credit work in academic subjects.

So about 1927, instructors from the junior college came over to Mines, and a professor in the junior college became the actual head of the school. He was C.A. Puckett*, who had a B.A. from Texas and a master's from Harvard. He did the hiring and firing. Of course Dean Kidd, as dean of engineering, was consulted on all matters pertaining to the engineering school. So when I came out here we had the old mining faculty and then about twice as many academic faculty, most of them being new and from the junior college.

53

The roads [on campus] were unpaved; you "rock-a-bye babied" as you drove a Model T along those roads. I had a son about two years old, and we lived out on Yandell at that time. He said, "I know how to go to Daddy's school. You go up a big hill and across the bridge, and you go out to the rocks." You parked at the "Magic Circle" there in front of the Main Building. They'd just drive up there and stop. Then when they got ready to go home, they'd just take off, right down through the sagebrush.

I parked there one day. I had a Model T, like practically everybody else that had anything at all, and came out to go to lunch at about one o'clock. The car was gone. I found it on top of a turtle-back knoll down just below where the flagpole is now, between the flagpole and town. My students had pushed it up there to tease me. I had no idea who it was, and I wasn't even interested in finding out. I wanted to enjoy the joke. And a whole line of buzzards [students and spectators] sat up there on the wall in front of Old Main and watched me go down and get it.

The first president was John G. Barry*, who had his degree from MIT in geology. After [World War I], Barry became a geology consultant and had his offices here when they elected him president. He came in 1931 and stayed until the spring of 1934. I was very fond of President Barry. I felt that he meant exactly what he said, and I felt he said the right thing. I had utmost respect for the man.

Now here's an interesting chapter that I've never seen written up. In about 1932 the legislature got a bill introduced to kill the College of Mines, just abandon it. Vamoose. The bill would cut about four or five of the teachers' colleges to junior college standing. In that way, the legislators hoped to cut down a great deal of tax money. Well, the bill failed to pass, but the next year a bill did pass to this effect: all state-supported colleges must get rid of 25 percent of their faculty. And those who remained, presidents on down, got a 25 percent cut in salary. That was an excuse on the part of a great many college presidents to get rid of some of the dead wood. They fired with a clearer conscience. If they wanted to abandon a department, why that would count toward their 25 percent reduction, you see. But then there was also the cut in salary; we all suffered a 25 percent reduction. Two or three years later they began to restore some [of the cut], $100 here, $200 there. It took me about six years to get my salary back to where it had been.

We lost about eight faculty members in the reductions. I was glad to stay. I thanked President Barry after he resigned. I went to him and said, "I appreciate the fact that I got to stay on at a 25 percent reduction in salary." He said, "You were doing a good job, hell's bells." Hell's bells was a popular cuss word in those days after a certain play that had been on Broadway.

Now President [Wilson H.] Elkins*, who came in 1949, was a four-star athlete and Phi Beta Kappa. He was a Rhodes scholar and got his Ph.D. at Oxford. He was probably the most sensational personality that ever hit the campus. No wonder he went to the University of Maryland and proceeded to make it one of the big universities. A pretty good golfer, too. I played golf with three heads of this school. Elkins was the best golfer of the bunch. Puckett couldn't play worth anything. And Wiggins was a little better than I was, but he wasn't as good as Elkins. The rest of them didn't play golf, as far as I know.

Dean Kidd was as gruff as an old grizzly, but I never did feel that he had a hard streak anywhere in him. It was just his way of talking. He had tuberculosis years before, and it had given him a kind of high-pitched voice that didn't sound quite natural. His students just worshiped him. They'd spit their tobacco and say, "Yes sir, Dean Kidd." He was the hero of the engineers, if they ever had a hero. When Dean Kidd dropped dead on the campus in Christmas vacation of 1941 and was taken to the mortuary to be funeralized, there were more handkerchiefs there than any other funeral I was ever in. They were those tobacco-spittin' engineers, too. They felt that a friend had gone.

Interviewed by David Salazar and Mildred Torok, February 27, 1973, El Paso.

"What is she going to serve her husband? Algebra? Chemistry?"

Maria Elena Garcia Connolly
Student, 1929-1936

I was born in Aguascalientes, Mexico, on August 18, 1914. I was two years old, and my brother was six months old, when we had to come all of a sudden to the United States. My father was superintendent of railroads in Aguascalientes, and one evening one of the workers came in and said, "Don Felix, Don Felix! Villa is sending men to kill you!" My father said, "Well, why would he want to kill me?" And then the man said, "There is a very wealthy miner and rancher in Zacatecas also named Felix Garcia, and he heard that you were here, and he is sending some men to shoot you immediately." So we got our things as quickly as we could. All the way from Aguascalientes to Juarez, I cried. Now, my parents did not have transportation, so they came in the cattle car.

First we lived in Juarez in a little boarding house [while] my father was gathering money enough to come across. We came across on the streetcar, and at the end of Myrtle Avenue one of my aunts and the cousins met us. They took us to their house on Magoffin, and we lived there for a while. We came to the United States on Halloween, 1916. And my mother thought that this place was crazy — all these kids dressed in black like witches, running back and forth on the street. My mother said, "What in the world is happening?" So one of my aunts told her, "Oh, this is *la noche libre*. It's Halloween."

When I was six years old, my father and mother decided that I was going to St. Mary's. My mother decided to take me on the first day of school. She dressed very pretty in a black taffeta dress and a black hat with a black feather. She looked very handsome. I think I learned English in a month. It was a case of necessity. I was the only Mexican child in the whole school.

When I graduated from St. Mary's, I received a scholarship for Loretto, but I went to Loretto [only] one year. It was during the depression, and my mother and father both told me, "Elena, it costs a lot of money to go to Loretto, even on a scholarship. So, I'm sorry, we can't send you to Loretto next year." I cried and cried. I had to go to El Paso High, which in a way wasn't so bad after all. Anyway, I graduated not with any unusually high honors, I just graduated, and I went on to college.

We must have been a very advanced family ideologically, because I went to college. In those days, Mexican girls, a lot them, didn't go to high school. I remember when my mother sent me to high school that these friends of mine told Mama, "That's wasted money. What is she going to serve her husband? Algebra? Chemistry? Is that what she's going to serve her husband? How is she going to iron his shirts?" And then my mother said, "Well, who said she's going to get married? She may not get married." My mother's relatives would say, "Hah, I guess you think she's a very studious girl. She's lazy. She doesn't want to help you. That's why she goes to school." And my father would say, "She's going to school as long as she's interested in it. When she isn't interested in it, she can quit."

I was sixteen when I was admitted to the College of Mines. In those days, college was not as expensive [as today]. My father gave me $100 and said, "Go register." I registered, paid my student activity fees, bought all my books for chemistry, math, Spanish, English — and had money to take home, about forty dollars. So, I went to school that year, and I did all right. I made A's and B's. I made an A in trigonometry, made A's in Spanish, and I made an A in English the first semester. I also took the first year of education. In those days you did your practice teaching the first year, and I did my student teaching at Beall School.

Mrs. [Isabelle K.] Fineau, who taught French and Spanish, was my favorite teacher. She was a darling. You see, there weren't many Mexican girls in those days in school. But she seemed to take quite a lot of interest in me, especially since my mother and father would take me to school every morning and wait there in the car until I finished, because by that time my father didn't work anymore. So my father and mother would go there and wait, and they would read the newspaper and read their favorite books while I was in school. So, even though I was not very brilliant, I was not pretty, I was not the best-dressed girl on campus, people noticed me because there was this girl, nothing unusual, who had her father and mother waiting for her every day.

When I would be invited to the school-sponsored dances, my mother insisted on going. Some were sponsored by the Newman Club, which is the Catholic club. There were some sponsored by Sigma Delta Pi, the honorary [Spanish] society. There was one at the Country Club. I remember that my mother wouldn't let me go [by myself], so she took me. Now my mother was a very nice person, very gracious, and she and Mrs. Fineau would sit together. The boys like Adolfo Trespalacios thought my mother was the greatest. In fact, I remember once I was dancing with Adolfo, and he asked me, "Is that your mother?" I replied, "Yes." He said, "I thought she was an American lady." I told him, "No, she's my mother. She doesn't speak English." And he said, "I've seen her driving a car!" I said, "I know, she brings me to school every day and waits for me." He [couldn't believe it]. "You mean she's a Mexican, and she drives a car?" I said, "Yeah, she drives her car." Then he went over and congratulated her and told her how wonderful, "That's the way more Mexican women should be."

That was my only year that I went to school [fulltime], that I was a "college girl." My father lost his job around May, and so we had no mode of income except the savings we had. And we were praying and praying that somehow somebody would get a job. My father was over fifty, so there was no chance of his getting a job. Anyway, all of a sudden I remembered, "I already took student teaching. I'm going to apply for a job." At that time, after student teaching, you could work. They didn't require a degree.

So I went and made my application, and they told me, "Sorry," they couldn't employ me because there was no place for me. But I was going to get a job regardless. I was there for two weeks every morning and every afternoon. I just sat there and waited for Mr. A.H. Hughey*. Now there is an elementary school here in El Paso named for him. He was a precious person, a very nice man. So Hughey would come in and say "Hello," and he would leave and say, "Good-bye." Finally, he must have said, "Get that girl out of my sight. Give her a job." So I went to Aoy School. And when I signed the contract, I was seventeen, so my mother had to come. I wasn't even a citizen yet.

When I had to go to work and support the family, that hurt my father very much. I used to tell him, "Don't worry, Daddy. Supposing instead of sending us to school you had put away all that money. Now, you'd be living off the interest. Imagine, you're living off the interest now." And then we'd laugh, and he'd say, *"Ay, hijita, ay, hijita."* And he'd pat me. It was a lot of fun. Don't think my life was sad. It was fun.

My brother says that there was a lot of anti-Mexican thought in those days. But I got a job when a lot of people didn't have it. Somebody said, "You must have denied you were a Catholic." I said, "Nobody asked me if I was a Catholic or not." In fact, one of my best friends that had been at Loretto, I noticed her mother didn't speak to me anymore. One day we were sitting down after Mass, and she came to me and says, "Elena, why did you denounce your religion?" I said, "I did not. Nobody asked me if I was a Catholic or not." She says, "Well, somebody told me you had become a Baptist." But I didn't have sense enough to know that anybody could be saying anything against me. I just never thought of it.

While I was teaching at Aoy, I went back to school. I would go to classes from 4:30 to 6:00, then take another one from 7:30 to 9:00. Now, my mother didn't come for me or anything, and I really didn't have any money to eat supper, but I didn't care. I just stayed there and studied. And in those days I couldn't buy books because they were so expensive, so we would borrow books at the library.

I used to borrow money from Gene Thomas*, who was an engineering professor. For instance, I would borrow twenty-five dollars in September to be able to register for my two classes, and then I would pay him my first payment at the end of September. This wasn't done through the office or anything. This was done through him and me. He would give me a check.

But I kept going, and then I graduated. My principal went to my graduation, and all my friends went, and they hugged me, and they hugged my mother. They said, "Mrs. Garcia, we know Elena couldn't have done this by herself. It was you that pushed her and that encouraged her." So they all hugged my mother and kissed her, because they all thought she was such a wonderful person, which she was. I tell you, our Lord must have been right there guiding me. I got my degree in 1936, which was not much later than the rest of the kids that I had gone to school with.

I always thought that one year of education courses was quite sufficient. When I was in college, I had an education teacher [who] insisted you could only teach a child one language at a time. Well, I argued with her and argued with her. And I think she finally gave me a C when I could have made an A or a B, but that was beside the point. She said it was a shame to teach a child two languages, because they became fluent in neither and they would always have an accent. [But] I knew better. After I got married and had my daughter, Patricia, by the time she was about three years old, she knew both languages. My mother spoke no English; my husband, her father, spoke no Spanish. So she learned both languages, and she didn't mix them up. A lot of my friends never taught their children Spanish because they said that would ruin their pronunciation. But I did. All my children are bilingual.

Interviewed by Debra Garcia, September 9, 1984, El Paso.

There was some consternation in that building after that rattlesnake had escaped.

Anton H. Berkman
[1897-1973]

Faculty 1927-1966

In 1927 I went to Austin to The University of Texas to teach. That summer, a telegram arrived from Dean [C.A.] Puckett* at Texas College of Mines, saying that the position of chairman of Biological Sciences was open. They were just adding academic work to the engineering school. Prior to that, I had heard of the College of Mines in El Paso. My idea of the school was that it was a frontier school and that it consisted of one or two buildings up on a rocky mound or hill. This attracted my attention. I thought, well, this is a pioneering place and that would be interesting, so I decided to take it. The salary was $3,000 a year. That was big money in those days. It went down to $2,000 during the depression.

As for facilities, we had one room in what is now Kelly Hall. It was a laboratory and lecture room together when I first arrived. It was very limited quarters, really the frontier. In 1930 we moved into another building, and we had half of the top floor. We had two labs then, and I had an office. This continued until 1936, when they gave another third of that floor to my department. Then we had two offices and three labs. We stayed there until they built the new Science Building. We were always

63

crowded. The interesting thing about when they gave the extra third to us, Dean [John W.] Kidd* said, "Now you have space." I never had enough space. It wasn't a year until we scarcely had room to move. That's how rapidly the students were coming.

To start with, the institution was really a technical school; therefore, our courses were largely zoology. We added the vertebrate anatomy when Dr. B.F. Jenness* was taken on in the department. He had been the school physician and a lecturer to the engineering students in hygiene and sanitation. They had to have that as part of their degree requirement. He continued in that capacity for nearly fifty years. The dominant work in the department was zoology, and botany was offered simply to satisfy the requirements for the bachelor's degree. Students weren't interested in the botanical; young people in the El Paso region wanted to prepare for schools of medicine. In 1931 or 1932 we added the third course, histology, and later embryology. These were the principal courses for the pre-medical preparation in the biological sciences. Eventually we started bacteriology, and after we got another laboratory, the students crowded in. So instead of having one section of lab, we had two sections, and this is where quite a bit of evening labs came in. Some days, I taught all day and then taught three labs at night; that added up to about twenty-three contact hours a week.

I would say that those who really wanted to go to medical school and were serious students succeeded in going. There wasn't much failure at all after they reached the second year. The place where we eliminated them was in the freshman year. The grades would tell, and they would know themselves if they should go on into the other course. I would say that 95 percent of the ones we recommended went to medical school and are practicing now.

The Pre-Med Club was a pretty good promoter of esprit de corps. Dr. Jenness and I started it. The first meetings we had were downtown in a restaurant on the second floor of a building now owned by the University. There were a few girls in that Pre-Med Club. One of them went up to the Chicago Medical College. Three went down to Galveston to take the medical technician's courses, and another got her M.D. degree at Southwestern Medical School in Dallas.

We always needed equipment. We benefited from contributions and donations. The main things we needed were microscopes. By keeping on the alert, we could find secondhand microscopes, sometimes from doctors who turned their lab work over to the laboratory in town and didn't need them anymore. So we got quite a number of very good microscopes that way for very little money.

We went out and collected rattlesnakes and brought them in. We experimented with them in reference to milking them to show the students how that was done and show them the venom that you get out of them. Once upon a time, one of them got away and turned up in Isabella McKinney's bookcase. It really didn't show up in her bookcase, but she thought it did! We did go through all of her books and everything. After that was all done, we settled down to the assumption that the snake had gone down the stairs and out.

It was about three weeks later that I was sitting in my office, leaning back in my chair at my desk. I had been reading, and I just happened to glance down into the lower shelf of my bookcase, and there lay the rattlesnake. So, I just got a stick and a jar and raked him out of the shelf and put him back in the jar. He didn't fight much; he seemed adjusted to his environment. He seemed glad to be home. I tickled him a little more to be sure he wouldn't get away again. But I tell you, though, there was some consternation in that building after that rattlesnake had escaped.

Interviewed by C.L. Sonnichsen, January 23, 1969, Round Rock, Texas.

There were not any girls in the engineering section before I bulldozed my way in. Nobody else was fool enough to try it.

Zora Zong Gaines
Student, 1931-1938

From the third grade on, I grew up in El Paso in Manhattan Heights. My father was with a construction company. I always wanted to go to college, but during the depression times, the only college accessible to me was the College of Mines. I graduated from El Paso High School in 1930, and all my friends were going off to college. They didn't have parents in the construction business. The bottom fell out for construction, so I had to stay out of school to work and make enough money to get back into school. But I won a bank night of seventy-five dollars. For seventy-five dollars I could pay my tuition and buy my books and go to college!

My family moved to Fabens, so I had to drive in. I had an old car that my father wouldn't let me drive past thirty-five miles an hour. I got up before sunrise, drove into Mines, [had an] eight o'clock class every morning, [had] labs every afternoon, and got home after sunset. That was the story of my first year, 1931-1932. I had taken botany and biology in high school, so when I came to college I thought, "I want something new." [I took] physics and geology. I got into that geology class, and all my

67

thoughts of majoring in mathematics went by the board. One year of geology put me on the road, and I wasn't going to study anything else. [Dr. Lloyd A.] Speedy Nelson* was teaching the class. Speedy didn't mind having me in his classes, so he let me go on. At that time you had to take geology to be a mining engineer. By the time I finished my sophomore year, why there weren't any girls [left] in my classes. My junior year, there just weren't any girls taking topography, pathology, and mineralogy.

I have a story about Captain [John W.] Kidd*. I can't remember what course it was, but I registered for it, and the professor was not gung-ho on having me. He reported to Captain Kidd that he had a female in his class, and he wasn't really interested in having her. I went to Captain Kidd, and he couldn't see any reason why a girl should be in that class. I went to the president, Dossie Wiggins*, and I said, "I want to take that course. It's a geology course, and I'm going to take every [geology] course you've got." He looked up at me, and he said, "Well, Z.Z., I can't think of any reason why a girl can't register for that class; there's no rule against it." So I got into the class. I never did hear any more from Captain Kidd, but I got dirty looks. He wasn't too fond of the women coming into the College of Mines, but as long as they stayed over in the history, English, and social studies end of it, that was fine. But when they wound up on the engineering campus. . . .

I had a little trouble with Norma [Egg*], who was the dean of women, for wearing pants on campus. She ate me out but good. Ladies didn't wear pants [in those days]. In fact, they didn't even make pants for women. I had to take the buttons off the front and put them on the side to get by with it. She complained about it. I said, "Look, what can I do? I cannot go on these field trips in a skirt." I couldn't climb mountains [or] get [lab] specimens on the top level off a tall ladder [in a dress]. You just couldn't do it, so I wore pants to school. I wore a brand new wool suit to school once. [I] went into the chemistry lab, sat down, started working, got up, and felt something funny where I had sat on the chair. Somebody had put sodium hydroxide in the seat, [which] ate right through my brand new wool skirt. I never wore a dress to school after that.

[The engineering students] were great about playing pranks on me. I was the butt of all their harassment. They'd take up for me against the academics, but among themselves they worked me over. They would open a window [in the classroom] in the Centennial Museum and set me out on the ledge, close the window, and lock it. Speedy would walk in and look up and say, "All right, let Z.Z. in." They locked me in the broom closet. He'd come in and say, "Where have you put Z.Z. today?" We had a concrete-lined pit on the campus, where they'd had some mining machinery at one time. Their big deal was to take me by the hands and drop me down in the pit, which was about ten feet deep, and leave me there until one of my professors asked where they'd put me today. If they weren't pulling one thing they were pulling another. It was fun. I lived through it. They gave me an education.

My sophomore year, 1932-1933, [I went through] the St. Patrick's Day [initiation] at Oro Grande. I crawled on a plank through the mine at Oro Grande. I got my butt paddled, just like everybody else. They only gave me one swat, but I got it. They had a nice gentle, separate thing for the girls, their dates. There were not any girls in the engineering section before I bulldozed my way in. Nobody else was fool enough to try it. It took somebody that was completely ditsy to do it. I was one of the boys, so I had to take [the full treatment]. They put me through all of it, except that they didn't get too rough. They let me live. I could sit down the next day.

Mining engineers were as ornery as they come. What they couldn't think of to do couldn't be thought of. [They wore] blue jeans, and their habits were beer busts. They liked to take me to beer busts. I didn't drink, and when you went to a beer bust they'd come around and fill your glass. Two of them would choose who was going to get me that night. The one on the right got the first beer I didn't drink. The one on the left got the second beer I didn't drink. So when it was time to go home, I had to drive. According to everybody that was sitting around and seeing my beer disappear, I had drunk everybody under the table.

At my senior prom in high school my date offered me a cigarette. By golly I liked it, so I started smoking, and I had tailor-made cigarettes. After about two months on campus with my geology field trips, the boys would come around and [say], "Hey, Z.Z., how about one of your tailor-mades?" None of them took snuff or chewed tobacco, but they did love to smoke my tailor-mades. It was breaking me, so I finally started smoking Bull Durham. I got even with them; I just gave them my Bull Durham sack. I didn't bring any more tailor-mades to class after that.

[Norma Egg] got to me my senior year. You went on a field trip in Colorado for your senior thesis in geology at that time. My parents gave the okay. After all, there were only about fifteen boys going, and they'd take good care of me. Well, Norma Egg heard of it. "Do you mean you're going up there for two weeks and take a woman with you?" Speedy said, "Well, why not?" She says, "Well, just think what those boys could do." Speedy said, "I'm not worried about what the boys will do to her. I'm worried about what she'll do to the boys." But she held sway. They wouldn't let the girl go on the field trip. I had to stay here and write a thesis.

I joined the College Players. Myrtle Ball* directed all the plays. My only contact with any girls was outside of classes, through the College Players. Johnell Crimen was one of them, and also Nell Travis and Louise Maxon. I didn't have any girls in my classes. There were fifteen to twenty boys and me.

I finally graduated with a degree in geology in 1938. Graduation didn't mean a thing to me. My parents had to fight me to get me into that cap and gown. I didn't see the use of parading down the aisle in a cap and gown, but I had to go. Speedy told me that there was an opening for a geologist at a mining company downtown. He made an appointment for me. I went down and walked in. I said, "Professor Nelson sent me down. He said you needed a geologist." And he said, "Yes, we do, but it's in Mexico." And I said, "Well, I do speak Spanish." He said, "Well, it's isolated. You can only get there on horseback or muleback." And I said, "Well, I ride out at the post, exercising the polo ponies, and horseback riding doesn't bother me." And he looked at me again, and he said, "Well, it's awfully isolated." And I said, "Well, I've been on many a mountain. That doesn't mean a thing to me." He finally looked up at me and said, "We just can't use a young woman." That told the story. I didn't try anymore. There just weren't any openings for women geologists in 1938. You were a man, or you didn't make it in geology then.

I had two uncles who were politicians over in Louisiana, and they got me a job teaching mathematics. I couldn't get one here in El Paso. The depression was still holding sway, and there just were no jobs. I met the man I married there. When we came back to Texas, I didn't start teaching again until we moved to Houston in 1950. I started out in an elementary school, and then I taught in junior high and finally at Bellaire High School. I was delighted to get there. It was the top school. [I taught] there seventeen years. It was a delightful experience, until students' rights hit the campus. It got to the point where it was all students' rights, and they expected to absorb [knowledge] by osmosis. They didn't have to do any work. They didn't retire me; I quit really. Now they are learning that I was right.

When I started here [at the College of Mines], there were only five buildings. And now I look, and the big crater where they dug gravel out and took us on our first field trip in geology has been leveled. And half the hills I used to walk over to get to class are gone. And they've changed the rock wall in front of Old Main where I used to sit and get into a bull session. I'm sure if I had to take classes out here again, I'd be a lost soul. Mines just fit me fine.

Interviewed by Charles H. Martin, October 14, 1989, El Paso.

Ross Moore threw the ball at one of the players. He ducked, and it hit the governor right in the stomach.

Cesar Arroyo
Student, 1935-1939

I was born in Parral, Mexico. My father was an accountant. He came from Spain when he was fifteen years old. He was a Spaniard from Bilbao. He studied and worked in Parral. My mother was half German and half Mexican, and [they] had thirteen children. While he was studying, [my father] worked in a merchandise store. A few years later he quit and put up a shoe factory. That prospered quite a bit, and he had a ranch near Parral.

[Pancho] Villa was after him all the time to get money from him [during the Mexican Revolution]. Finally, that's why he had to leave — our whole family had to leave — during the Revolution. I was about three years old when we left. That must have been 1914. He left alone from Parral to Ojinaga on a horse; he sent for the family later on. There was no trouble with immigration. There were a lot of people going into El Paso at that time; they just let them in. They took your name and a little information, and you were a resident. The Schaefers stayed behind. My grandfather, Felipe Schaefer, got along well with Villa and never had any trouble. My dad never did want to go back because Villa destroyed his home. I'm the only one who came back to Mexico.

73

[We lived] in Sunset Heights on Mundy Avenue. I went to grammar school at Vilas. I didn't speak any English; I learned it there. I picked it up fast. Then I went to [old] Morehead Junior High and El Paso High School. We had very good teachers, and they were very kind to us from Mexico. There wasn't any discrimination among the teachers. Some of the lower class people working in El Paso, they were discriminated [against] a little bit. A little discrimination is a big loss.

I took ROTC at El Paso High, but I didn't drill much. I was on the rifle team, and we spent our time shooting. I didn't go out much for sports there [because] I was working a delivery route. I had to go on a bus toward the smelter to pick up two big five-gallon cans of milk. I'd go on the bus and leave the empties and pick up the full ones. I had to do that about six o'clock in the morning, and then I'd deliver my route. I had to be at school at eight o'clock.

After I graduated, I worked for a year and a half before going to college. Bob McKee got me a scholarship with the New Mexico Aggies. I went there my first year and was captain of the [freshman] team, captain and quarterback. They had a good engineering school. I started to take mechanical engineering, but then the coach at Texas College of Mines offered me a better scholarship. I'd be at home, so that's when I changed schools. I went out [for football] a week or two, but then I was getting way behind on the labs, so I had to quit. I had too many labs. But I took part in basketball, track, and tennis.

[Pulls out 1938 *Flowsheet*.] When I was on the varsity basketball team, we had a lot of good athletes from Louisiana, back in the bayou country. They always had Copenhagen [snuff] in their mouths. Ross Moore* played. This boy [Salvador] Mora was a very good player, and [Riley] Matheson was too. He turned pro. I only made 43 points in the [1937-1938] season. Holliday Hall* is where we played. We traveled by bus, a college bus. We never did fly around the Southwest; it was either by bus or by car. We played Socorro and lost 33-24. New Mexico University — we lost that game too. We beat Tempe 42-35; Tempe beat us in another game. We lost to the University of Arizona. The Aggies beat us. Texas Mines — last place in the [Border] Conference! We didn't have a very good team.

We played in Chihuahua one year in a tournament for local teams. We won one and lost one here in Chihuahua. One of the games was awfully rough. The score was tied 50-50. Ross Moore went dribbling down the sidelines. The gym was packed, and [someone] stuck out his foot, and he tripped Ross Moore. That started a riot. The governor was there. Ross Moore threw the ball at one of the players. He ducked, and it hit the governor right in the stomach, the governor of Chihuahua. [It] hit him right on the stomach, so we had to leave. The coach asked me, "What'll we do, Cesar?" I said, "We'd better go."

When I was in track, I used to run the 100, the 200, and broad jump. Harry Phillips was the coach. And I played tennis. There were two boys from Monterrey [Rodolfo and Federico Villarreal] on the team. They were twins, but they didn't look alike. At one of the matches that we played against Arizona, this fellow [John] Beaty stuffed himself with sandies and a bunch of junk before the game. Boy, he was puking all over. We lost that match quickly.

[Pulls out a faded clipping from *The Prospector*, which reads:]

Feeling in a good humor we decided to pay tribute to someone this week in our sports column. After a bit of a search we selected Cesar Arroyo. . . . Cesar is that short, stocky, quiet individual who has all year managed to bear up under an engineering course on one hand and big athletic program on the other. He has worked hard at each one and has done well in both.

Overcoming the handicap of small size, a real handicap in this day of sports, Cesar has played basketball for the Miners and lettered. . . . Cesar was one of the hardest working men on the team, and he was hard to stop when shooting for the basket.

But if you think that Cesar was busy then, listen to this: track season came on and so did tennis. . . . He was a shark at tennis and was the leading man of an all-too small squad of dash men out for track. . . . Track and tennis meets often came on the same day, and Cesar would take part in both of them. He would run his hundred yard dash and then slip out of his spiked shoes into his best pair of tennis kicks and then meander on down to the courts to play his matches. Then it was back to the track to see if he was needed on a relay squad or in any other capacity.

Cesar kept that up for three years, and his grades are still average. For any athlete his grades are unusually good.

Mining [was my major], with a minor in geology. Dr. [John F.] Graham taught us metallurgy, and Prof. [F.H.] Seamon* taught chemistry. Lots of engineers were from Mexico, since it was cheaper to go to [TCM]. The Mexican mining schools were too far away. Tuition wasn't very high. In engineering we were pretty close together, the Anglos and the Mexicans, the Hispanics. We got along pretty well. We called the other [students] "Peedoggies."* John Holguin graduated six months before I did. He was a very good student, and he turned out to be one of the best mining engineers in Mexico. He lives in Torreon now.

My social life stayed usually on the weekends. In the evening they'd have a dance at school. On Oregon Street [was] a casino; it used to be the old Army "Y." They sold it to a group of Mexicans who converted it to a casino for dances. [John Holguin was president of] Phi Beta Mex. That was a Mexican fraternity. I was [a member]. Most of our dances were at the casino. That was where most of the Mexican people went to dances. Probably [there was] more drinking on the campus. You used to go outside Holliday Hall, take a swig, and go back in. They had their liquor in the car. It was the students that were taking other courses who had a better time at the dances. The engineers were more serious.

I remember one time I parked my brother's car, a great big ole Plymouth, right in front of the office of Dean [John W.] Kidd*. He came into class, and he says, "Who's got that big moose out there in front of my office?" I raised my hand. He said, "Get it out of there!"

At the time I got out of school there were quite a few jobs available. Very few of the Latin/Hispanic engineers stayed in the state, very few of them. Most came to Mexico. They were scattered all over Mexico. They started getting top jobs when [the mining companies] Mexicanized. That's when a lot of the Americans started moving out.

[I finished] in '39. Very few engineers finished in January of '39. When I changed from mechanical engineering to mining [engineering], I lost a few credits, so I actually was in college five years. [Graduation] was in May of '39. They only had commencement exercises once a year, so I had to come back for my diploma. [It was] at the Scottish Rite Temple, near the El Paso Public Library. [I changed majors because] I wanted to come back to Mexico. The best career was mining, and my dad had a few mining properties. They were originally sold to his aunt.

I wrote out three applications, and I got all three accepted. But I took the one up there in Santa Eulalia [above Chihuahua] because it was close to home. I worked there three years, and then I went to Santa Barbara with AS&R — American Smelting and Refining Company. I worked there until I got to be a mine foreman. I quit to go on my own. I started a small mine in about 1947 and worked about twenty years, small scale. I was cofounder and president of the equivalent to AIME in Mexico — Asociación de Ingenieros Metrologistas y Ecológicos en México.

After I quit mining on my own, I went back to Industrial Minera México, which was partly AS&R. I used to go out in the hills quite a bit to look at prospects that the company might take over. I was traveling a lot, riding a mule a lot, walking a lot. The last time I went out in the sierra, I was perspiring all the time. I was on a mule. I got soaking wet and caught a bad cold; it turned into a drunken pneumonia. That's when I quit. I was getting too old anyway to go down mines. These old abandoned mines, they're not safe. So I figured I should stop.

Interviewed in English by Charles H. Martin and Cheryl E. Martin, June 25, 1989, Chihuahua, Chihuahua, Mexico.

The deal was to grow a beard, but boy, the day after the dance, everybody took it off.

Pollard Rodgers
Student, 1936-1941

I went to high school at Barstow, Texas, near Pecos, about 200 miles from here. When I got out of high school — of course [it was] the depression — I worked three years on construction and saved enough to come to school. I lived in the dorm my first year. The dining hall was in the girls' dorm, so we'd walk across this rough ground. The pavement wasn't in.

[The student body] was so small that everybody knew everybody else. The profs knew you; you knew the profs. In fact the profs knew everything about you, which was fortunate in some ways, because we needed help. I mean, not on the school work, but financial help. It was still depression days, and sometimes these profs helped you out of their own pocket [with] a loan. I graduated as a mining engineer. At that time, what they tried to do in mining engineering was prepare you to go out to a mining district, an isolated mining district. So, my gosh, we had a first-aid course that was practically like a premed course. What Cap [John W. Kidd]* was so good on was teaching us practical things. I didn't realize it at the time. I realize it now. He instilled in us high standards.

I think one of my favorite Cap stories was: He had an eight o'clock class in surveying, and there were two students called the Mitcham twins,

79

who lived up the valley. Of course, they had a hard time getting to school for an eight o'clock class because they caught a ride. So they were usually late. Well, Cap didn't like anybody being late for his class, so one day he gave us this talk about that. "Now, boys, when you get out of here and you go to work in a mine, the cage to go down into the mine will leave at a certain time. If that cage goes down and you're not there, you've just lost a day's work." So, okay. A couple of days go by and the next eight o'clock class of Cap's, we were there, and the Mitcham boys weren't there. So old Cap got up and marched over to the door and slammed the door closed and locked it, and then he looked at the back of the door, and we'd printed this big sign, "The cage has gone down!"

Now, at that time there were lots of students here from Mexico. My gosh, nearly all the mining engineers in Mexico were graduates of the Texas College of Mines. A few years ago we had a little convention of our own down in Mexico City. Oh, that Salvador Treviño, that's the best friend I ever had. We've kept close contact through the years. Sal rounded up these Mexican graduates, and we had a real reunion. One night we got together for a banquet, and there must have been twenty-five people.

These Mexican engineers, they had a lot of stories, too, about Cap. And one of them was: There was this fellow Morales that Cap used most of the time to help him dynamite, and you've heard about all the dynamiting on the campus. Once in a while he'd need some help, so Morales would get two or three people. Now this is the way the Mexicans tell it. One day Cap called him in and said, "Morales, I've been looking over the list of these people that you have helping you, and I see Garcia, Valdez, so forth. I have to turn in this list. We're going to have to get an O'Reilly and a Jones and a Smith in here." But see, the Mexican engineers, they loved him, like we all did.

Dr. [Howard] Quinn* and [Lloyd A.] Speedy Nelson* were the Geology Department, just the two of them. They got such small allotments to carry on their work. One year Dr. Quinn had $700 available, and he was trying to hoard it so he could buy a couple of microscopes that he needed. You need lots of samples of minerals for mineralogy class, so when anybody graduated and went to work in a mine, Doc Quinn told them, "Well, send me a sack of every type of ore they're mining." And, of course, postpaid! Doc Quinn had some great big shelves that he'd found down in another building that were about ten feet high and twenty feet long. The students moved them from that building up to the third floor of Main. They were so long, to get one around the stairwells, you had to lift them up over. And we always said that moving those damn shelves was the hardest part of Doc Quinn's mineralogy course. But he was a great fellow and such a gentleman. I'd say Doc Quinn kind of smoothed off some of our rough edges and tried to get us to act more like gentlemen.

When I first was here, the library* was on the third floor of Kelly Hall. As I remember, it was just half of the floor. It wasn't much. Baxter Polk was the librarian, and one day when the new library was finished, he needed to move the books over to the [new building]. As soon as we heard about it, various ones of us started helping him. He had an old flatbed truck that he loaded some books on, but then a lot of it was just carried by hand. And anybody that came by the building, we hollered out the window to come up and get a load of books to take over there. My gosh, when I think about that new library they're getting now! There was practically nothing in that old Kelly. On the mining research, down at the Public Library, there were some good files. Engineers in the Southwest and Mexico had turned over their files to the Public Library. And, boy, they were real valuable. They were sure a big help to us.

Nearly everybody had some kind of a nickname at that time. There was a John who was a great big, heavy-set guy — not fat, just big. He worked up in Alaska a couple of years before he came to Mines. So somebody referred to him one time as "that Alaskan moose." Well, [the name] stuck, and to this day, any of us who know him call him "the Moose." Now Bill was a nickname for me, but this is how I wound up with the "Barstow Bill" nickname. When I first went [to Mines], there was another Bill Rodgers there. My gosh, with only those few students, there were still two of us! People were always getting us mixed up. But this fellow Trevino started calling me "Barstow Bill" Rodgers and the other one "Wink Bill" Rodgers.

Both of us were living in the dorm that first year. The phone rang one Sunday morning, and somebody hollered, "Hey, Bill, there's a phone call for you." So I went down and answered the phone. And this girl says, "Is that you, Bill?" I said, "Yes." And then, boy, she started chewing me out. Well, what had happened was that this other Bill Rodgers had a date with her to take her to a dance the night before, but he'd gone over to Juarez with some of his friends, and he missed picking her up. I think by the time he got to her house, she had given up and gone somewhere else. At any rate, she missed the dance. And I kept trying to tell her, "I'm not that Bill Rodgers." And boy, she never let up. She kept going. I don't know how they ever solved that, but later on they got married.

Oh, that poor Holliday Hall*. It was everything! We registered in the gym, and there was plenty of room for everybody, all 700 students. And, of course, the regular basketball was in there and all the physical education classes. It was [also] the only place, really, to have dances in. Seemed like nearly every Saturday night there was a dance in Holliday Hall. They had a school band that played dance music — the Varsitonians, they called them.

The student activities fee was ten dollars, [and for that amount] I think they listed twenty dances, thirty-two issues of *The Prospector, The Flowsheet,* six football games, and I don't know how many basketball games. It was optional, but nearly all the engineers paid that activity fee, because you had to pay that to vote in the student elections. At that time the academic students were already outnumbering the mining students, but the engineers still liked to hold the offices. So there was really a lot of politics.

There were a lot of girls that backed the engineers, and they called themselves engineers. There weren't any [girls] taking engineering at that time, but when some girl said, "Well, I'm an engineer," she meant she voted for the engineering ticket. Then it was turnabout [during contests for] the most popular girl or this or that. We backed them to the hilt.

Nobody had any money then. Gosh, it was unbelievable how poor everybody was. But we were all in the same boat, and we still had a great time. Now that Scientific Club was the student chapter of AIME, the American Institute of Mining and Metallurgical Engineers. They handled politics, the painting of the "M" on the mountain, and the Hard Luck Dance. Nearly anything to come along, well, they'd push it for the school.

We held the freshmen responsible for painting the "M" on the mountain, but, by gosh, everybody went there. Everybody. Right at the top of Scenic Drive where the lookout is, there's a path that goes right up to the mountain. And that's where we painted the "M." We usually got a water truck from the city, which the city never admitted loaning to the college students, but that's where it came from. To carry sacks of lime and barrels of water was a real job. You expected every freshman to be there, but actually everybody helped out, even including the girls. The Coed Association saw that there was some food and drink and so forth up there, and we'd have the picnic and all.

We used to have St. Patrick's up at Oro Grande at the old mines there. St. Pat's Day was to initiate the freshman engineers, but of course the girls went along. Each year we'd have the Hard Luck Dance. This was something that went way back with the early engineering days, and it was put on by the Scientific Club. And the deal was to grow a beard, but boy, the day after the dance, everybody took it off.

When my wife Pat was a student, the year '47-'48, we tried to take movie reels of activities through that year. At that time the stables were still up north of the Kidd Field, and the swimming pool wasn't covered, and they had the beauty contests. The students rode horseback on these little trails around the hills. Some of these movies showed where they had horseback musical chairs, where they'd ride the horses around in a circle. When the music stopped, well, they jumped off the horse to sit in a chair. And then they had the sombrero races, where they'd put these big Mexican hats on, and you raced your horse down to the line, but you had to get there wearing your hat. And at that time, too, there was a little golf course right where the Special Events Center is. It was kind of a draw there; it couldn't have had nine holes, but there were certainly five or six holes.

What I've always thought about so much is the closeness of everybody. All the students knew each other. Even after we graduated from there, we always tried to keep the old profs informed of what we were doing, and they had a real interest. If you came to Homecoming a few years after, well, these profs knew your wife's name. If you had some children, they wanted to hear about it, and the next time you saw them, they remembered the names of the children. Just unbelievable.

Interviewed by Rebecca Craver, February 14, 1984, El Paso.

I'd just go through the campus yelling "book return day!"

Baxter Polk
Librarian, 1936-1973

During the depression I graduated from high school in Abilene, Texas, in 1932. I wanted to go on to college, so I went to Hardin-Simmons University, which I thought was the best of the three colleges in Abilene. And I got a job as secretary to the librarian on the NYA [National Youth Administration] program, which is comparable to the Work-Study Program we have now. That's where I got interested in becoming a librarian.

At that time, Dr. D.M. Wiggins* was dean of Hardin-Simmons and a professor of education. Although I had not had a course with him, he used to come to the library to get books, and he always asked me to wait on him. In my senior year, he applied for and got the position as president of the then College of Mines. Before he left he said, "Baxter, what do you plan to do for your future? You have been so wonderful here in the library, and [I've been told that] you have such a potential for this profession. I really think that you ought to go on to library school." And I said, "Well, Dr. Wiggins, I just simply can't afford it. I don't have any money. I've got to get a job as soon as I graduate."

He said, "Baxter, how much money would you need to go to library school? Where would you go?" So I said, "Well, the closest one is the

University of Oklahoma." And he said, "Well, find out much it would cost to go there and let me know." I thought, "What is he up to?" It all sounded very encouraging. I looked into it, and I called Dr. Wiggins to tell him I had all the information that I needed about Oklahoma. So he came up to the library, and we decided I needed about $1,200. Well, he didn't really have the money himself, but he borrowed it from somebody on his own name and loaned me the money and promised me the job as librarian here when I got my degree. And all of that came true, just like a Horatio Alger story.

I came here in September, 1936, and took over the job as librarian at the College of Mines. Everything was rocks, greasewood, and cactus. It was *much* prettier than it is now, simply because they had left it in its natural state. We had blooming ocotillo, and we had blooming yucca and devil's crowns and all these beautiful things. They were all over the campus, on the hills. We just had trails; we didn't have sidewalks or paved streets. [There was] just the little mass of buildings up here on the hill, plus the president's home, which was on College Avenue. I believe College was paved. In between, there were just hills and rocks and stones and rattlesnakes. There really were snakes on campus at that time.

The lady whom I had replaced was pregnant. And in those days pregnant ladies were considered . . . well, you just didn't stay in a job until your *accouchement* was upon you. And this lady *did*. She stayed until the very last day and then had her baby the next. Well, in those days, when a lady went around with a swollen belly, people were embarrassed by it. It wasn't like it is today. We all accept the fact that children do indeed come out of their mothers. But this disgusted everybody, so she had to go. So when I came, I met Dr. [C.L.] Sonnichsen* on the campus. I guess he just realized that I was probably the new librarian, because they referred to me as "that kid running the library." Although I was twenty-two, I appeared to be about fourteen. So Sonnichsen came up to me and thumped me on the belly and said, "I hope you're not pregnant!" It just shocked me! That was my introduction to Sonnichsen.

At this time the library was on the top floor of what was then Kelly Hall, which became the Mass Communications Building [and today is Old Kelly]. The outside staircase on the west was the entrance to the library. And the reading room was on one end and the bookstacks on the other. I had a sliding panel between me and the kids. When we started getting things, we had no room to shelve them, so I'd pile things up by the wall in the reading room. And I'd go out there and say, "You roughnecks, keep your paddy paws off those things — they're valuable!" We were so *small* that that's the way we ran things. "Okay, Polk," they'd scream.

But they were very nice when it came to bringing their books back to the library, because I'd go through the dormitory on my way to work saying, "All books are due today!" I'd even call the names. "Albert, you have fifteen books overdue!" At that time the fine was a penny a day. And I'd just go through the campus yelling "book return day!" People would apologize, "Hey, Baxter, can I bring them back this afternoon? Will that be okay?" I'd say, "Get them in there before five o'clock." And we got our books back; everybody was friendly and nice. If we ever did have a problem, the kids were reasonable about it. I could call them in and say, "Now, look, you're keeping somebody else from these books," because we had so few.

Of course, the kids used to call me up from the dorm, where they were lying around drinking beer and smoking, to bring them a book. They'd call and say, "Hey, Bax, bring me so and so; I need it for a theme." They'd give me the title, and frequently I'd do it. Lazy so-and-so's! Then later on they'd take me out and buy me a beer or a sandwich. But it was fun, and I really had a good time. I was close to the students and close to the faculty.

When I first came to the campus, one of my favorite people was Captain John W. Kidd*. The poor man had this bad throat, and he kind of whispered. He came over one day and he said [in a hoarse whisper], "Baxter, are they treatin' ya right?" I said, "Cap Kidd, I don't know. Everybody's mad at me because I can't get any money for the library*, and I can't get the place straightened out. I don't have any help." The job was not considered a full-time job when I first came here. They made me teach four classes plus run the library with four student assistants. Yet people wanted the library to stay open more hours, because they had been closing at noon. I extended the hours until five o'clock in the afternoon. I had to teach these classes, grade papers, run the library. Oh, I was going out of my mind! So Cap Kidd went to bat for me, went over to Wiggins and said, "That young fellow over there is trying to do a good job; why don't you let him do it? Relieve him of all that teaching; give him some help!" He was just marvelous, and I was finally relieved of teaching. Everybody respected the man because he would say anything he felt like saying. The engineers absolutely adored him. They really did.

When we started to build this new building [now the new geology building] in 1936 and 1937, Cap Kidd was working with the engineers and the architects on the physical design of the building, because he was in charge of buildings and grounds. So he came over to ask me what I wanted. It was to be a combined Administration-Library Building. We had a WPA grant from the federal government to build the building. Do you know how much that old building cost? One hundred thousand dollars! We would go through the building when it was being constructed, and he'd get mad about something. He chewed tobacco, and he would spit on the walls to mark where he'd want something changed. And the workmen would say, "Well, Cap, what do we have to do now?" He'd say, "Go up there, and where I've spit tobacco juice, do it all over." And they'd look for the tobacco juice stains on the wall to put more plaster on some damn thing.

He was just a marvelous person. He lived in this little house up here on campus, because he was so honored and revered. And he used to give parties, and he'd roll up the rug and want to dance. He was just a short, pudgy, bald-headed man. Well, the four student assistants that I had were very pretty girls, and he had quite an eye for pretty girls. So he would invite me and tell me to bring my four pretty girls. And I'd say, "Now, girls, dance with him." His dancing consisted of getting up on the floor and just shuffling, flatfooted, back and forth from one end to the other. But these girls would all dance with him.

When I came here, we had 13,000 or 14,000 volumes. I recommended that for a college this size a basic collection of 100,000 volumes would be a good [start]. We *never* got it! We're still struggling. But you see, everything took priority over the library. Space and facilities were absolutely *lousy*. If he had gotten the volumes, we wouldn't have had any space to put them. We occupied the new building in '38, I believe. It was a combined Administration-Library, which was ridiculous because those two things are not compatible; they have *nothing* to do with one another. We had the top floor in the back annex. I called it a little carbuncle on the back of our neck. So we put up with that until 1956, when the administration built themselves a new building. It should have been the other way around.

People got very hysterical, particularly just before [World War II], because there was a great deal of Communist propaganda in this country. The Martin Dies Committee sent a group of people down here to check the curricula of all the public institutions and all the libraries for their holdings on pro-Communist literature. So the head of the school at that time, an acting president, came up in great panic and said, "Baxter, you better hide all these things you've got," because we were getting at that time the *Daily Worker*. I was not paying for it out of state funds. As a matter of fact, we weren't paying for it at all — the Communist Party was sending it free to libraries all over the country. I kept it because it was representative of that group of people. I thought everyone had a right to read. Well, he asked me to hide these things while that committee was here. I wouldn't do it, so he did it. He just gathered up all the publications, the current ones, and took them down to his office and locked them up, which I thought was ridiculous. But when the committee came and went, he brought them back.

But I didn't get into any kind of trouble at all. They looked at some of the faculty check-out files. I told them that this was confidential information. But this committee primarily wanted to see what certain people here were reading, particularly if they were in the classroom teaching, and whether or not they were promoting any of this propaganda in their classrooms. I protested very strongly, but these people said they had every right because they were federal agents and appointed by the federal government to do this. So I just sat there and let them do it. I don't know what they came up with; nobody got in trouble. But I was branded later by the community as a "pink."

We had other things come up. When the John Birch Society came into existence, I accepted all their publications from a lady here in town who would bring them to me. She just brought the packages of publications and dumped them and said, "Baxter, I'm just amazed that you would accept these things, because you're such a liberal, such a pink." I said, "I'm taking this stuff, and I'm going to put it on the shelf, but I assure you I'm not going to read it. I'm taking this stuff because it represents a bunch of *nuts* in this country and what they think." Of course the McCarthy era was *very* bad because there were people who were self-appointed censors, and they would come around, talk to you, and try to find things.

Censorship takes all kinds of forms. There were lots of people who objected to miniskirts, pantsuits, and particularly hot pants, which I never liked either. I was told that I should absolutely make it a rule that the people working here should wear dresses at least down to their knees, or just above the knees, and no pants. And I said, "Good heavens, I can't dictate to these people what they wear. I don't allow them to come to work in bathing suits or barefoot, and that's as far as I can go on restricting this."

I have enjoyed what I've done here. It's been rewarding for me. People have been extremely good to me and extremely tolerant of me. I have liked El Paso. I liked the Spanish-Mexican-Indian elements here. I felt that I melted into the community. And I feel that I am as equally loved among the minorities as I am among the majorities, whoever they are. I don't know which is which anymore. [Incidentally] I employed the first full-time black on the staff at UTEP. The personnel section at the time was very upset. Quite a number of people were. Some of the faculty were horrified. One faculty member came over to ask this girl if she were French. She was quite dark, and she said, "No, I'm Negro." And of course that just [really] upset that person.

This school was not terribly friendly toward people with what they called Spanish surnames at that time. You didn't find many of them on the faculty. Texas was still coming from the Revolution. There's still a problem. But it would have remained the way it was if a few people like myself and others had not been bold enough to sound off about it, and just simply say, "It's grossly unfair, and you're letting a lot of talent go to waste." Well, I think I am loved by those groups. I have some good enemies, too, and I intend to keep them!

Interviewed by David Salazar and Mildred Torok, April 27, May 4, 1973, El Paso.

He jumped back! So did the rest of us! And the alli-
gator then started trying to get under his desk.

William S. Strain
[1909-1986]
Faculty, 1937-1974

In August, 1937, I came here as director of the museum and an instructor in geology. I taught geology laboratories and ran the museum as a combined sort of thing. I had the museum job until 1946 and [eventually became full-time in] the Geology Department, and I remained there until I retired in '74.

When we came here we knew all the faculty, and I knew most of the students. I see students now that tell me they were on the campus at such and such a time. Maybe they majored in English, but I remember them, though I didn't have them in class, [because] the school was so small. The Co-op was a bookstore up in the east end of the ground floor of Old Main. Everybody met in the Co-op. You got your mail in there, and so everybody sooner or later went into the Co-op almost every day. You saw everybody on the campus. That's one of the reasons you got to know them so well.

The kids pulled a lot pranks in those days. They engineered quite a few things around campus, and their initiations were always a bit color-ful. They'd dress up the boys in all sorts of outlandish getups, and they'd send 'em downtown to beg [or] to try to catch a carp in a pond down there that they had with the alligators. Some of the APOs [Alpha Phi Omega*] were mixed up in the stunt. They had one member who was a geology student, Herbert Tune. Herbert could play the guitar a little bit. So, when they initiated him, they gave him his guitar, put some dark glasses on him, and put him downtown with a tin cup. They had him walking up and down the streets singing songs. Anyway, he collected quite a bit of money. Every time he'd get a little money in his cup, half full or something, why the upper classmen would go take the money out and duck into the nearest beer joint and have a beer. Somebody saw this and turned them in to the police, and they arrested them for robbing a blind man! That sort of thing was pretty common.

I was standing behind Dr. [Howard E.] Quinn* the morning he opened the door, and the alligator was in his office. The kids were always playing jokes on Dr. Quinn. He carried a running banter with them, and of course they'd do their best to get even with him somewhere. So they went down to the Plaza and got an alligator about six feet long and put him in his office overnight. When Dr. Quinn came in the next morning, I had a question I wanted to ask him. I met him at his door, and he opened the door, and here was this big ole alligator's mouth going "krssshhh." He jumped back! So did the rest of us! And the alligator then started trying to get under his desk. Dr. Quinn had a very expensive microscope sitting out on the corner of the desk, and he was afraid the alligator would knock it off and break it. So he slammed the door and called the authorities, and they sent the [city] park people out. The park people tied the alligator up [and] hauled him back to the park.

On St. Patrick's Day the students used to go up to Oro Grande and have their initiations in the old abandoned mines there. They would always set off dynamite on the hills around the campus, about five o'clock in the morning, to start St. Pat's. And they got a lot of complaints about that after they built [Providence] Hospital. They frightened the patients over there.

I think what maybe finally capped it for us was they got off a pretty good shot in behind Old Main, over on that hill, and it was a little overdone and knocked out a bunch of their windows. I think that's the last time we ever shot the dynamite. Well, the police caught them a time or two with dynamite in the cars, and they thought it was pretty dangerous, which it was. On the other hand, they forgot that these students took courses in explosives. They knew what they were doing. And a number of them helped [Dr. John W.] Cap Kidd*. Cap Kidd was an explosives expert, to the extent that he blasted out rocks under Old Main while they continued to have classes in there. And nobody, as far as I know, ever stopped a class. Cap was a real good "powder monkey," as they called them in the mining business. I never heard of anything getting away from Cap to the point that it did any damage.

Cap Kidd had tuberculosis. He had a funny, peculiar little high-pitched voice. As I understand it, the disease affected his voice, and he came here for his health. Dr. [B.F.] Jenness* was another person who came to El Paso with tuberculosis. Mrs. Jenness brought him to Alpine, Texas, on a stretcher, and they lived in a tent. He regained his health, and they came to El Paso. They hired him at the College of Mines as a school doctor. The interesting thing about it is he lived to be ninety-six. Dr. Jenness is a shining example of someone who came out here expecting to die, was near death, and lived to be way up in his nineties.

Dr. [D.M.] Wiggins* interviewed me for the job out here. One of my professors at the University of Oklahoma had told him that he thought I would make a good research man. Dr. Wiggins said, "Now, I want you to know that we don't want you to do any research. We want you to teach." And so what research we did in those days, we would just get on our own time and bootleg, so to speak. But it is certainly vastly different now. Research is an extremely important thing in the university system. This worked a hardship on some of us, too, because later on they wanted to see what you published. Well, in a lot of those years you didn't publish anything. You couldn't! And they didn't want you to, but people didn't understand that.

We had heavy loads in those days. I had as many as twenty-five contact hours a week. That's just the way everybody did it in those days. We went up there at eight o'clock and we stayed until five o'clock every darn day. And we went until noon on Saturdays. They wanted you to devote your full time to teaching, which I think was all right in those days. I think the energy should have been strictly on teaching. I'm not too sure [but] that we put too much emphasis on research now and we ought to put more emphasis on teaching.

[In] the earlier days, our mining engineers and geologists were practically all from out of town. As a matter of fact, we trained nearly all the mining engineers in Mexico for a good many years. And up until about now, most of the mining engineers in Mexico were trained here. Salvador Trevino is a good example of that. So our numbers from El Paso were relatively small in those days. But then the town grew, and the school grew with it, especially on the academic side. It burgeoned because the city was growing so rapidly.

Dr. Wiggins didn't want the school to be large. He said one time in fact that he didn't want to see this school ever get to be more than 2,500. Well, that would be a controllable unit, I'm sure. So in those days they weren't very farsighted, as far as campus expansion. At that time they could have bought a lot of that property which is between the University and North Mesa now for very cheap prices, but they didn't buy it. They didn't think we were going to expand that much. To get it now would be terribly expensive.

When I came, the museum was just really the bare walls. I was the first curator they had. For a long time the museum had a tough time, because it wasn't one of these things that developed from funds at the University. It was forced on the College in a way. When the State of Texas gave the money — $50,000 — to El Paso for a museum for the Texas Centennial, there was a great squabble about how to spend the money. The city wouldn't take it, wouldn't agree to perpetuate. The county wouldn't take it, wouldn't agree to perpetuate. The Pioneer Association had a collection; they'd like to have it, but they couldn't agree to perpetuate.

So the College of Mines agreed to perpetuate, and that's how it got out there. Some of the administrators had said they wished to goodness we didn't have it, because we didn't want to spend the money on it. It was hard to try to convince them that the new museum had teaching value. And every time we got a new president, why, we had to go into another campaign to try to convince him of the value of the museum. We didn't have much money to run the museum when I was over there. My maximum annual budget was a little over $2,000, and I had to hire students for janitors.

[During] the days when I was running the museum, upstairs in the right wing, that would be the northeast wing, Miss [Vera] Wise* of the Art Department was in one room, and in the opposite wing, upstairs on the left side, which would be northwest, Jackie Williams was the voice teacher. And I had a terrible time with those women in the wintertime. Jackie would go up there, and she wanted to sing and keep singing. They wanted fresh air, so they'd open all the windows. Miss Wise would come downstairs [and say that] her kids were up there with their hands wet, and they were freezing to death. Oh boy, did I ever have a hard time! I couldn't keep both satisfied to save my soul. Miss Wise wanted it warm, and Jackie wanted it cold. The poor ole boiler wasn't big enough to handle it.

During World War II, troops were over there at Mt. Cristo Rey guarding those railroad bridges. Because we were so close to Mexico, they feared planes might fly in from the West Coast or down in Mexico and bomb those bridges. If they did that, they would destroy all the east-west traffic across the southern United States. With Fort Bliss being a very important military base, there was a tremendous amount of rail traffic in and out, moving troops and bringing in equipment. So these bridges really were important targets.

They had machine-gun nests all around and observation posts, so that if any plane flew over, it would be identified. Any person who went out there had to identify himself. I found some little coral [fossils] out there before the war, and I wanted to go back to find some more. They had a command post down across the street from the cement plant, right on the road there. I went down there and talked to the corporal, and he called the officer of the guard. They finally told me I could go up to the place I wanted to go, which was around Cristo Rey Road. There was another machine-gun nest up there, and I reported to those fellows and told them what I wanted to do. I went down about 200 yards or so to reach the locality I wanted to go to. All the time I felt like I was looking right down the barrel of a machine gun.

After the war was over, oh, my stars! We were swamped with people going to school on the GI Bill. And it was the best group of students we ever had. Those people had been out in the world, and they'd come back to school, and they knew why they were here and what they wanted. They got in there and got after it. We had some awfully fine students. Some of these people now are prominent; they're presidents and vice presidents of oil companies and mining companies. They were a fine group of people. They had the intelligence to start with, but they had motivation when they came back. It was the best group of students we ever had at this university.

The vets and their village were down there where the multi-story dormitories are. They had a bunch of old barracks, and they transported them over to the campus and made housing apartments for married students. They also brought some old two-story, barracks-type buildings and put them on the campus where the present Fine Arts Center is. They were wooden structures. Everybody was scared to death they'd burn down. Fortunately, they didn't. But a lot of the people going to school on the GI Bill lived down there in those old apartments, and they served us very well for a number of years.

Charlie Steen* is one of our old illustrious graduates of some fame. He discovered uranium up in Utah and developed a national reputation. He was selected Outstanding Ex, and the Outstanding Ex made a speech, which was customary. But his speech was a little off-color, to say the least. He used some rather common, ordinary, mining-type terms, which you don't usually hear in polite society. You see, they had changed the name of the school [from College of Mines to Texas Western]. Charlie and others were terribly upset about it, because they felt that we had a fine reputation as a mining school all over the world and [that] the school had lost its identity when they changed the name. And then when they did away with the mining program, that capped it, and we lost a lot of loyal ex-student support.

The way this thing was written, it was the School of Mines. And then the town grew, and people who couldn't afford to go away would come to school out there, and they wanted a broader program. One thing that brought about the name change is a lot of people who graduated out there wanted their degrees recognized in a different way from that of a mining school. They had liberal arts backgrounds. They felt that with a liberal arts background, a degree with a mining school didn't give them the recognition they should have. So that side of the campus outgrew the mining people. That was the reason the tail got wagging the whole school, and so they changed the name. That precipitated an ill feeling to begin with. Then Dr. [Joseph M.] Ray* did away with mining school entirely, because the number of enrollees dropped to a point where it wasn't economical to keep the program going. The engineers started painting the green line after they changed the name. It went from over by Quinn

Hall right across the campus. It cut off the engineering and geology parts on the west side of the campus from the other side, [whose students] they called Peedoggies*.

When we came here, Dr. Wiggins was living down on Montana Street. The faculty used to go down there for the Sun Carnival. They'd have coffee and doughnuts and stuff, and we'd sit out there and watch the [parade]. Then the University bought the old house just across the street, [to the] south, from the present Student Union. There was a homestead in there. At one time it had been used as a house of ill repute. The University bought it and moved the president up to that house. I guess they tore down that old house to build the present Liberal Arts Building.

I don't know what people in general thought about the architectural style of the first library building*, the "Hay Barn." Nearly everybody I talked to was dissatisfied because they thought it ruined our motif. But I noticed that with all the newer buildings they have gone back to at least some elements that have a hint of the original architecture. The new library building is out-and-out Bhutanese. It really has given our campus a distinction that few campuses have. The type of buildings we have and how they fit nicely into the setting is unique. There's not another one in the country like it.

Interviewed by Rebecca Craver, November 1, 1983, El Paso.

*So what do you do with Golddiggers when there is
no football team?*

Catherine Burnett Kistenmacher

Student, 1944-1948

When I began [in 1944] it was a woman's college for sure, because
there were 400 girls and 100 boys. These boys were the seventeen-year-
olds who were not yet eligible for the draft, some veterans, and a few
4-F's. That was the era of gasoline rationing, and not many people had
a car. That's why we depended on the bus to get us to campus, or we
carpooled. If we took the Highland bus, we got off on Arizona Street and
Mesa. These were the good old days when the motorists were extra friendly,
and if they had a gallon of gasoline they wanted to share it with as many
people as they could. Motorists would see a lot of college kids standing
around, and they would just stop for us and take us up the hill to college.
It was wonderful.

I started majoring in journalism because I planned to go into advertising. That was when Judson Williams* was dean of students at the college. He had the brilliant idea to go around the various businesses in
El Paso, including the American Furniture Company, the Popular Dry
Goods Company, and KTSM. He asked if they would offer cooperative
scholarships to some of the graduating seniors from high school. And
they said yes. That gave me a chance to apply for the scholarship in which

I was interested, and that was advertising. I won a four-year scholarship from the Popular Dry Goods Company. I had labs there to learn advertising all four years that I was in college, and then on the holidays and during the summer I had a job waiting for me if I wanted to work. So it was really great.

When I was a freshman, we didn't have a football team, [because] this was right in the middle of the war. There wasn't anything for the Golddiggers to pep for. So what do you do with Golddiggers when there is no football team? We went and sang for the soldiers out at Beaumont Hospital. Mainly because we did not have a very good instructor in the Journalism Department, my sophomore year I changed my major to art. Vera Wise* was head of the Art Department. I learned watercolor under her and am still partial to it, and that's what I paint in today, watercolor.

[On campus] the students congregated in front of the Co-op. It was actually just the bookstore, and it was located in the end of Main Building. That was the place where you went to buy your books, and they also had soda pops and sandwiches, which weren't very good. I don't know who supplied them with the sandwiches; they were always wrapped and rather tasteless. But they filled the bill if you hadn't brought your sack lunch from home. You went to the Co-op to socialize, and in our El Paso weather, most of the time we sat out on that wall in front of the Co-op to talk and visit.

We wore what was in style at that time, and that was bobby socks and saddle oxfords and skirts and sweaters. We certainly didn't ever wear blue jeans — that would've been unheard of. Nor would we have considered wearing any type of trousers; the women just didn't wear any kind of slacks of anything to the campus then. That was just not the thing to do.

The sororities were quite active on campus then. We had three: Tri Delta, Zeta [Tau Alpha], and Chi Omega. The Chi Omega and the Tri Delt lodges were next door to each other [where the present Education Building is located], and the Zetas* were on the other side of the campus. We never permitted any boys [inside] the sorority lodge. If they wanted to come to pick up their date or their girlfriend, they would come to the front door, and whoever answered the front door would say, "Well, just a minute, I'll call her." But he could not come into the house or into the foyer or anything. That was one of the rules I best remember about the sorority. I pledged Chi Omega when I was a freshman and went all through four years with the sorority. This was a good thing, especially [my freshman year] when not too much was happening on the campus, because with [only] 500 students you don't have too much going on.

Our social life centered around the campus. We used to have dances at Holliday Hall*. When I was a high freshman, the Chi Omegas sponsored a dance that had a circus theme, and it was really quite nice. Our colors were yellow and red, so we draped streamers from the very top and brought them out as a giant circus tent. Then we decided that we would have horses like a real merry-go-round, and I drew all of the different horses that were on this merry-go-round. Well, if you can, visualize this giant tent, with the streamers establishing the size of it, and then all of these horses going around as if it were a giant merry-go-round. It was beautiful.

I guess it was the spring of my sophomore year when the war ended. All the men started coming back, which was nice, because then we could have a football team, and the Golddiggers could actually be a pep squad and march as they were supposed to do, instead of singing. The enrollment at the college went up tremendously, and we had many, many veterans on the campus. They brought a note of seriousness to the campus. Some of the students felt that they didn't pay enough attention to campus life as such. Maybe they took some of the fun and joy out of going to college. A few of them were bitter, you might say, but the majority of them seemed to fit in very well.

I was in the pioneer radio class at the college. Never before had they had any radio instruction, and KTSM gave us their old equipment. We had all of these wonderful turntables and consoles that they gave us, plus they gave us our first radio instructor, who was Virgil Hicks*. Well, our mascot is *el burro,* and I guess it was primarily my idea to put this program on the air is if *el burro* was talking. In this day and time they wouldn't like it because *el burro* had a Mexican accent, but it was so funny. He'd interview some of the students, and then we would play music. Once a week we aired it, and it was good experience to teach us copy writing and how to put a program together.

All campuses have their politics, but in those days you were either an academ or an engineer. Even the sororities were lined up accordingly. At first, the Chi Omegas voted with the academs. Then something came about that they didn't like, and they changed their allegiance to the engineers, and for the rest of the time the Chi Omegas voted engineer. Whoever the candidates were that the engineering party was running, that's how we voted.

Our classes were on Monday-Wednesday-Friday, or they were on Tuesday-Thursday-Saturday. Now, there weren't any labs scheduled for Saturday afternoon, but we still had classes on Saturday mornings. We went to school six days a week. I was busy. For instance, when I was a freshman, I had a chemistry lab. Then I would go to the Popular the other afternoons and learn layout and copy and things like that. Then during my succeeding years I used to actually prepare ads for the Popular. Besides advertising in the *Times* and *Herald-Post,* they did a lot of advertising in *El Continental* and *El Fronterizo,* which are two [Spanish-language] newspapers. By my junior year I was doing a lot of the actual ad preparation for these papers. I really got, in my labs, what the course itself meant and what I would be doing later on, because I had a job waiting for me as soon as I graduated.

Interviewed by Rebecca Craver, March 20, 1984, El Paso.

Vet Village was for married GIs, but it was heaven. We had a beautiful view of the cement plant and ASARCO.

John A. Phelan
Student, 1945-1948

We really had a congenial group out there. Our friends that we made there are lasting friends.

Elouise L. Phelan
Student, 1946-1947

John: I had been a newspaper reporter before I went to war, and I really planned to go to the University of Missouri and get my degree. While I was a patient at Beaumont Hospital, and I wasn't real sure what I wanted to do, I took a creative writing course with Dr. Burgess Johnson. This was in 1945. He was a visiting professor. I was taking him home one afternoon after class, and he pointed at Mt. Franklin, and he said, "You see that mountain? That's a beautiful mountain." And I said, "You know, I guess you're right. I never really thought about that." And maybe that was the beginning, because it was a beautiful mountain, and somehow that mountain attracted not only me and my family but so many other people here.

103

Anyway, I was getting rather restless at the hospital because they were operating on me about every six weeks, and I had nothing to do. I thought I would like to go back and take another course, a few courses, anything to transfer to Missouri. My doctor, Willard Schuessler, encouraged it, so I and some of my friends in the burn ward went out and got in line [to register]. Dr. [C.L.] Sonnichsen* got ahold of me, and I told him what I wanted to do, and he said, "Well, why don't you take fifteen hours? You can transfer all of them. No need to waste your time." So we sat down together and looked at the curriculum, and I saw there was a course in radio. I thought that a newspaper reporter ought to really know something about his competition, so I took radio more or less as an elective. That was the beginning: the mountain and Dr. Johnson and my doctor and Dr. Sonnichsen.

I hadn't been in class too many weeks [when] KTSM needed somebody as a night man in the news department. So I came down here and worked at night in the news department for a dollar an hour. Of course, I've been here ever since. I wound up getting a degree in journalism and radio broadcasting, and I never gave another thought to the newspaper business.

Here I am — someone who's not planning to go there — and [I wind] up with an entire career because of the school, quite honestly. Not only me but a lot of my friends also got their degrees there. We were still in uniform, going to school [while] patients of Beaumont, and bandaged up a lot of the time because of operations and various things. It was a little difficult sometimes for us to get out in public, but the school just eliminated all of that and took us in and really helped us to rehabilitate ourselves in a rapid manner. When the war was over and I was back in school, I realized that I really wanted to do something for myself and my family. All [the returning veterans] felt the same way. We were quite different [than before the war]. We had grown up a lot faster than some of the other people. In 1945 I was all of twenty-four years old, but I was a very old twenty-four.

Our oldest son was born during the war in 1943 out in San Diego, and our second son was born in Beaumont Hospital in July of '46. Elouise and I [and the two boys] had been living in an apartment. We heard about Vet Village being constructed [on the campus], and we applied. The first thing were the trailers. And back in 1945 and 1946 a trailer was really a trailer. A mobile home today is a mobile home. That was a trailer; believe me, it was a trailer. Now, we couldn't get our family in a trailer, plus the fact they didn't have any available to us. So we just waited until they built the apartments.

We lived in Apartment 17-A, two bedrooms. Elouise and I had a bedroom. The two boys had a bedroom with bunk beds. We had a bath, a living room-dining room in front, and a kitchen. That was it. I had an old replica of a bomb I hung out over the front porch with the address on it. During one heavy snowstorm one winter, the snow came through the cracks in the windows. But it was a lot better than most of us had been living in, because housing was acutely short, and you took what you could get. Another thing, the people in town used to give furniture to the young couples out there. They didn't give it to Goodwill Industries or the Salvation Army. They gave it to us. Boy, it was great!

Elouise: That apartment was a mansion to me, because I had a bedroom for the boys and our bedroom and a kitchen. The kitchens were quite nice. They did put new sinks in for us, and the stoves were new when we moved there, and the iceboxes were adequate. We had iceboxes in the beginning, but the second year we bought a refrigerator.

The buildings were wooden, and the floors were wooden. I do not know who came up with the idea of putting linseed oil on the floors! We didn't have any kind of a rug, no carpeting, or anything at the beginning. I remember this oil was black, and my children's pajamas just would get so dirty. Well, finally we bought linoleum and put it on the living room, and I believe we put some in the children's room.

John: Vet Village was for married GIs, but it was heaven. We had a beautiful view of the cement plant and ASARCO. It was a beautiful sight to see that slag when they'd pour it and to see the trains come by, and I'm not being facetious. We had a view of something. We could see the mountains. We never complained about anything. We were just grateful to have it.

In 1948 *Parade* magazine wrote an article on us as young married couples living in Vet Village and how we looked upon our marriage and how it affected our marriage by working and going to school. Elouise and I were one of the couples. We'd all get together and help one another, and we'd put yards in for each other and grass. We'd borrow a truck and borrow shovels. We'd go down to the river and dig up the riverbed and bring it back, and we'd build yards with grass. We'd go get stones and make stepping stones, put up a picket fence and a gate and paint it. This was fun for us. This was our first real, honest-to-goodness home since getting out of the service. We were one big, happy family. The girls thought we ought to have a nursery, so we went out and begged and borrowed material and [combined] skills, and we built a nursery. We were donated the material, and we built it. Then we hired a babysitter to take care of all the little kids. I'd say that was a cooperative effort. We had a washeteria, and the girls used that. It was a very happy existence, believe me. It was fun.

Elouise: We had a little grocery store between Vet Village and Paisano, which was [within] walking distance if we needed milk or bread. I think the [owner's] name was Bustamante. We could just run down there and get what we needed, but the last week of the month we probably didn't have the money to go down there and buy what we needed. We had a limited income. The last week of the month many of us would run out of certain staples, but we could always go to our neighbors. We did a lot of borrowing. We'd go to a neighbor and say, "Well, I've got the meat. Do you have spaghetti?" We'd get together, and we'd come up with a pretty good meal.

One thing about us, we were all in the same boat — poor. Most of the husbands worked, and we wives would get together and play bridge or just visit in the evenings. On the weekends we would have covered-dish suppers and have lots of fun. We always took the children, and we'd gather in somebody's yard. We had a yard, and John even put up a picket fence around it. We would sit out on this small, little porch and in the yard. We enjoyed that view of the mountains and the area very much. Frances Humphrey lived across the road. Both our husbands worked at night. We would put her little boy to bed, and because my yard had grass, I can remember sitting there on that grass many an evening just visiting until the husbands would get off from work. My children would be asleep, and she would watch them while I'd run down to the station and pick John up.

John: When you're young you can do a lot of things. We all studied hard. I'd shut this place [KTSM] down at 11:30 at night and then get home by midnight. Usually I didn't try to study at midnight. I'd go right to bed. [I'd] get up at six o'clock in the morning when I was fresh and clear, and I'd do my studying. That's the way I operated. We had to study on the weeknights and Sunday, but on Saturday, that was our night to really have a good time together. Somehow we'd manage a case of Mitchell's beer, and the girls would bring covered dishes, and that was our party.

I became a fraternity man. I was in SAE, and many of my GI friends were SAEs. We were not accustomed to politics at the collegiate level, and at one fraternity meeting the eminent archons of our fraternity announced who we were going to support for student body president. They didn't ask us who we'd like to support. They just told us who the fraternity was going to support. I would say we were the activists of our time, and we didn't think that was the democratic way to do it. So we got together, and we decided we'd put our own candidate up against our own fraternity candidate. Our own candidate was Raymond "Sugar" Evans, who was the star tackle on the football team.

Of course, the engineers had their candidate, and it became a three-way race, and that's when it really heated up. I was the campaign manager. The women would make cakes and various things, and we'd have rallies. Once we conned a dance band to come down and play at a big rally. Come election day we lined up the entire football team at the polls, and they all voted one way. Well, to make a long story short, our candidate Sug pulled more votes than the other two put together. He was an independent, and it was the first time, I think, at Texas College of Mines [that an independent candidate won the presidency]. We were proud of that because the students rallied around us.

I don't know how it all came about, but [I became mayor of Vet Village]. Later my friend Sug Evans became the mayor. As mayor of that village, my most immediate contact was with Gene Thomas* of the Engineering Department. Now, everybody was scared of Gene. He was a little rough on the outside. He was crusty and growled a lot. I was the go-between between the administration, being Gene Thomas, and Vet Village. But Gene and I hit it off just great, and in later years he and I became very close friends. Gene got us a lot of things down there that we probably wouldn't have gotten from somebody else.

Everybody's life is changed not by one but a series of events and a series of people. I believe that very strongly. You don't get where you are without somebody helping you. Nobody gets there on his own. No such thing as a self-made man. A person that probably had as much influence [on me as anybody] at that school was Clarice Jones in Speech. I had a really burning desire to be an announcer, [but] I had grown up in Galveston, and I had an accent that you could cut with a knife. I said "dese" and "dose" and "Toity Toid" street. I didn't know how to say "I." I said "Ah." And I didn't know how to say "running." I said "runnin'." I didn't know how to say "room." I said "rum." Everything that was bad I said, because it was a combination of Brooklyn, New Orleans, and Deep South.

Clarice got ahold of me in a phonetics class, and I probably worked harder on that than anything. I managed to correct it to the point where I could continue a career as an audio person in radio and TV. But that's a contribution of that school, you understand? That's what it did for me. And then Virgil Hicks* [allowed me] to practice play-by-play football with a wire recorder. Then on Sunday mornings I'd get my football player friends up there with me. We'd listen to it, and they'd critique it. That's how I learned to do play-by-play. But I'd have never gotten that shot if I hadn't have had the facilities and the encouragement to do it. That's helped me tremendously in my career. I owe that school a lot, believe me.

Elouise: We really had a congenial group out there. Our friends that we made there are lasting friends. We still keep up with the ones out of town, and when they come to Homecoming we're always so glad to see them. We really try to keep up with each other. I think that this experience has been such a great blessing because we were all so happy. Our husbands had been to war and had come back, and we didn't realize that we were doing without anything. We were just happy people all in the same boat, very thankful that we had a place to live and very thankful that our husbands had the GI Bill to complete their education.

John: We moved out [of Vet Village] in the fall of '48. I was [sorry], particularly because the rent was so low. We were able to buy a home. I had $200 cash and a GI loan, and I was able to get it for nothing down. The $250 cash paid some back taxes on it. I paid $7,800 for our first home. That was a step up, you see. Everything from Vet Village, for most of us, was a step up.

We were the beginning of changing the nature of the school. I graduated in '48, and it was 1949 when they changed the name to Texas Western College. So I got one of the last diplomas that says Texas College of Mines and Metallurgy. And my oldest son got the last one that said Texas Western College.

Interviewed by Rebecca Craver, February 20 and 24, 1984, El Paso.

Part II:
Texas Western College
1949-1967

Fernando Valenzuela said it. . . . "In sports you win and in sports you lose, but in education you only win." And it's so true; it really is.

Rudy Tellez
Student, 1948-1952

I was born at home in 3222 Frutas Street. My mother was afraid to go to the hospital. She didn't want them to give her the wrong kid. That's the way my mother was. I went to Beall grammar school, Vilas grammar school, and Dudley grammar school; I went one year to El Paso High School. My mother and I moved to California, and then I came back and graduated from El Paso High.

I entered this college primarily because they had a very good radio department. And since the age of nine I knew exactly what I wanted to do. I wanted to be a radio announcer. When I was a kid I used to listen to the radio full blast, and I loved my imagination. There was no television then, so I would tune in all the radio programs I could. There was "Jack Armstrong the All-American Boy" and "Lux Presents Hollywood" and "Inner Sanctum." That's growing up with imagination!

I'm Chicano, in the true sense of the word. I'm born in this country of Mexican parents and spoke Spanish at home, learned English at school. But like young kids who speak Spanish, I didn't like my accent, so I practiced. I got every newspaper I could and read it out loud so that I could try to sound like the radio announcers that I heard on KTSM and on

111

NBC. So my dream was to [be like them]. My dream was also that some-how along the way I would be able to leave my own mark in this business.

When I graduated from El Paso High I came right to the College of Mines. I got a music scholarship from this college, and I've always felt grateful for that. I played in the orchestra; I played in the band; I was the drum major my last year. You know, the guy with the tall hat, with a baton, and all those pretty girls marching behind him. I was a sight, I'll tell you. I loved that.

We had the radio department in Kelly Hall, at the top of the hill. I found a marvelous, wonderful instructor there in Mr. Virgil Hicks*. A lot of equipment wasn't state of the art. It was gift to the art, because radio stations would give it to the college. In my sophomore year I began to get the practical application of working at the radio station. I went on the air on KVOF, the [college] FM station, [which] was heard only on campus. Then we got a ten-watt [transmitter], and you could hear it maybe a mile away. I guess I was born with a certain vibration in the voice, and it seemed to please the microphone. I didn't come out scree-chy, and I didn't come out with an accent. I worked as many hours as I could at the station. That experience at KVOF, pulling a shift, reading commercials, playing records, doing a program, was the singular most important thing for me in my career.

Forty-eight through '52 we saw the "end of innocence," I think. I don't know if I could go through college with all the [temptation] that's available today. When I was going to college here, I remember participating with all the other guys, and the thing of the year . . . was panty raids! That was the thing to do. And we were foolish enough to try it. I was also a member of the drama club; I was in every musical thing there was. There were lots of sororities and fraternities around. I did not join a frater-nity, and I never felt lesser than anyone else. Later on I was asked to join the Tekes [Tau Kappa Epsilon], primarily because my mother ran the Teke house. I became an honorary member.

I don't remember in my entire life ever being degraded except once, and that's when I went looking for a job at a radio local station. The guy said to me, "What would you say if I told you that I wouldn't hire you because your name is Tellez?" It shocked me. I never heard that before. I said, "Well, to tell you the truth, I'd feel sorry for you." He said, "What do you mean?" [I said,] "You might miss the chance of working with someone who really could do a good job for you." By the way, I got the job, but that's the way I answered. That's the only time I remember that ever happening to me.

There were three professors who [really] inspired me: Virgil Hicks in the radio department, Dr. [C.L.] Sonnichsen*, and Dr. [Eugene] Porter*, my history professor. Those three men, through their "one-on-ones" with me, inspired me and got my imagination cooking. Porter ran a strong, hard class. He wouldn't put up with any B.S. He would sit there, and he would make it interesting. His knowledge impressed me tremendously. He would talk about Russia, and when I left the room I would feel like I had been a part of that somehow. He made history come alive for me in a way that no other professor had.

Sonnichsen was funny and humorous. Sonnichsen had a warmth about him that was unlike any other professor. He is one of my heroes, too. His method of teaching inspired me to read voraciously. Today I read as much as I can, because that's the way one gets knowledge. I would make jokes in class, and he would laugh louder than anybody else and wouldn't cut me down for it. He made English Lit come alive for the student and got me excited about what was behind the writing.

Hicks was good. He allowed you to take chances. He would say, "Okay, the assignment tomorrow is so and so, and you come in prepared." If you [didn't] you still went through the thing on the microphone, and they would critique you. "Okay, what did he do wrong; what did that sound like?" We would try to do the best that we possibly could. He would go home, and he wouldn't listen to local radio stations. KVOF was on his dial at all times. He'd come back the next day and say, "That's not the way you pronounce that word." Or, "This is not what you do. How come there's so much dead air?"

I'll never forget that he was able to get a couple of tape machines. We learned how to play with them, and we learned how to make an echo. [What] you do is K . K . K . K . K . V . V . O . O . F . F . Sometimes we'd do it so loud that we'd damage his speakers at home, and he wouldn't like that. He said, "You can overuse that device; let's not make it into a religion." I always felt as though he cared. He wasn't just a professor who came and sat down and said, "Okay, here's the lesson plan, go do it and then turn off." One of my happiest times was in 1970. I came back as the Outstanding Ex-Student, and he walked up at the banquet and gave me the microphone that I used to speak on over KVOF-FM with. I still have it at home.

I came back after my two-year stint in the army in '54 and went to work for radio station KEPO. Then KTSM called offered me a job, and I was with them until 1959, when I left to go to San Francisco. I worked for every radio station and television station in that town. I began as a radio announcer, then started to produce my own radio show. I realized that my strong suit was producing. I did not have Hugh Downs' [deep] voice, but I could be around as long as I want to if I *created* my own shows or produced them. Finally I created a program called the "Les Crane Show." I'm said to be one of the "grandfathers" of talk radio; I helped invent that entire call-in show format, although I had done the caller format here at KTSM.

I went to New York with the "Les Crane Show" in 1964. It was the most successful television show in the history of New York, for in ten months the show was on the ABC network. It was the first competition Johnny Carson ever had. We failed in sixteen weeks, and I went to work for the Carson show. I was there for five and a half years, culminating as his producer and inventing a lot of different things that he still does today, including the anniversary show. No one had gotten as high ratings on "The Tonight Show" as I helped it to get. As a matter of fact, the highest rating in the history of broadcasting still belongs to a show I did on "The Tonight Show" — Tiny Tim's wedding. Believe it or not, that show got an eighty-nine share of audience at 11:30 at night, the highest share ever in the history of broadcasting for any entertainment show.

I got one of my Emmys for "Both Sides Now." It was a local program in Los Angeles that [featured] this guy who leans a little to the left and a guy who leans a little to the right — conservative/liberal. Then you put a controversial guest in between them and let them go at one another. And in eight days the two guys began to kill each other on the air; it took eight days for them to hit venom. The show lasted only a month after that, but it was spectacular, and the idea was right. I've been ahead of my time a lot of times. Now I'm ready to pull back and play catch-up and do some other things.

I was nominated for five [Emmys]; I won two. I know I won two of them because I've got them — as door stops! The second was for "John Barber's Other Show." John Barber was a critic in LA, and I did a show with him that would take on a different subject, from Steven Spielberg to whatever we came up with nightly. Then I did a one-hour special. Remember when New York was in such trouble they were going broke? Well, we announced the First Annual Telethon to Save New York City. What I did was a take-off on all the bad telethons. Guess what we raised? $623. In Los Angeles! And we took it to Mayor [Abraham] Beame in New York. And he was very gracious; I have a picture of him accepting the check from John Barber. It was tongue-in-cheek, but it was done well enough that my peers thought it deserved an Emmy.

This is my fortieth year in this business. The first twenty years were in radio, the next twenty were in television, and my next twenty are going to be back in radio but as an owner. I am now trying to buy licenses and put my own radio stations on the air with my own choice of programming. I look back at times with a great deal of favor and happiness. I never regretted being what I am, coming from where I came. I've watched this campus grow. I've watched with pride some of the things that have happened. It's unfortunate the scholastic side doesn't bring as much honor to the university as sports does. When UTEP was number one in the nation [in basketball], my God! When Bob Beamon broke the [world long jump] record, my God! Yet when the football team does badly, the university seems to suffer along with it. I wish there was some other way to get around it.

I am asked to speak before students now, students at risk. And I find that what they really are looking for is some kind of inspiration. We used to live in Hollywood, and there's a school there, John Marshall, that is probably the greatest mixture of Hispanic, Filipino, Asian, and blacks. If there are 10 percent WASPs, I'd be very surprised. And that school won the Olympics of the Mind last year. You should see those kids walk down the street; they're talking fifteen different languages. But one teacher inspired them so much that they got the knowledge, and they beat everyone else in the United States, which shows that knowledge is real power.

I just think we need more role models and fewer sports [stars]. I'll tell you something that I told the kids at Roberts grammar school. Fernando Valenzuela said it. He says it to all the kids that he meets. He says, "I'm in sports, and in sports you win and in sports you lose, but in education you only win." And it's so true; it really is.

Interviewed by Charles H. Martin, October 13, 1989, El Paso.

*The Twirp Dance was your one golden opportunity
to invite a boy.*

Esperanza Acosta Moreno

Student, 1951-1954
Librarian, 1976-present

I attended Texas Western College between January, 1951, and May, 1954. I was lucky that my parents were supportive. My mother had always told us that she would send us to school as long as we wanted to go to school. So my sister and I were the two that decided that we wanted to go to college. She was a year older than I, and she went on to college. This was before Work-Study grants, and so you had to work your way through whatever way you could. She ran out of money one year, so she had to stay out a year to have money. So we graduated together, because I caught up with her while she had to stay out to save enough money to go back to school.

The tuition was a lot lower and the books were less expensive. Would you believe [that] on fifty dollars I could pay my tuition, pay my student association fee, and buy second-hand books? I wasn't making that much at the El Paso Public Library. I was only working twenty hours a week. My mother was [thrifty], and she sewed our clothes. I still have some things she made. So we were able to go with her help and our jobs. We wanted to go, and we made up our minds that we were going, and it never occurred to us that this was anything unusual or that we were anything different.

117

We lived at home, and we had to help around the house. We weren't just sitting pretty there. We had to help clean, wash, and cook. So it wasn't as if we were just little Lord Fauntleroys sitting around waiting for somebody to wait on us. We weren't pampered in the sense that just because you're going to school you don't have to wash the dishes.

As a matter of fact, there were six of us at home growing up, and television had just come to El Paso, and if the TV wasn't on, the radio was on. There was always some activity going on, so I couldn't really study. I learned to go to bed early and sleep, and then I could wake up at five o'clock in the morning and get a lot done between 5:00 A.M. and 7:00 A.M. My daddy and I would be the only ones up, but everybody else was sleeping, and I'd get a lot of studying done.

I had learned to do that because summer classes were at seven o'clock in the morning. I'd get up real early and run up and catch the 5:15 A.M. bus at Five Points, so I could transfer downtown to the college bus in order to be there by seven o'clock classes. This was before any air conditioning. You were glad to get a seven o'clock class, because if you got anything later you would probably melt before it was over. After I got a car, it wasn't so bad. I didn't have to [get up] quite that early, so I'd pack all my books in the car and ride off to the park and sit and study in the park, because I couldn't study at home. There was too much commotion. But somehow or other I managed. I even made the Dean's List my last semester.

Dr. [Joseph M.] Roth was one of my favorite teachers. He was a true scholar. Dr. [Eugene] Porter* taught history. He knew his material, and he made it fascinating. It was just one of those things that you could hardly wait to go back to the next day, [just] like a mystery story. And Dr. Anton Berkman* was such a disciplined gentlemen. He had such a dedication to the teaching profession and to his field, zoology.

I think the University had some areas in which it could have expanded. We had dissected frogs in biology class in high school, and we dissected them again at the University. Now, the premed students used to dissect cats — and this is before they bought them — so they'd run all over the alleys chasing cats for dissection classes. The only reason I knew was because I knew a premed student that did it.

Before I changed majors, I had been in the choir with Dr. [E.A.] Thormodsgaard*, who was the head of the Music Department, a fantastic

118

musician. Dr. Olaf Eidbo at that time had just come in from Minnesota, St. Olaf's Choir, [and was] a very gifted teacher. He was also a musician, but I thought of him more as a teacher. We did all kinds of programs. We did "Il Trovatore" at Magoffin. We did "Faust," 'Of Thee I Sing," and "Finian's Rainbow." I can still remember some of the choruses. I did not consider myself a singer. I just liked to sing because it was fun, and I've always enjoyed music. And the choir met at noontime, when I didn't have other classes. We had a lot of rehearsals, [but it] was a lot of fun.

I was in the choir, and I was in the Golddiggers before they started wearing [those] very, very short skirts. We wore culottes down to our knees. We had the white cowboy shirt with mother-of-pearl buttons on the cuffs and on the front, and then we had white cowboy boots that were hand made for each of us and the white Stetson hat. I kept [the outfit] for a long time.

I got goose pimples when we were practicing for the Golddiggers. Gene Lewis was the trumpeter for the band, and he would play one of the bull-fight songs on the trumpet out in the desert while we were practicing. We practiced out there at Kidd Field. We marched in the New Year's Day parade, and we went to all the football games, [even the] out-of-town games, to Lubbock, Midland, Albuquerque. The football team wasn't a winning team at that time. It hasn't changed too much, [but] the main purpose of the school wasn't football. I was also in Sigma Delta Pi, which is the honorary Spanish fraternity. You really have to learn Spanish to learn about Cervantes and de la Vega. Then, of course, [I was] still in the CYO, which is the Catholic Youth Organization.

The University used to have Twirp Dance every December, and back in the older days, the girls didn't ask the boys to a dance. It was supposed to be the other way around, and you just didn't do things like that. But anyway, the Twirp Dance was your one golden opportunity to invite a boy. [I asked] an engineering student. And, you know, the engineers were the kings of the jungle, and to get to go to the dance with an engineering student, you had really made it. You got all dolled up in your long dresses; you had corsages. The boys got all decked out in their tuxedos. Girls looked like girls, and boys looked like boys. And you had little dance cards, and the boys would sign up as to who had the first dance and the second dance. I still have my little card. I had the whole thing booked and had a ball.

119

But I didn't really do much dating in college. When I wasn't going to school, I was studying or I was working. I had gone in as an education major. I wanted to be a high school teacher, but I couldn't see taking that many hours of education courses. I switched majors my junior year. My [new] major was Spanish, and I minored in English. What happened was that spring I was aiming to get a job at the El Paso Public Library. I got interested in libraries, and the more I thought about it, the more I decided I really wanted to be a librarian. When I changed majors, there were not library courses as such at the University, but library schools would accept a major in something else as long as your credits or your grades were acceptable. So I switched majors and went ahead with it. Then I took off to library school at the University of Illinois in Urbana.

Interviewed by Rebecca Craver, March 9, 1984, El Paso.

[The blast] was probably a little stronger than he had anticipated. It blew out all the windows on the north side of Old Main.

Ralph M. Coleman
Faculty, 1947-1982

At the time I came here there were sixteen buildings on the campus. Dr. [D.M.] Wiggins* was president, Professor [C.A.] Puckett* was the dean of arts and education, and Professor [Eugene M.] Thomas* was dean of engineering. Judson Williams* was dean of student life, and Mrs. [Cordelia] Caldwell was the dean of women. [Marshall] Pennington was the business manager. Most everybody is familiar with the name of Pennington. He did such a wonderful job while he was with us here.

Baxter Polk was the librarian, and Dr. [John L.] Waller was chairman of the Graduate Council. Col. [M.H.] Thomlinson was curator of the museum, and Dr. [B.F.] Jenness* was in charge of the health service office. There were eighty-seven faculty members, two visiting faculty, twenty-three administrative assistants, and three people on the dormitory staff. You can see that's quite a change from the present number that we have.

Dr. L.A. Nelson* was chairman of the loan committee we had at that time. One hundred dollars was the maximum amount that a non-resident student could borrow, and a resident could borrow fifty dollars. This fund was operated entirely by Dr. Nelson. Tuition for residents was twenty-five

121

dollars for twelve or more semester hours, and a nonresident had to pay $150 at that time. Room and board in the dormitory was $233.75 per semester.

I think the evolution of the Engineering Department is very interesting. Believe it or not, when I first came here there was no degree in engineering. I saw the influx of all the GIs returning from World War II; in fact, my classes ran forty-five to fifty mature people who knew what they were coming to school for. Those were the years I had the best students, and many of them are now doctors and are teaching in the Engineering Department. It was such a surprise to me when I first came out here to find that we had that many students taking engineering, and they'd take two years and [have to] leave. I just couldn't see that type of thing happening to El Paso, so I did suggest that [a four-year program] be established. I said, "Mr. Decker, we can't permit these people to leave here [after two years]. Let's give them a four-year degree plan."

Professor [Floyd A.] Decker and Dean Thomas said for me and Professor [Eugene J.] Guldemann to get busy and set up some degree plans. We went to work on civil engineering. We secured catalogs from all of the engineering schools that we could possibly locate, some seventy or eighty. We then sat down and analyzed their courses and set up our program. The university system approved the civil engineering degree and the electrical engineering degree. Then the following year after that, other faculty got busy on the mechanical engineering degree. So that's really how it got started, and that was about 1948. I think the degree offerings have done quite well.

I designed the first addition to the [old] Engineering Building. I had asked Dr. Wiggins for $7,000 for lights and new desks, but they couldn't dig up that much money. I used to go to the end of one of the old drawing rooms and look out over the old Power House. I saw a vacant space back there, and I thought, "Gee whiz, you know that could just go on up and put a roof over that, build another drawing room." So I designed that one and put in my request through Dr. Wiggins, and he said, "Yeah, that sounds like a good idea." So they came around with $77,000. I guess the moral there is, if you want something, don't ask for $7,000, ask for $77,000! That was the first addition to the old Engineering Building. It was over the old Power Plant. The second addition was the wing that went to the south, which is still there.

Then this building became too small, and we had to move to Globe Mills across the freeway. Fortunately, I didn't have to stay down there very long. I had the summer [of 1970] down there, and I believe the fall, and then moved back [to the campus] to the new Education Building. I wanted it to be called the Education and Engineering Building, but the Education Department overruled us. Then we moved out of the Education Building to the new Engineering Building [in 1976].

The St. Pat's celebration started early in the morning before daylight with a big blast in the gullies and arroyos around the dormitories. They'd always set off dynamite and wake everybody up. That was against all rules and regulations. The culprits would disperse, and they never did know who was doing it. One year the culprit was the chairman of Civil Engineering Department, who hadn't been here very long. He was an ex-paratrooper, [a] very daring type of individual. He took some dynamite to the hillside just north of Old Main and set the blast off up there. It was probably a little stronger than he had anticipated. It blew out all the windows on the north side of Old Main. Of course he had some help. He had a bunch of seniors and students doing this with him. I might say he paid for the replacement of the windows.

My first experience with the initiation was at Oro Grande. They used to hold all the initiations at the old mine shafts and tunnels. Dean Thomas always delegated me to be one to go. I'm thankful that the initiation is no longer held [there]. I was always afraid somebody was going to get killed, because there was beer drinking and sometimes even hard liquor, even though it was against the rules. I know in some instances some of the students got a little bit too much to drink, and chances are they were driving cars back to El Paso. Fortunately, we never had a wreck. Nobody ever got hurt; nobody even got hurt at the mines. But I think [that] if it had gone on much longer it could have really proved a disaster.

The thing that I remember the most was the Hard Luck Dance. The dance was held after the St. Pat's initiation and was quite an affair, attended by a few faculty and practically all of the student body. You would dress like a tramp or an Aggie. This was before the days the students started wearing long hair and beards. We always had a beard growing contest. We would have a judging, and awards would be made to the longest and the prettiest beards.

123

I think one of the greatest assets we have had here was the Schellenger Research Laboratory. It was established about the time I was hired. The first director was Dr. Thomas C. Barnes. The others that served on the board were Professor [Robert L.] Schumaker, Professor Decker, Professor [Oscar J.] McMahan, and later Dr. Anton Berkman* and Dr. Floyd O'Neal. They had a staff of more than fifty working in the Schellenger Research Lab, and the people that could work had to have top secret clearance, because the lab worked on government contracts with White Sands and William Beaumont Hospital. One of the first grants that were received was from William Beaumont Hospital [to design and build] a machine for testing hearts.

There were five installations on the campus that were part of the Schellenger Lab. I designed the environmental chambers personally and had a great deal of fun in doing so. We needed to take the smoke and gases from the building. To get the duct through, I found out that the walls of Old Main were approximately four feet thick, solid rock and concrete. So instead of going through the wall, I went down the edge of the wall and piped the fumes out from the climatic chamber to the trees just east of Old Main.

This created quite a disturbance because people would come out and see this pipe sticking up out of the ground with smoke and fumes coming out of it. They were always curious to find out where this was coming from and why. The acoustic research chamber is still on the campus. It is the finest one between Dallas and Los Angeles, and it was built by the faculty under the direction of Dr. Barnes and Professor Schumaker. It is located at Kidd Field, under the north stadium seats. We also had an electronic research lab, a data analysis center, and the optical and mechanical test center.

The Schellenger Lab was able to receive enormous grants. In fact, the first two or three years we had two million dollars in grants. That may not sound like much in today's prices, but if you think back to 1948-49, two million would be equivalent to six or eight million a year in grants at the present time. And I really think that Schellenger was one of the biggest assets that was added to the University.

My son graduated from this institution. I thought if it is good enough for me to teach in, it is certainly good enough for him to go to. And he came here by choice. I told him he could go wherever he wanted to, and he selected Texas Western. I enjoyed what I was doing — working with young people, seeing them get an education and making a success out of their life. That's what education is all about anyway.

Interviewed by Rebecca Craver, November 1, 1983, El Paso.

All the paint on the window sill, where they crawled
in and out, had been worn off.

Louise Resley Wiggins
Student, 1938-1940
Faculty, 1942-1957
Dean of Women, Assistant Dean of Students,
1957-1973

I was going to school with no idea of ever teaching math. I was majoring in education and hoping to just get a job teaching in a public school and had not decided what subject I'd rather teach. I was taking math from Dr. [E.J.] Knapp, and at that time the football boys were nearly all failing their math. They needed a tutor, so Dr. Knapp asked me to tutor the football team. I entered here in the fall of '38 and started tutoring in '42. I was living in Benedict Hall then, and the football boys would come down there. We'd take over the living room, and I would teach them the math that they were taking under somebody else.

Dr. Knapp offered me a job teaching math if I would go ahead and take my master's degree, which I did. I took it in education with a minor in math. As soon as I got the degree, I went on the permanent teaching staff. I taught math for many years under Dr. Knapp and learned a lot more from him and teaching it than I ever did in a class. I was his protege, and, frankly, he taught me all I ever knew about math.

In those days we had assemblies of the entire college population. We used to meet up in Holliday Hall* once a week on Wednesday mornings, I think, at eleven o'clock. They had programs and brought in speakers. Everybody, students and faculty, were supposed to go. I can remember one instance that sticks in my mind. I'm sure this has no value as a historical item, but the word got out that they were bringing Clark Gable in to be speaker at one of the assemblies. Somebody asked Gladys Gregory* if she was going, and her response was that she just wasn't interested in going to see Clark Gable. But he didn't come. I don't remember Clark Gable ever appearing up there.

It was a close group of faculty in those days. We knew everyone, and the old faculty lounge was the gossip mill. Everybody went in there at least twice a day. We must have consumed barrels of coffee. There were long tables down the middle of the room, and over in the corner there were tables of chess players. It was the hub of the campus for faculty social interchange. It was never empty in the morning. Those people who didn't have eight o'clock classes were in the faculty lounge at eight o'clock, you can be sure.

I went into administration in 1957 or '58, but I know I was still teaching math the first year that black students were enrolled. I believe that Texas Western was the first Texas college to admit black students. Someone called me one night, I think it was the vice president, and said, "When you go into your Math 304, Section 9, in the morning, you're going to have some black students. Make as little show of it as possible." I had ten or twelve black students in that freshman math class, and I soon forgot that they were black and the others were white. Some of them have gone on to do some outstanding things. I can remember one girl in particular who was in my freshman math class, who is now teaching at the medical school in Galveston. And we had some very brilliant black students who have gone on to do a lot more than just play basketball.

I became what was then called a dean of women. It was later called assistant dean of students — that was my title when I retired — but the function of the office did not change. To me the main purpose of that office was to provide an extracurricular program so that there would be something available for every woman student who wanted to belong to any kind of an organization. Also, [I was] responsible for the behavior of the students in the dormitory, and that was a big job. We had a staff of officers who assisted in making the rules and enforcing them. It was largely their responsibility, and in those days it was a tremendous organization, the way those young ladies handled their many problems. It was very seldom that the problems were solved in my office. We had a marvelous dormitory head resident then, Mary White, who understood young ladies. We didn't have coed dorms. We had the men's dorm, and we had the women's dorm.

Later on, the function of the Dean of Students Office changed. The administration of the scholarship program was moved to my office. I was even in charge of commencement one year and had to make all the arrangements. We did most anything in those days that needed doing and nobody else wanted to do. Students were then beginning to want, whether they needed it or not, less and less counseling, so the idea of a dean of women being a woman to whom women students went for help gradually disappeared.

There were dorm hours back in that time. At one time curfew in Benedict Hall was ten o'clock. We had a lot of unenforceable rules, let's face it. There was no way on earth to enforce some of the rules that we had, so we just got by and didn't have any serious problems. As far as trying to enforce curfew, there were always ways to get in and out of that dormitory.

I remember one occasion that has always given me a great deal of laughter and enjoyment. When we had six or seven residents in Benedict Hall, and I was the head resident, I think curfew was ten o'clock. Well, on the bottom floor there was one room that we never put anybody in, because there was a window [in it] that all you had to do was raise up and go out, which was being done constantly. All the paint on the window sill, where they crawled in and out, had been worn off, because they'd crawled in and out so many times. One night I went into the room, and I turned out all the lights. I knew they had all gone out; everything was quiet. I don't think they stayed out very late; it wasn't past twelve o'clock when here all six of them were climbing in the window. I turned on the light, and there they were. It was too funny. I remember the startled look on those gals' [faces] when the light came on and I was down there!

About that time we started having the panty raids. The boys would get in one way or another and leave messages on the mirrors in the girls' rooms. They got in from the top of Bell Hall; they learned some way of getting in there. We could tell they had gotten in because you could see the footprints. I don't remember anybody being terribly disturbed about it, because it was just their way of showing us that we had unenforceable rules. You just couldn't do anything about it. Nobody worried about it very much.

When the move came to integrate the dorms, and the boys and the girls stayed in the same dorm, those of us in the administration more or less just said, "Well, they're doing it everywhere else. They're doing it at The University of Texas. The students are pushing for it. We have no choice." And that's the way it happened. Of course, about that time we had to do away with curfew. That gave us a lot of problems because of the two new dorms that were built right there on the border almost. We never felt that it was safe to leave those doors unlocked all night long. So, that gave us some problems.

In the '50s the social life on campus really revolved around the sororities. That was one of the things that I was trying to change, because that's all there was. There weren't any other women's organizations. It was very difficult to get girls interested in a sorority, because the majority of them lived at home, and their ties were to their churches and their high school organizations. So it's always been a battle to have enough girls in the sororities to justify the number that we had on campus. At that time the three main groups [Zeta Tau Alpha, Chi Omega, and Delta Delta Delta] had houses on campus. Well, that almost meant the end of any other group that didn't have a house on campus, because naturally a girl was more impressed with the lodges. They never housed the girls; they were meeting places.

For a while the Greek sororities did not take girls with Mexican names, but later they did. Now I would say half of each group is of Latin origin. As far as the students themselves were concerned, they would have taken them [Mexican-Americans] anytime, but the sororities were governed by the alums. There was no feeling among the students themselves. That feeling was generated by the alums because nobody could take a girl into a sorority until the alums agreed that she could be in there.

There was another group that was interesting that we brought on, Phrateres, which was a organization of girls who either could not afford the Greek sororities or did not want to belong to them. It was patterned after the Greek sorority, and it was a tremendous organization because at that time there were no Jewish sororities, there were no black sororities, there were no girls of Syrian descent who could belong to anything, because they were barred from sororities. But they could all belong to this Phrateres. [The name] meant friendship, and it was organized solely for the purpose of giving the girl an opportunity to have a part in campus activities and belong to some sort of an organization. Now, that's been gone for a long time, too.

Of course, when the student revolutions and uprising began, nobody wanted to belong to anything. There was a time when Mortar Board girls were turning down invitations to belong to Mortar Board*. Sorority girls didn't wear their pins out in public. Nobody wanted to belong to anything. It was difficult to keep those organizations alive during that time, and a lot of them went by the board.

I was thinking this morning about, "Well, what did I really contribute when I was in that office?" And I suppose that if I had to put anything at the top of the list, I spent a great deal of time bringing in organizations. Mortar Board was my greatest pride, but I did not begin that. To become a member of national Mortar Board there had to have been an organization for so many years functioning on campus which promoted scholarship among women students.

Dr. [Wilson H.] Elkins* and Maxine Steele in 1952 formed an organization with the sole purpose of having it become Mortar Board at some time. It was called Chenrizig, and I was their sponsor. Somewhere in the library they found a book on Tibet and Tibetan architecture — that is the story, really, of the University — and in some of the research that they did they learned that there was a princess in Tibet called Chenrizig, who was a very learned, studious, person. So that's how the name Chenrizig got attached to Mortar Board.

Interviewed by Rebecca Craver, February 23, 1984, El Paso.

We would start at the entrance to the mine. They would blindfold you and roll up your pant legs.

Hector Holguin

Student, 1953-1958

I started college in 1953. At that time, it was very unusual for a Hispanic to leave town. I could not afford to go away to school; I knew I had to work. The only alternatives were Texas Western College or New Mexico State. At that time Texas Western had [less than] 5,000 students; it had the feeling of a small community. You really got to know everyone, and the classes were small. We received a significant amount of personal attention from the professors, and we had a lot interaction with our classmates. I think that it was an excellent setting for learning. We had good professors, not only in engineering but in all of our basic courses.

I just naturally gravitated towards engineering. Engineering gives you an excellent base, especially today, because you can move in so many different directions. In my case, I was able to move from aerospace to consulting engineering and then to a computer environment. Engineering continues to offer just excellent opportunities. I was fortunate that college was important to my parents. Two of my uncles were college graduates; one was an architect and the other an engineer. I think that their influence also helped me to proceed with engineering. At that time, I don't really know what the Hispanic population was at UTEP. It certainly wasn't the 50 to 60 percent it is today.

133

The thing to remember most about campus is that engineers tended to really stick to themselves. Maybe a few entered fraternity life, but I didn't see this happening within the civil engineering group that I associated with. We didn't really make time to participate in extracurricular activities. At that time Hispanics were not allowed to participate in fraternities or sororities, but I don't think we felt excluded. I think it just wasn't important for us to participate. Most of our activities were centered around the Newman Club, which was a Catholic organization on campus. We were also involved with the civil engineering technical society. We interacted with the professional community though this organization. We didn't have much time for anything else. I graduated in a class of twelve, so you can see that it was a very close-knit environment.

I'm sure that you have heard the stories about the alligators. College students were always playing around with the alligators in the downtown plaza. Before my time, a professor in the Geology Department walked into his office, and you can imagine his shock upon seeing an alligator that had been placed there by his students. I do remember going to campus one day and finding an alligator floating in our swimming pool. They had to close down the pool. I guess the Health Department was a little concerned. How they got the alligator in there I'll never know.

Well, my favorite professor was my next door neighbor, Dr. [Joseph C.] Rintelin. He was a professor of metallurgy. I was not too interested in metallurgy, but it was a mandatory course. Dr. Rintelin being my neighbor, I knew I had to do well in this course. He had a way of needling you to excel. In my second year, I was having second thoughts about engineering. He was instrumental in coming in and you might say hitting me over the head with reality. I decided to go ahead and stick it out at a critical point in my life. I remember another event that occurred in his classroom. One day the bell rang and nothing happened; he just kept on talking. Finally, he caught on, and he said, "Hey, when the bell rings, you all walk out, because I hear bells all the time." He came across as a very rough individual, but under that rough exterior was a gentleman. He cared about teaching, and I learned so much from him. We had many good professors there.

I was working, and I didn't make it to St. Pat's my freshman year. The next year they were out to get me, because they knew that I hadn't gone. I couldn't back down, so I went. The mine was located at Oro Grande.

We would start at the entrance to the mine. They would blindfold you and roll up your pant legs so you really didn't have much protection. Then they would stuff as much tobacco as they could in your mouth. It was very hard not to swallow. Many people got very sick; some of the tobacco was spiced with chili. We started out by crawling through the mine, but you're constantly being stopped; at least I was. They would ask you questions; even if you gave the right answer, they would still give you a good solid hit in the behind with a wooden board. So it was quite an experience.

It just seemed like we were in there forever. Everybody's crawling, one behind the other. You feel that you are wandering, not knowing where you are. That's when you really test your friends. I think that I would still be in that mine today if it wasn't for Kiki Bustamante. Kiki was a good friend of mine, and he finally got me out of there. If not, I would still be there crawling around! When we came out, they told us to kiss the Blarney Stone; it was just a big rock with a tremendous amount of green paint. We were so happy to get out there that we instantly forgot all the pain and the frustration. They still do a version of it, but I don't think it can compare to being in the mine.

I guess looking back on it, it seems childish, but I think it's an important tradition. I think it helped to bring people together. I think it reminded us about the College of Mines and Metallurgy; it reminded us where the University really came from. It takes many years to develop that kind of tradition. I think that's what UTEP offers today. Its roots really go way back, and there's a flow of tradition that is very important. In my business, I have traveled to many campuses. I've been to MIT, Stanford, Harvard, TCU, and SMU. UTEP is very unique. And how about our Bhutanese architecture! Not too long ago, we were very fortunate to visit a museum where we saw many pictures of this architectural theme. Looking at some of these photographs, I swear that I was looking at some of the buildings on campus. It's a shame that we have a couple of buildings that stand out like a sore thumb. It disrupts the uniqueness of the Bhutanese architecture. We have a campus second to none.

I graduated from UTEP in June, 1958, and I went immediately to graduate school at U.T. Austin. At that time it [had] only 25,000 students; it's twice that now. My first time on campus, I felt like a little ant. I was overwhelmed when I attended my first football game. I felt that I had lost my identity. There were so many people, and you just felt like one of

100,000. It was very different. I don't know if I could have been as successful in undergraduate school in that large an environment. There're so many activities at U.T. Austin, so many things to do and so many distractions. I am glad that I went to UTEP, where I could focus my attention on what we were there for.

My first taste of discrimination was when I was very young. I wasn't invited to certain birthday parties. After you go through it once or twice, you just sort of form a shield against it. At [TWC] I think it was low-key. I didn't really see a harshness to it. We knew that the fraternities and sororities were set up a certain way, and we just accepted that as a way of life on campus. No one really came out and tried to fight the system or change it. At U.T. Austin it was a little harsher. For a while, I was dating a sorority girl, and it caused some problems in that environment. I think that it was more evident at Austin than [here]. I wasn't an undergraduate; I think the undergraduate students would probably have felt it more than we did in graduate school. I don't think we were that far removed from the time that our buses said "colored section in the back," or blacks could not go to local restaurants or theaters. We knew it was there. So I guess maybe my attitude was we were here first, and I never did let it bother me.

I think that an important priority [should be] to keep our best high school students at UTEP. Our best students tend to leave El Paso; they tend to find better opportunities outside of El Paso. It's a job not just for the University, but it's also a job for the community to keep our best students here. But there's no point in keeping them here unless we can also offer them the best opportunities. We have to be very aggressive but also very careful to properly plan the future of this community. It is a shame to see our best students leave to Houston, Dallas, California, et cetera. I think there have been dramatic improvements in that area, but I think we've got a long way to go to change that. We have to attract the right kind of industries that can offer our graduates the optimum levels of achievement.

When I graduated, there were few major companies here in El Paso. We knew that they would not employ Hispanics, so it even limited us further. I went to California to work in aerospace for six years. I got married in 1964; my wife, Rosario, is from Mexico City. Our roots are really here, not only in El Paso, but also in Mexico. Our first daughter was born, and I had just finished the project I was working on. I knew that if I didn't leave then, it was going to be very difficult for me to leave later because of the many opportunities in California. I knew I didn't want to bring up my family in California. I just didn't feel comfortable, so we packed up and moved back. I'll never regret that decision. Even today, in our business, everybody tells me, "Why aren't you in Houston or Denver or Atlanta?" But we find the world's getting smaller, and we can work very nicely from El Paso. We have excellent people in El Paso.

Interviewed by Rebecca Craver and Vicki L. Ruiz, February 17, 1984, El Paso, Texas.

They said, "If you can't eat, then we won't eat." And no one ate, and that little town just lost a lot of business.

Edna Nixon McIver
Student, 1956-1960

Texas Western had been integrated just a year [when I started in 1956]. There was really just a handful of black students there. I think there were only fifteen of us out of a student body of about 3,000 students. By the time I graduated there were about twenty-five black students. I think there were more black students in the Music Department, not necessarily majoring in music, but participating some way in band or orchestra or whatever. There were about seven or eight of us there.

I didn't have any problems on campus from teachers or students either. I found just one instance with one of my teachers, who was a very lovely person, and that was Mr. Ralph Briggs. He was my piano teacher the whole time I was there. I had the feeling that this may have been the first time he had ever taught any black students, and there were things that he wanted to know. I had an inkling that he was learning a lot of things that he hadn't known before.

One spring day it was just so gorgeous, and we didn't have to wear even sweaters anymore, and I came in all bubbly and said, "Oh, my, isn't this a gorgeous day, and the weather is warm." And he said, "Oh, yes, it is beautiful." And he says, "By the way, I've always wanted to know, is it true that blacks like hot weather and fare better in hot weather than they do in cold weather?" And I said, "No, that's not true. Some like warm weather, and others can't stand it and like the cold." I told him that we all come from different parts of the country, naturally, and are used to different things, so it really doesn't make any difference. He said, "Oh, well, I just wanted to know." So there were people who just were curious, and this was their first time to go to school with black students or to teach black students and to find out that they can be as brilliant in many subjects as they could be dumb.

I think my upbringing was different [from] many young black students, [because] in my family, from the time I was a baby, my mother and father had friends from all over the world who were literary people, who were artists, who were politicians, who were State Department representatives from other countries. Our house was just always filled with all kinds of people. And then I grew up in a Mexican neighborhood, and my mother had grown up speaking German and French, and so I just had a growing up with all sorts of people and things. So I didn't feel like a fish out of water.

But then I did have a sense that, gee, this is the first time. Everybody couldn't help but feel that way. I think I felt a little [added pressure] because — I never talked to Mama about this — when I was growing up, every now and then, Mama would say, "Now always remember — people are looking at you, and you have to do your very best, especially because, in this particular instance, you're the only black child." The only other thing that really made me quite uncomfortable, and that's just me, was my senior year when I was elected to Who's Who in American Colleges and Universities. That was one of the most unhappy days of my whole life, because I had always been a very good student and I felt, "Oh, my goodness, now I have to prove myself even more."

Being a music major, I was in the choir; I was in band. In high school I had played flute, but in college I played clarinet and contrabass clarinet — clarinet in the marching band and contrabass clarinet in the concert band. I was also a member of the Texas Western-El Paso Community Opera Chorus, which I really enjoyed. I guess it was my sophomore year in college we did "The Merry Widow" and then my junior year "Il Trovatore."

I was also a member of the band sorority. When I was there it was the first time Texas Western had the national band sorority and fraternity, and I was president. Then I was a member of one of the service organizations. It was all girls. Anyway, I was a member of that, and from what I can remember, we weren't that active on campus. We did little things, like one year we helped build a float for the Homecoming parade, and we helped with little fund raisers and passing out literature to freshmen students.

[One activity] that I enjoyed was painting stage sets. Art has always been my first love, and I didn't major in that [because] I hadn't had any background other than just working on my own and growing up in galleries and museums and what have you. I helped with the scenery for "Faust." And I remember "Dr. Thor" [E.A. Thormodsgaard*] asking me if I would paint some of the scenery, and I said, "Of course." And this particular time was the first time that I was given a job to paint a really large piece of scenery all by myself. And it was a huge stone wall that was partially destroyed, with a huge arch in it.

Well, I was given a sheet of paper, and it says it has to be so wide and has to be so tall. I had always had good eye for sizes and doing things without taking out a tape measure and marking off inches and feet, and I painted the whole thing without measuring. It was perfect. I was so proud. I hadn't even taken any classes in painting or designing, but I had always known that even for public speaking, for singing, for acting, you had to exaggerate some things. If you wanted a certain feeling, you'd have to exaggerate that particular feeling, so that you would emote that feeling to the furthest corners of the theater. I thought [that] it stands to reason, with such a huge stage and with such bright lights, you have to exaggerate stones. I exaggerated the corners of these stones with real black, black paint. And when it came out, it was perfect, and I surprised myself! I think I surprised Thor, although he must have had a lot of faith in me when he said, "Paint this."

Of course, Dr. Thormodsgaard was the first and only person I have ever known to have hypnotic powers, really and truly. I would go to class, and I would think to myself, if I see Thor walk down this hall towards me — because usually when you ran into Thor he talked you into doing something — I am not going to do it. I'm just going to tell him, "Dr. Thor, I don't have time. I am sorry. You will have to find somebody else." And lo and behold, there's Thor. Next thing I knew, I would say, "Oh gee, Thor, I would love to do that. When do you want it done?" And that's how I got talked into music education rather than applied music. Just like that [snaps fingers] I changed my mind. Thor talked me [into] it.

I was a very good typist, and I liked to do office work. Every time I saw Thor walking down the hall, he'd say, "Edna, I need you to type thus and such." And I'd think to myself, "Oh, I can't do it. I just have to tell him I can't do it." But lo and behold, in the matter of five minutes, I was in his office just working away. And that's the first paying job I ever had, and that's when I got my Social Security number. I worked in the Music Department. It wasn't a full-time job, but sometimes it felt like a full-time job, especially when Thor had loads of stuff to get caught up with.

One of the first times that the band went on a trip for a big football game, we stopped to get something to eat at one of the little restaurants where the bus driver said, "This is a nice place to stop." There were about four of us black students who went in that restaurant, and we all sat down with everybody — we were all good friends. And everybody orders, and then the waitress turns and looks at me and my friend I had grown up with, Billie Newman (we used to trade comic books when we were little) and said, "I'm terribly sorry, but we don't serve blacks in here."

So we said, "All right. Thank you." And we got up and walked out and went on to the bus and turned around and looked, and the entire band had quietly gotten up and walked out, including Mr. [John] Carrico, the director. He got up and walked out. And we said to them, "Oh, that's all right. Go ahead and have something to eat, because it's going to be a long time." They said, "No, we're not. If you can't eat, then we won't eat." And no one ate, and that little town just lost a lot of business.

This was the first time that black students had gone to Texas Western, and back then I didn't have the courage to speak out. I would just always keep very quiet. And I've often wished that I had said something, especially when one [particular] incident came up. We had a huge band show where we utilized all of the high school bands. We had several rehearsals with everybody there. And one of the things that we were supposed to do was to play "Dixie" and salute the Confederate flag. There was just a handful of us black students in the band, [but] for black people the waving of the Confederate flag and all [that] is like the waving of the Nazi flag for Jews, and none of us wanted to play "Dixie." We just hated it. I don't blame anybody, because sometimes people just don't know these things, but the director kept saying, "It doesn't sound right. Play it with all your heart, like you have your heart in it." And I thought, "Good grief, how can we do that?"

One more thing. When I did my student teaching my senior year in college, I couldn't do my high school student teaching at an El Paso high school. Even though the high schools were integrated, the teaching staffs were not integrated. All of the black students who were secondary education majors had to do their secondary student teaching in the one predominantly black school in the city, and that was Douglass. So I had to do my high school student teaching out at an elementary and junior high school.

Once I had gotten out of college, I thought to myself, now that I'm a teacher I'm going to make such a big difference in everybody's life, and it just doesn't work that way. In our education classes we were basically taught to teach in the ideal situations. I didn't expect to teach school and find whole classes of children that didn't smile and children that were underfed. That just wasn't for me. Now I feel that since I've raised five children of my own, and I understand firsthand what the learning process is all about, I could go back and be a much better teacher.

Interviewed by Rebecca Craver, February 4, 1984, Albuquerque, New Mexico.

I always said Texas Western was going through integration; I wasn't.

Charles T. Brown
Student, 1956-1959, 1960-1963

I was born in East Texas, in Longview, and spent most of my childhood there. Later my family moved to Atlanta, Texas, and then to California at the time of the Second World War. Then they moved back. I was involved in football, basketball, and baseball [at] Pruitt High School of Atlanta. After I finished high school I attended junior college for a year, then spent three years in the Air Force. After the military, I attended Amarillo Junior College. My nephew Cecil drew me to Amarillo; his mother was my oldest sister.

At Amarillo College [there was] a very small number of black students. I think Amarillo integrated in 1954 [or] 1955. There might not have been a great rapport between some of the white students and blacks, but I never really had any conflict in school. At that time all the motels were segregated, but there were places that [the basketball team] traveled to where special arrangements were made.

I entered Texas Western in June of 1956. To be truthful, I had driven through [the city] on the highway, but I had never stopped. So I knew absolutely nothing about El Paso, except the things you hear about, Juarez and Mexican food. Basically everything that was done, in terms of

145

me being recruited to El Paso, was done by telephone. I had never met [basketball coach] George McCarty in person. I talked to him numerous times, and I formed an opinion on the telephone about him, his program, and the school. He explained that the school hadn't been integrated as far as athletics and that the first black student had just enrolled the previous year. That really wasn't a factor for me.

When I arrived here, he had Alvis Glidewell, who was a senior, meet me and more or less be my mentor. I enrolled in summer school, and Alvis helped me get familiar with a new environment. There were areas of El Paso that were completely integrated, and there were areas that were not integrated. At the time I came here, [blacks] were not able to go into [all the] movie houses. Glidewell and I tried to go to a movie together downtown, [but they wouldn't let us in].

Cecil came in the fall [to join the basketball team]. The situation on housing was that no black student could live in the dormitory, so we lived in an apartment. But we always ate at the same training table as the other players. Also, we did have a room at [Miners Hall] that was unofficially set aside before games, so we could be part of the team. In later years we did move into the dorm.

I had good relations with the black students that were attending [TWC]. Several of them became long-term friends — Edna Nixon, Donna Brooks, Joe Atkins, and John Jimmerson. I was involved in a lot of social activities. A small number of the students were involved in the BSU [Baptist Student Union] on campus. Mostly people gathered at different people's homes. Many of these students had attended Douglass Elementary and became more or less like an extended family. I became good friends with their parents, and I had some white friends [and] some Mexican-American friends. I always said Texas Western was going through integration; I wasn't.

During the summers I participated in basketball games and baseball games. Union Furniture was sponsoring a basketball team to travel through Mexico. Saul Kleinfeld was the person that organized the team each year. We played the Mexican Pan American team. Some of the players back then were Sam Adams, Alvis Glidewell, Jim Babers, Wayne Jones, and Nolan Richardson. I taught [Richardson] everything he knows. And he completely ignored everything I said and did whatever he wanted to.

I can say that I never had an incident with any of the players on any of the sports teams. As far as the professors, there were a couple of minor incidents or disagreements, but a very minimum. Of the people that I remember that were concerned for me, the most supportive was George McCarty, the coach. Mike Brumbelow was extremely helpful, [as were] Ben Collins, Ross Moore, Jimmy Walker, and Steele Jones.

By far my most successful season was my first year here. I'm not sure why. There were more seasoned players, more seniors, that [first] year. The total number of wins was about fifteen per year the three years I was here. My first year [I won] the scoring championship and the rebounding championship. [I was selected as] the Most Valuable Player for the Border Conference, and we won the championship. Our senior year we tied for the championship. We weren't an up-tempo team, but we were probably a little more up-tempo than some of the early Don Haskins* teams.

We played the Arizona schools each year, and we also traveled to New Mexico. The traveling conditions in New Mexico and Arizona were no problem as far as accommodations and restaurants. But in Texas there were problems. Actually, in Texas the accommodations were prearranged, and as long as you stuck to the arrangement, there were no problems. If you wanted to go to some other place, [then there could be problems.] Some schools were more difficult than others, from the standpoint of fans and players. West Texas State and Texas Tech were difficult. We played at Washington University in St. Louis, which was very difficult, especially the players. We also played Tennessee Tech, [where we were given] a nice reception by the fans and the team. In the heat of battle I had a tendency to ignore many of the things that you'd hear. You just close your ears to it. I never discussed it with the others, but sometimes my nephew and I would sit and talk about these things. Because Cecil was not a starting player, he would hear on the bench a lot of the things that [players on the court] would not pay attention to. His being there was a positive experience and made the transition much easier.

There were several times I became discouraged, especially during the beginning of my senior year. The senior year is when you get your student teaching [assignment]. And I was not able to do my student teaching in the El Paso school system. The certificate that I was pursuing was what they called an all-level certificate, which means I would be able to teach K-12. I had to do part of my student teaching at a secondary [school]. They simply weren't going to allow me to do it in high school, and I refused the elementary part at Douglass Elementary. That became my first really serious problem since I came to El Paso. All the others were minor things. My first reaction was to drop out of school. The reason why I stuck it out was because [Texas Western officials] made arrangements for me to do student teaching here at the college. So I did student teaching under Jimmy Walker, with the freshman and sophomore classes.

I never really looked at El Paso as being in Texas, because other parts of Texas were so different. Even though the schools were not [very] integrated, the living conditions of many Mexican-Americans and blacks were integrated. People would talk together on the sidewalks and on the corners and on the playgrounds. In the time I was in El Paso I became friends with as many Mexican-Americans as I did black Americans. Many of those people I still communicate with. I think that if I'd gone to any other place in Texas, say Texas Tech or The University of Texas or SMU, I never would have gotten beyond the first semester, because in those environments things were black or white.

[After graduation] I was unable to get employment. I'm sure a lot of people had the same problem. There just weren't any jobs available. The exception was one company that hired me part-time when I was in graduate school. I had graduated in May, 1959, and I attended graduate school for a year. I majored in history.

I was finally employed for two years at Jefferson High School as a PE instructor and frosh basketball coach. It was a very difficult experience. I couldn't advance within the school system, so I decided to move to the West Coast. I started working for the San Francisco schools in September of 1964. I started with social studies, PE, and drivers' education, which I did through 1969. From 1969 through 1977 I was in personnel administration, and from 1978 until now I'm involved with funding problems. Our department receives about 90 percent of the state and federal money that comes into the school district, and we administer that money to both the public and nonpublic schools. In the past five years I've been heavily involved with computer education for teachers and administrators.

[Growing up] I basically had an advantage that a lot of kids today don't have. I had a strong family background, a mother and father that were not rich but [who] provided for their kids. We had an opportunity to go to church, and my parents taught us how to relate to people. Those kinds of things are a foundation no matter what you do later in life.

At the time I entered Texas Western, I had no idea that no other [black athletes] had participated in any form of sport [in any major southern college]. I knew that there had been a recent Supreme Court ruling; I was well aware of that. And I was aware that history was being made with integration, but not really in the context of student athletes. In looking back, even with all the problems, I still would do the same thing. I have no regrets in attending the college.

Interviewed by Charles H. Martin, July 14, 1989, El Paso.

I opened the door, and I look, and these guys have got a nine foot alligator!

Donald S. Henderson

Student, 1952-1956

In 1952 I graduated from high school in Alamogordo, New Mexico. There were a whopping sixty students in my graduating class. I had no idea about coming to Texas Western. A couple of things happened. At that time the University of New Mexico had a big deemphasis on athletics. New Mexico State had some scholarships, but they were cutting back as well. I attended a meeting with about seven or eight other athletes in our high school [about going] to New Mexico Military Institute, where we would play all sports. My father had moved back from California to El Paso. He'd remarried, and [he invited me to] spend a long weekend with him. The following Wednesday I was to go to Roswell to sign on the dotted line.

My dad said, "I'd like for you to stay here." We hadn't had much time together over the last six or seven years, and he said, "I'd like for you to go to school here." He called Dale Waters, the basketball coach at Texas Western, and I met him over at Holliday Hall*. He remembered seeing us win a couple of tournaments here in El Paso. I dribbled around, took a few shots, and he said, "I'll give you a [partial] scholarship, books and tuition, and then maybe next year we'll give you a full scholarship."

I told my dad, and he said, "You can live with us, have that scholarship, and go to school here." So I agonized for two days and Monday made a determination to come, which I thought was an excellent decision. I played [on the] basketball team as a freshman. I can say that I had the privilege of playing on the worst team the Miners ever had. I think we beat Crockett [Elementary], Coldwell [Junior High], and Loretto [Academy].

The following year, my sophomore year, [George] McCarty showed up from New Mexico State as the coach. He recruited some good basketball players, so I was through. I went to the other side of the campus and began to be more involved in [nonathletic] activities. I switched halfway through my second year from being an engineer to business.

The interesting thing about the school at that time was there was no parking problem. Very few people had an automobile. When I was president of the student body in '55-'56, the full student body was about 3,900 students and that included night students. In '52 it had to be less than 3,000 students. A fellow by the name of Gene O'Dell was president of the student body. I remember his freshmen orientation. He came around and welcomed the group. He had a tie on, and he looked so nice. I thought that's where I'd like to be three years from now, so I set it as a goal. Almost three years to the day I had the opportunity to do the same thing.

I joined Tau Kappa Epsilon my second year. TKE had been on the campus, and then it had faded out. I was concerned because a lot of [the fraternities] wouldn't [accept] friends of mine who had Spanish surnames. TKE was the only one at that time that did not have a discriminatory clause, so two or three friends of mine started TKE back again in 1953 and built it up. Texas Western at that time was such a neat place. The school was so small that it was like a fraternity. If you were a business major your association with that department and the faculty and staff [was] like one big fraternity. You knew your professors and the staff, literally on a first-name basis. If you had problems you went [directly] to them. As the student body grew it got away from that. It was great for me. I was a high C, low B student, because I was the last guy [to go to bed] in the dorm. When everybody else went to sleep, then I'd go study. It wasn't so much partying; I just liked people.

Some of my contemporaries at that time in the early to middle 1950s were very close to their professors. Dr. [Anton H.] Berkman* had such a tremendous reputation with medical schools in the country. He went to bat for so many students that probably could have been pushed aside. But through the doggedness and the reputation that Berkman had built up with the people in these medical schools, when he put the word on them about [a particular student], they [concluded that] this was a person they should have in this medical school. Well, it put a tremendous amount of responsibility on the student. Those students knew that he went out on a limb. Mike Finerty was in the business school for three years. Then one day he decided he's going to become a doctor. He went back and set it up with Berkman and the people in premed. He went through that program. Then [Dr. Berkman] got on the phone for Mike. I knew from being very close to several of those people what that meant. Now Mike is a neurologist in San Francisco. I think that speaks well for them and for the institution they came through. From that standpoint I think [the college] measured up.

The [most influential teachers] that come to mind were Dr. Wade Hartrick, Don Freeland, and Mrs. [Lelah] Black, who was a business letters and typing teacher. She was tougher than dirt, but she was really a neat gal. She was always very encouraging. I still refer to [the College of Business Administration] as a department, and the dean gets on me all the time. It's a college now. We didn't have [more] Ph.D's than other schools, but they did have people who really cared. They talk about dedicated professors and what that really means. To me it means that somebody goes a little bit out of the way to help you. If you wanted help you could get it.

I took a course with Dr. [Rex] Strickland in history. He was one of the most fascinating people that I have ever met; [he] could captivate you. A lot of students look at their watch after about twenty minutes, [but] he could get on a subject, and you would want to stay another hour. Students tried to get him on "The Sixty-Four-Thousand-Dollar Question" [a television quiz show], because he knew the batting average of every baseball player in the history of baseball. But for some reason he wouldn't do it.

Pearl Ponsford [was] one of the most fascinating lecturers that anybody could have, [even] if they went to Stanford. When the bells sounded, the door [to her room] was closed; nobody got into her class after that. She got after me one day. She kept looking at my feet, and I had one

153

green and one red sock on. (I'm color blind.) She said, "You can do a lot better than that, Mr. Henderson." She was really an extra [special] person.

I lived at home my first year. Then my sophomore year I moved into Benedict Hall, which was like a fraternity in itself. There were only twenty-eight or thirty guys that lived there. The first week I was there, two incidents happened which set the stage for my life on the campus. One, I was awakened one night about two o'clock in the morning, and I heard them say, "Hold him up, don't drop him, hold him up." I think somebody's coming in drunk. I open the door, and I look, and these guys have got a nine-foot alligator! They put that alligator under [Dr. Howard Quinn's*] desk. Poor Quinn comes in [the next morning] and almost has a heart attack.

The second [event was] a panty raid on Bell Hall. The president was [Wilson E.] Bull Elkins* at the time. All wrapped up in one human being is a guy that is president, had been a Rhodes Scholar, an All-America football player, and [a member of] the U.S. Olympic track team. We all migrated over to Bell Hall, taking our cues from the upper classmen. We get over there, and some of the gals were hanging their laundry out of the window and encouraging everybody to make a run into the place. About half a dozen guys got around the back of Bell Hall and got inside. One guy pops out of a window, waving panties to everybody, and a big cheer goes up. About that time, up on the balcony, there was Bull Elkins. He said, "Guys, it's over. The next group [that] comes through has got to go through me." Well, in about three minutes it was over. Everybody left. I don't think there was ever another panty raid while I was there.

I lived there with some fellows that were mining engineers. These guys were the "hippies" of their age. They let their hair grow. They wore dynamite caps on their belts. They never bathed. They were just awful. One of them I met [years later], and I couldn't believe it. He had a three-piece suit on and was the vice president of one of those mines up in Colorado. I was astounded. I figured that he [would be] in jail.

Of 3,000 students [back then], probably 80 percent lived at home and really didn't have a lot of school spirit. It [was] very difficult to get that going, so you got it through the fraternities and sororities. You had your homecoming events, which were a lot of fun. A lot of the students participated. We organized this Spring Festival when I was a sophomore; it ran for three years. We put together a deal with New Mexico State for intramural athletic contests in conjunction with that festival; that came off very well. Intramurals was a big deal. There were a lot of guys like me who liked athletics [but] were not good enough for the varsity. We had some real competition among the fraternities and independent organizations in intramurals.

I held two [of the few] paying jobs [on campus]. As intramural director you got paid twenty-five dollars a month, and as president of the student body you got fifty dollars a month. I didn't have a car until I was a senior. I worked in construction jobs in the summer, and I could pay my room and board [from] that. Then I would run out of money in April. My folks helped when they could. Everybody that I knew in those days had some kind of job. They either worked construction during the summer, or they went to the wheat fields in Kansas, or they worked on the ice docks. Everybody had a job of some kind.

Nobody even knew what marijuana [was]. I didn't even know anybody that knew anybody that smoked marijuana or any other drugs of any kind. [But the students] did pretty good with the KPT Bar and the Hacienda Bar. In the dorm, they didn't serve on Sunday night, so you had to fetch for yourself. We used to go to the Alcazar in Juarez. You could get a steak that would fall off your plate for two dollars. We'd get two plates and split the steak. One got to eat the soup, and one got to eat the salad. Literally for two dollars you could have a pretty good evening over there, if you could get a car. That was the problem.

In the dormitory there were six guys out of thirty that had a car, so mobility was a real problem. Four of us in Benedict decided we were going to [buy] a car, so we saved our money. We put in thirty-five dollars apiece and bought a car for a hundred and fifty dollars. We were going to take turns. I drew the short straw, [so] I got it last. I had a date with a sweet girl who lived over by Austin High School. I forget where we went, but I took her home, and then I'm driving over Scenic Drive. I'm coming down through Kern Place, and that sucker died just like somebody shot it. Those guys never let me live that down. They said, "You did something to our car."

A lot of the hopes and dreams that I've had — for instance, getting accreditation for the business school — have become a reality. That's a monumental event, to get that recognition. I think the last few presidents have done a good job of singing the praises of [UTEP]. We're doing some research on Alzheimer's [disease], which is fantastic. It's been recognized all over the country. Now that sort of thing should be encouraged.

When you look at the budget of the [U.T.] System, 3 percent of that budget is for research, and 90 percent of all that research money winds up in Austin. It's going to take a tremendous effort to change that, but I think we can. We've concentrated on providing all of the facilities here relative to teaching, providing all the support systems to get [a student] to graduate. I think that's primary. But I also think that there are people who would want to be on the faculty of UTEP and [who are] interested in doing research, as well as being a teacher. Why can't we get more of those funds? We have to be diligent. Everybody that loves that school like I do says, "We want to do our part to see that we're getting our share and that 90 percent of the research money doesn't go to Austin." They don't have all the mines down there. This is the school of mines.

Interviewed by Carole Barasch, July 12, 1989, El Paso.

*I mean it was every night a big beer party [while]
making the floats. We made thousands of little flowers
to put on them. It was a lot of fun.*

Martha Lou Florence Broaddus

Student, 1957-1960

There was just an awful lot of socializing, there really was — just
a ton more than what they have now. Because the campus was so much
smaller, everyone was very close; everyone knew each other. They were
all good friends, and there was something going on all the time. Your
college life focused there at the University. [Even if you lived in town]
you were not a commuter, in other words. You went to school, and you
were there most of the day. I sometimes didn't get home until 6:00 P.M.

A lot of your life at Texas Western revolved around the sororities and
fraternities. They were the biggies. At that time there were two sorority
houses on campus over where the Education Building is, the Tri Delta
house and the Chi Omega house. The Delta Gammas were right down
below. And the Zetas [Zeta Tau Alpha*] had their house [across cam-
pus]. The fraternities were all together except for the TKE's.

The sorority houses were social gathering places. We had a living room,
a meeting room, and a kitchen. We had other smaller meeting rooms.
But that was it. There was an awful lot of rivalry between the sororities.
[There was] a very strong rivalry between the Zetas and Tri Delts. We
were always at each others' throats. Boy, you were after them all the time.

157

And in any election that came up, we were always campaigning against one another and trying to get our girls in and their girls out. We had friends who were excluded from sororities. When we went to college, it was completely taboo for Mexican girls to be in a sorority, and the same way with the fraternities. We had several friends [who were Jewish]. But they couldn't go through rush because we did not have a Jewish sorority [or] a Jewish fraternity. You had guilt pangs over the friends that you had who were excluded. I can remember that we didn't like it at all, and we used to fight [with the alums about] that all the time.

The Student Union Building was a great deal smaller [than it is today]. Everybody would hang around in there. It was packed all the time, and everybody played bridge. It was just the wildest place, and everyone went there. Of course, they would hang out in the sorority houses and fraternity houses, but the big gathering place for all of us was the SUB. It was small, and then eventually they built a new SUB; it was on the same floor as the ballroom.

They had the Coed Ball at Christmastime, and it was always at the Student Union Ballroom. It was campus-wide. It was all the Greeks, and it was all the Coed Council, which was a non-Greek organization. They elected a court, but it was all boys. You put them up and voted on them. That's how it was. A lot of Hispanics were involved in the Coed Council. One year Orlando Garza was the Coed Ball king. The Coed Ball was formal, and we wore formals that you stood in, and your body could move right or left, and your formal stayed where it was. You had all those bones and lots of net.

You were supposed to be a lady at all times. I remember that there was a certain etiquette about smoking. You couldn't smoke on campus, or walk across [campus] with your cigarette. That was just really tacky and low life. There were a lot of things that you weren't supposed to do. Pants or shorts were not allowed on campus. I mean they definitely had a dress code. Everything you went to for sorority rush, you were always dressed up. When you had your little teas and things, it was hats and gloves and the whole bit, dressy cottons and heels.

They did have very strict dorm rules. The girls couldn't stay out past one o'clock, even on special nights. Anybody who lived in town who had a home would open it up. We'd take everybody in on those nights. The girls would sign out of the dorm, and then they could stay out as late as they wanted to. My mother would just open the door and say, "Who's coming?" At night there would be thousands on the floor here and there.

Everybody went to the football games, and you dressed up. You did not go to the games in your Levis. You wore your really nice clothes, sweaters and skirts. And we did win some games. We weren't always losing. It was not the WAC Conference; it was the Border Conference then. We were never at the top of the heap, but we were never at the bottom either.

Homecoming was a huge thing. Everybody used to build floats, and then you'd decorate your [sorority and fraternity] houses. Most of the time the fraternities built the floats, and all the sororities helped them. They would rent warehouses to put the floats in, and they had parties there for weeks ahead. I mean every night it was a big beer party [while] making the floats. We made thousands of little flowers to put on them. It was a lot of fun. We spent every waking hour working on them. The parade went all the way through [downtown], and it was a big deal. Our society wasn't as fragmented then as it is now. At that time I think the community gave total support to Texas Western because that was the focal point.

Everybody could park on campus, but you had to have a sticker. By the Tri-Delt house there was a little hill that was our favorite parking place, up there behind Graham Hall. All the Tri Delts would squish every car they possibly could get into this little area. If you didn't back out just right, you got stuck. One day I didn't back out just right. I was in my boyfriend's car, and I stuck it straight [in]. Seriously, the back fender was in the ground. Oh, God! It looked like a Nike missile, sticking straight up. It was like it was going to take off. I was scared to death. They had to have practically every Kappa Sig [help] dig the thing out. It was terrible!

At the time my dad loved to trade cars, so I always had some different car every year. One year I had the cutest Thunderbird; it was darling. It had a black hardtop that you could lift off and then ride around as a convertible. My dad said he used to have heart murmurs, because everybody in the world drove that car except me. I'd just leave it there with the keys in it, and everybody took it. He'd see it riding around, and he'd think, "Oh, my God, no insurance, no anything." Everybody was driving my car, everywhere. It was a very popular little car.

159

Oh, gosh, we *lived* in Juarez. It was our second home. I think I spent more time in Juarez than I did on this side when I was in college. We went there all the time. We never drove over; you always walked over. We hung around a lot at the Lobby, which was a joint. I mean a *joint*, but we loved it. The Lobby always had a good band, and so we went there [to dance]. The Submarine was another place we often went to, and [also] Cavern of Music. La Fiesta was really a very nice nightclub. They used to bring in big name stars — the Kingston Trio, for example. I mean big [stars] came there, and so you went there when you were really going first class.

I didn't go to college because I thought I wanted to be something. I just wanted to go to college because I knew my mom and dad wanted me to, and I sort of wanted to. I thought it was neat. I wanted to get an education because I would have something to, as my parents said, fall back on if I ever needed it. That was the only reason. I didn't go to become some super career woman; [it] never entered my mind. I thought I'd get married and have children and be at home, just like my mother.

But it was really neat. We enjoyed it. A lot of my friends went away to school, but I started there and never did want to go away to school after I started. I loved it. I had wonderful friends there, and we had a marvelous time. I do not think we were deprived one bit as far as education is concerned. Not at all. [I had a friend who] went to Stanford. He came back here and took courses, and he said, "My gosh, the courses here are just as good, even better." You really could get a good background.

Interviewed by Rebecca Craver, November 13, 1983, El Paso.

We used to water ski, driving along the levee with the ski rope . . . and the river didn't have any more water in it than it does now.

Richard D. Overley
Student, 1962-1967

Benedict was so small that . . . in order to get to the closet, you had to climb over the beds.

Carolyn Fisk Overley
Student, 1962-1966

Richard: I graduated in January of '67 [with a degree in] metallurgical engineering. Two years before I graduated, they decided that since they had only two mining engineers that they'd discontinue it [as a major]. So there were no mining courses that I took. I probably could have, but I had no interest in them. That's the old hard rock and pick and shovel guys.

When I first came here from Odessa, I lived at the trailer park there across from the Phillips station on Thunderbird. I got fed up with that after the first year, and I went to the dorm after that, Hudspeth Hall, the one where the rowdies lived. The smart ones lived next door at Worrell, and then the jocks lived down there at Animal Hall, [which is what they] called Miners' Hall.

161

Carolyn: I lived in Bell and then at Benedict, and then back at Bell. Benedict was so small that [if] you put two beds in a room, in order to get to the closet you had to climb over the beds. It was just wild. Campus life on the whole was very boring, because there were so many commuter students. [But] you really felt a comaraderie with the small amount of kids that actually did live on campus. In the spring there was always spring fever, and that's when we had snake dances out in the street. There was lots of closeness between the kids, and we'd sit and talk and chat. That's how I met Richard, of course, because he lived in the dorms, too, and I was dating a friend of his.

Richard: Alpha Phi Omega* was established back in 1919, when the boys from World War I came back to school. The guys that were in hard rock or [mining] engineering decided that they wanted to establish a fraternity. For years and years it was just the engineering fraternity, then they spread out to [include] the geologists, the chemists, [and] the physicists. [When I was a member] the monthly dues were a dollar, and that went towards river parties. Kegs of beer didn't cost but fifteen dollars, so if you got twenty members you could have a couple of kegs each month. The rodeo used to pay us anywhere from $300 to $700 to usher. For a week during February we were the nicest guys in the world, because people liked to go to the rodeo. We'd allow them to work at the rodeo for us, and we would have a beer party afterwards. We gave some of our money to a milk fund for underprivileged kids, but that was how we collected money for river parties and stuff.

We'd have the river parties anywhere on the levee. We'd turn down Frontera Street and head for the levee and go and find us a tree, or maybe two trees. We used to water ski, driving along the levee with the ski rope attached. The very proficient in water skiing were the valley boys from Ysleta. They learned how to ski on Ascarate Lake, so I guess they knew their stuff. I would never try that in a million years. Later on, the fraternity had big steak fries out there, steak barbecuing plus the water skiing. That was when we got more civilized. We had to take up an extra donation for the steak. We finally got to the point where we couldn't use the levee, because the police would patrol it, and they would frown at a lot of fast driving. Finally they just ran us off. But we had a lot of good times out there, and the river didn't have any more water in it than it does now.

Only the Greeks and the APOs did the Homecoming Parade. Not very many other people got involved with it. [One year] the theme was "Greek Gods." We stole a toilet, and we put it on the back of a cotton trailer. I got sent [to ride it]. I was the god, the Thinker. We used to have a real good time building floats down in some barn at the Coliseum. Once we [built a float] over at Seamon Hall because it had an electric welder over there, and we could weld and wire everything. I cut my thumb off practically, cutting crepe paper.

Carolyn: These were the years — I don't remember if it was '62 or '63 — when we had some California football players come in. It was these guys, the new football players, that brought something new to UTEP, something we had never experienced before. They mooned! We had never had that at UTEP, and all of a sudden here are these guys mooning out the windows of their cars as they drove by.

There was a lot of Juarez-hopping then. Carta Blanca had a big brewery and a beer garden, and you could go over there and have a party. The Lobby was kind of a wild place to go to. You'd try all those places. You'd go to the Cavern of Music and the Alcazar Bar and the Manhattan Club. I never have liked to drink. It just has not been my cup of tea. But invariably your date had too much to drink, and you would pray, when you came back to the border [checkpoint], that he was going to say "American," because they used to yank you out of the car and hold you if you said "German" or something real cute.

Richard: I never went through St. Pat's Day when it was held at Oro Grande, New Mexico. Those were some real tough times. We had our own mine. Where you walk from the Sun Bowl, around Seamon Hall, going towards campus, about fifty yards up the hill was an old mine. I think it's all caved in and closed up now. Those geologists and the mining types would always have some dynamite, and they'd save it for St. Pat's Day, when they'd set off a charge back inside the old mine. They'd set off the charge, and it would ricochet off the Juarez mountains, come back, and smack a few windows in some of the dormitories. I would say that '65 was probably about the last year that they set off the dynamite at the mine. They also did a trick on Kidd Memorial. That seismograph was real close to where they set out the dynamite.

[Our St. Pat's] was in a big gully, just behind Seamon Hall. You would go through the initiation any year you wanted to or felt that you were safe to do it. There were some seniors whose professors said, "If you don't go through engineering initiation, you don't graduate." There were a few people who went blindfolded for the whole crawl, and they had to do whatever the person who was administering this initiating requested them to do, so it was very involved. Sometimes they would make you crawl in the opposite direction of everybody else. You'd bump heads, and you'd have to then crawl back the opposite direction.

The Blarney Stone was just any old rock down there that they painted green. You had to kiss it, and then the St. Pat, with his gloves on, would smear you with green paint on the face and all that good stuff. You had to eat or to chew anything [they] wanted to feed you. It was painful. Something I had was very, very dry when I put it in my mouth. They said, "Chew it up," and the longer I chewed, the hotter it got. I don't know what it was, but I would have loved to have been able to figure that one out.

Interviewed by Rebecca Craver, February 9, 1984, El Paso.

We were Number One! I was part of a team that was the best in the United States.

Nevil Shed
Student, 1963-1967, 1973-1974
Assistant Coach, 1980-1981

I was born in New York City in the South Bronx. It was bad then, and it's worse now. I attended one of the city schools there, Morris High School, where I was an All-City player and an All-American. My freshman year I attended a black college, North Carolina A&T. After one year there, I decided that I wasn't learning anything. It was all basketball and nothing else.

After counseling with my mom and my coach, a gentleman by the name of Hilton White, who was credited with sending myself, Willie Cager, Willie Worsley, and Nate Archibald [to TWC], I started school hunting. Willie Brown was a ballplayer here who played for Coach [Don] Haskins*. Brown told Coach Haskins about us, and Coach Haskins got in touch with Hilton White. I never had a visit down here, but I just came, and by golly, this is the best thing that ever happened to me. It had its ups and downs, but it was one of the best moves I ever made.

When I left New York City to go to North Carolina, it didn't seem I was a long way from home. I knew that Greyhound bus could get me back in New York City in about twelve hours. But when told that I was going 2,450 miles away from home and flying for the first time, right there I began to feel culture shock. I was [expecting to see] cowboys and oil wells. The Mexican population did not affect me much, because we have a large population of Puerto Ricans [in New York]. As far as getting out of [the South Bronx], the first time I set foot on El Paso soil I was glad; I was leaving a hell of a place.

Coach Haskins and Coach Moe Iba met Willie Cager and myself at the airport. They welcomed us and fed us and were nice to us. [Coach Haskins] was a young, handsome, easy-going, mild-mannered guy. I said, "Hey, I'm going to like this guy." When we left New York it was cold, and here the weather was beautiful. I said to myself, "Hey, I'm going to like it here." I remember the first day in the gym. He shot around with us and told me certain things he expected from me. This may sound funny, but he seemed like the ideal TV coach.

At the first day of practice, though, he was a different person. He started putting me through a couple of little drills, and I figured, "This is going to be about five or ten minutes." And five minutes became ten minutes and ten minutes. . . . To make a long story short, we were out there about forty-five minutes. He really got into basketball. He was tenacious, that's the word. And he used that word a lot — tenacious. I couldn't spell it, I didn't know what it really meant, but as time went on, I had a good idea of what it was. I mean, he got *down*. Work, work, and work. You didn't have time to think about being tired. The name they gave him — the "Bear" — was a good name. We had other names for him, but we do not want to put them in a history [book].

He never cursed at us, but he had a talent for saying certain things to you that [made] you wish you were cursed at. He said, "Shed, you wild man, if your brains were dynamite you'd blow up this gym." Or he'd call you, "You big sissy, you don't have the guts to get out there and work." He had that beautiful knack of challenging you. "If you're not a sissy, you show me! . . . Moe, you get a dress for that big girl." And he was a slave driver. I really thought he was a slave driver. I thought this was the worst man on two legs.

Our practices were harder than some of the games we played. When it came time for games, I didn't know what pressure was, because I knew that if I made a mistake in practice he was going to come down on us. We could withstand the pressure. We had several rebounding drills. I used to go through these antics on the floor, and a couple of times he got mad at me. This one time I wasn't rebounding, and then I was going through my little facial contortions and tossed darns and durns at everything. He finally got enough of it, and he said, "Shed, get the hell out the gym. Just put on your clothes and get out of here." So I went and took my shower and started back over to the dorms. The next day in practice, when it got to the rebounding drill, a little flash came over me. I was six foot eight, 100 nothing pounds. David Lattin was six foot six, a muscular 244 pounds of Titanic strength. And I remember the first time that I went to confront Lattin on a rebound, he broke my nose [POW!]. I mean David got me right square in the nose.

At that time Coach Haskins only had one assistant. Coach Moe Iba had a little Mickey Mouse voice. He would sometimes yell at us. He'd say [imitating Mickey Mouse], "Nevil, get over here. Get out on the court." The thing I liked about Moe Iba was that even though he tried to yell at us, the man knew his X's and O's. You'd listen to him because he definitely knew the game. The mightiest man of all was Ross Moore*, the trainer. God bless Ross Moore! He kept us walking under all circumstances. He made men out of us. He instilled in me, "Nevil, you can play with pain, but you can't play with an injury, and by golly you better know the difference."

[The style of play here was] totally different from New York City's fast pace. I remember a scrimmage game we had. I grabbed the rebound and pitched out to Bobby Dibler. I took off down the floor [yelling], "Throw the ball! Throw the ball!" And I'm looking at Bobby Dibler. Bounce, bounce, bounce, pass, pass, pass, and some more bounce, bounce. I [yelled], "What you doing, man? Hey, pass the ball here." And I remember Coach Haskins saying, "Son, in this program we pass the ball. You're not back there in one of them city slicker places. We pass the ball." That first year was a big transition.

We got off to a pretty good start [in the 1965-66 season]. The media were saying, "Well, this team is promising, but they are only playing Twiddly-Dum University. It's going to be different when they go up against better teams in the near future." As time went on, Coach Haskins started putting together his combinations. We never really blew anyone out, but we [kept winning]. Our last game was against Seattle. At that time we were, along with Kentucky, Duke, and a junior college, the only teams in the United States that were undefeated. And it just so happened that earlier that day, Kentucky, Duke, and the junior college [were] defeated. He said to us, "Right now you're the only team in the nation that's undefeated," and for a minute a little butterfly [got in my stomach]. It just so happened that we lost that game, and it took the pressure off of us.

There was a curfew [after the game]. We said, "Hey, this is the last game of the season. We're going to hang out a little bit." Coach Haskins came by the rooms at twelve o'clock; everybody was there. The minute he left, we got off the beds and went downstairs. I trailed behind them. By the time I got there, the car was full, and they left. They were going to come back for me. I was standing out there waiting, and all of a sudden I see Coach Haskins and Coach Iba coming back into the hotel. I made this mad dash, running up ten flights of stairs, trying to beat the elevator. With the grace of God I did.

I heard them knocking on a couple of doors, and no one answered. [Coach Haskins] came to my room, and I was in bed. He said, "Where's Hill?" And I said, "I don't know. Isn't he down in Flournoy's room?" He said, "No, nobody's in the room! Where's Lattin?" And I said, "Coach, I don't know. I've been in my room." He was steaming mad. He started out the room, paused, and turned back around and said, "Nevil, why are you still here?" I looked up at him with this sad look and [pretended to cry], "Coach, can't you realize that we were the only undefeated team in the United States, and we lost this game. I'm really upset!" I snuggled back down and put the cover over my head, fully dressed. He put his hand on my shoulder and said, "Shed, you *will* play the next game." He walked out of the room, and the first thing that came out of my mouth was "Whew!" I got away with that, and it took years before I told him the truth.

I remember [playing] Oklahoma City [in the first round of the playoffs]. He told us, "You better get out here and play this team tough right from the start. If you don't, before you know it, you'll be quite a few points behind." We took the game seriously, but they came out shooting the ball, and we were [behind] at halftime. Fortunately, we came back and won.

I remember playing Cincinnati [in the NCAA regional tournament]. This was the game where I became Cassius Clay. This one athlete got my goat. He was bumping me and grabbing my shorts and everything. I remember one play when this guy had a hand full of my shorts. I saw one referee looking at Willie Worsley, and I didn't see the other referee, so I just squared off and hit this guy right in the nose. Of course they — beep — blew the whistle on me, and I was ejected from the game. Coach Haskins went wild. If it was left up to him, he would have thrown me out of the state of Kansas. He didn't even allow me in the room at halftime. I stood out on the ramp, and that's where I watched the game from. With the grace of God we won that game, too.

Then came the last one against Kansas to get to the finals. That game really got tough [at the end]. There were a few seconds on the clock, and Kansas had the ball. I remember Jo Jo White took one step across the half-court line and let it go. I saw the ball in flight, and I knew it was going in. My knees got weak, and I said, "Oh no!" And bingo, it went in. But a referee by the name of Rudy Maritch (God bless Rudy Maritch!) was right on top of the call and saw White's foot out-of-bounds, and they called it no basket. We went to overtime, and as usual we came out on top. After that game it was on to College Park, Maryland, for the Final Four.

I couldn't believe that I was going to the Final Four. In my heart I always thought we'd get into a post-season tournament, but to go that far was a surprise. The pressure wasn't there. We defeated Utah that first game, and Kentucky defeated Duke University. Going into the finals the next night, I was the one who was the most jittery on the whole team. We didn't take [Kentucky] lightly. We respected the man who was coaching there — Mr. Adolph Rupp, the Baron of Basketball. We knew that any team he put on the floor was going to be a tough team. I remember the game. We handled them pretty well, particularly with those two steals by Bobby Joe [Hill]. [We played] physically and with poise, things that we did all season long. I thought the Utah game was a little tougher than the final game. Most definitely Kansas [was a tougher game].

Oh, how I can remember those last seven seconds! When that clock started ticking off, it seemed like the whole world just stood still, and the only thing that I could see was that five, four, three, two, one. Hey, we were Number One! I was part of a team that was the best in the United States! And that's a feeling you cannot imagine ever happening to you. We won it, and we won it because of all those things [Coach Haskins] did in practice. It was a well-put-together team, well-trained for the ultimate goal of an NCAA basketball championship.

The media made a big deal out of the [racial angle]. They would say, "Kentucky, an all-white team, will be playing this team that consists of white players and seven black players." [Later] it really got ugly. They said that Coach Haskins was a "nigger lover" and that he had a bunch of misfits that didn't graduate. That is a lie, because practically all of us are now college graduates, and some of us are working towards our master's. We all have good jobs. It's altogether different from what they said. And it really, really hurt me. Each year when I go to the playoffs, if I see one of those sports writers, [I say], "Hey, I'm here. I'm one of those black misfits. I'm one of them, the ones you said didn't graduate. I graduated." We weren't misfits.

I really think that [the victory] was a big stepping stone for the black athlete. A lot of doors were opened, and when you really look at it, you've got to thank a guy like Coach Haskins for being a pioneer and giving qualified athletes a chance to participate at the major college level. Right after that, you started seeing a lot of your southern super white programs start getting the black athletes to play for them.

We knew that the challenge was even going to be harder [the next year]. Everybody we played [wanted] to beat the national champions. Most of our team was back, and we felt we had a good chance to win again, but we lost to Pacific in the post-season tournament. I stayed in El Paso until the end of the year. I guess I was athletically and educationally burned out. I was waiting for that phone call, and I did get it. I was told that I was drafted by the Boston Celtics in the second round. That was the beginning of a new era in my basketball life. That fall I went and played [with Boston]. Unfortunately, after all my high school and college [games], I had a bad knee injury — torn cartilage and a damaged tendon. I played there for one year, and the team won a world championship. Just having the opportunity to play with a Bill Russell and a Sam Jones and a [John] Havlichek was something that you just can't forget.

After that year, I went back to New York City. I got married, and I worked at a community center right around the corner from where I lived. I had a pretty decent job, but as time went on, it was rough without that degree. I couldn't advance, so I decided to go back to school. I called up Coach Haskins and asked him, "Hey, big daddy, do you think I can come back to school?" And he said, "Well, hell, you should have [already] been back here."

He gave me a student assistantship. I stayed on until I graduated, and he helped me get my first coaching assignment at the University of Wyoming. After Wyoming I moved to the University of Wisconsin in Milwaukee and then to Milwaukee School of Engineering. After that, I got a call from Lindsay Holt, who was a good friend of Coach Haskins, asking, "How would you like to come down to El Paso and work with your daddy?" I asked him, "When do I leave?" I worked here with him as his assistant. After one year, this new university was opening up — the University of Texas at San Antonio — and at the present time that's where I'm at.

Interviewed by Charles H. Martin, February 28, 1986, El Paso.

I came here to be president of the damned place and do the best I could.

Joseph M. Ray
[1908-1991]
President, 1960-1968

This was the biggest job I had ever had, and I was concerned about doing it well. I had come twice to the presidency of an educational institution, once at Amarillo College and once here. Whatever I was able to accomplish in reshaping the academic focus of [the college], I brought with me. It wasn't in my pocket; it was in my head. I was an academic man from the very first. I had never been anything from the time I graduated except a professor, and I had deeply ingrained in me the various areas of understanding that all academic people have with a minimum of convictions about how I was going to do this or that. I didn't come here to sweep with a new broom. I came here to be president of the damned place and do the best I could.

I think Mission '73 is the biggest thing that happened in my years of the presidency. I think the idea came in a suggestion from Vice Chancellor Lawrence D. Haskew, who was my advisor in Austin. Mission '73 arises from the fact that 1963 was our semicentennial. We were going to celebrate our Golden Jubilee. As a part of the celebration, we were going to have a citizens' study group, and so we appointed thirty-six citizens

173

of El Paso, big names in the community. Our mission was to project where our institution should be in 1973, ten years hence.

We met in the Union Building, at 7:00 P.M., once a month, for several months. Haskew came out every time, by air. The executive director of Mission '73 was Milton Leech*. That's how I got to know Leech, and my admiration for him never flagged. He's a first-class man about getting jobs done. I had at that time an assistant to the president, Ray Small. Small and Leech and I were the three from the campus who were most active in Mission '73. Judson Williams* was chairman. [We had three] women members: Hilda Kitchen, Maxine Steele, former dean of women at the college, [and Mrs. J. Burges Perrenot].

We published the recommendations of Mission '73 and a little volume called Jubilee Papers. The most important recommendation was that we should abandon the then-controlling assumption that we were a community college. We were a cut well below the university level. Before we would become a university, we would abandon the community college concept and work in all things toward quality. It's a simple fact that if you've got a university class of twenty students, and ten of them shouldn't be there, the standards of the institution will be lower. If you've got a faculty member who is not well trained and is not imbued with proper attitudes, the institution will be cheaper. If you've got a library with paperback books in it and no substance in the library holdings, you'll have a cheap university.

We were for full accreditation. For example, we were accredited in engineering only in one program — that was mining and metallurgy — and Professor William G.N. Heer [held] the only doctor's degree in engineering. We didn't hire anybody else except [applicants with] doctor's degrees for a long time. We finally got a quality establishment in engineering. All of our systems are now accredited.

The main point is that we got a grip on our goals. In other words, we would work toward quality on everything. We did some very difficult things. One of them was limiting admission. We set up a system: Higher-ranking high school graduates would get in automatically, but we never did close the door. Anybody who graduated from a Texas high school or from any accredited high school could go to summer school, take two courses, make B's, and be admitted to the University in September.

Mission '73 didn't bring about the name change. The name change was brought about through the virtuosity of Frank Erwin, [a member of the Board of Regents]. He drafted that scheme. We did it just like the Californians had done. They've got nine or ten state universities, [but] the mother university at Berkeley is still the [diamond] in their crown. They changed our names, all of us, made us The University of Texas *at:* The University of Texas *at* San Antonio, The University of Texas *at* the Permian Basin, *at* Arlington, and *at* El Paso. We used to call U.T. Austin "the Main University." It was "the Main University." It still is. But it's disparaging to the others to call it "the Main." They are all full-fledged branches.

[The name change] was all plus. For many years people wanted something like that. The prestige of the University at Austin goes in a good measure with the name. We're a more important institution. I thought we were when this job was first offered to me. I thought Texas Western was a premier state college, and I was delighted to be invited to preside over it. I didn't have the hope that we would ever get the name University of Texas at El Paso. I didn't think we could primarily because the people at Austin would rebel. Most of them didn't even know us. We had a committee from Austin come out here, and one member of the committee stood in my presence and expressed amazement when he was told that we were part of the University System. He just hadn't known it until I told him.

Some people say football has no part in the University program. It does. It's a simple fact. If things are going well with the football team, everything's lovely and the goose is hanging high. If they are doing poorly, you're damned if you do and damned if you don't. You're in the doghouse on everything you try. As a matter of fact, football is our main moneymaker, [but] every university on our schedule has a program better financed than ours. When Bum Phillips was our coach, he had a successful season; [he] won maybe seven of his games. He showed up in my office one day and says, "Dr. Ray, I've got to resign." I said, "Bum, what are you talking about? You don't have to resign. There's nobody after you. We want you." He said, "There's no chance of my ever winning consistently in this conference. They all get more money than us." In those days, the legislature of New Mexico gave $150,000 a year outright to the athletic program at New Mexico State and the University of New Mexico. We never got a dime and never will.

I wouldn't know when people started talking about building the Sun Bowl. I never paid much attention to it early on because I didn't think that we could do it. The single person most responsible for the bond issue was County Judge Woodrow Bean. He just flat did something that was popular for the county to do. It wasn't the county's business at all. In the bond issue election, there were eight items on the ballot, and seven of them lost. The Sun Bowl [proposal was the only] one that carried.

What I had to do was to get a deed of the land for the county. And we had to get the Board of Regents to approve the transfer of the land to the county. And then the county, all in the same deal, would agree to lease to the University the Sun Bowl for one dollar a year, for ninety-nine years. Well, that shows you how much business it is of the county. And the money comes from the taxpayers paying it off the bonds every year. Bob Kolliner actually hustled the arrangements for the Sun Bowl bond issue. Mike Brumbelow, the former football coach [who] died not too long ago, helped with getting the location. Marshall Willis was the one who made sure the work went right.

The Peace Corps was a program of training workers to go to foreign countries and help countries lift themselves by their bootstraps. President [John F.] Kennedy inaugurated the program. One of the enterprising members of our faculty was Clyde Kelsey, who was then dean of students. He and I, mostly he, went to work on Lawrence Dennis, who was the educational director for the Peace Corps. They wanted to send fifty or sixty young men and women to Tanganyika. We went to Washington and had breakfast with Larry Dennis in the Mayflower Hotel, and it was there where he succumbed to our blandishments. I really think it was my talking that was most persuasive with him. I recall distinctly that I was talking when Dennis threw down his pencil and says, "All right, we'll do it." We were elated, because we would be the second Peace Corps program. The only one that had already been announced was [at] California-Berkeley.

One advantage we had was that the language spoken in Tanganyika is a generic language from that whole part of the world, [Swahili]. At any rate, the foremost person who was teaching that language [in the United States] was spending the first six weeks of the summer term in Austin at The University of Texas. At our insistence, they agreed to let him fly out here two times a week from Austin to teach language to the corpsmen.

The program went fine. Kelsey was the director; [W.H.] Bill Timmons was the assistant director. We got fifty or sixty people in here. It went fine. We had them quartered in the old house to the northwest of the Union Building. Most of the lecture sections were held in the old Union Building. The planning of the curriculum was entirely Peace Corps. It came to us, and we executed as best we could. There was a big to-do about the language, and they just had time enough to get a working knowledge of it. They also received training in highway, road, and bridge construction, geology, [and] a smattering of carpentry.

The Peace Corps program at Texas Western lasted just sixty days. We had Sargent Shriver, who was director of the Peace Corps, here for the graduation exercise. I figured he would have a written speech. Most politicians do, and they refer to it as an address. We had lunch in the athletic dormitory, but as we walked over to Magoffin Auditorium when the people had gathered, he said, "Dr. Ray, you referred to my address. I don't have any address. I was going to write one last night, and I asked [this reporter] here if he could help me, but he begged off. He wanted to play poker. So I haven't got an address." Well, that just floored me. No first-line politician would come to an important engagement with no formal preparation, but he did.

Anyhow, we went on over to Magoffin Auditorium. We were about ten minutes ahead of time. I sat in the third row. In the second row was Sander Vanocur and two or three more aides, and [Shriver] sat on the front row. The [group of aides] bunched around him and talked to him for ten minutes, obviously pumping him up with things he should say. Then he and I went up on the stage, and I presented him and sat on the stage while he talked. He made the best speech I ever heard in my life, all pat phrases taken out of the lexicon of the Peace Corps. It was perfect; it was truly perfect.

After the program was over, our boys and girls [were invited to Washington to be congratulated by the president]. Bill Timmons and I went to Washington for the ceremonies, and we both met Kennedy and stood in his office and were congratulated by him. Kennedy is one of the few men I have seen in my lifetime who was larger than life. He just effervesced an aura. When we were in the Rose Garden, two classes were meeting the president at the same time, the one from Berkeley and ours. We heard Kennedy make a speech. I was possibly ten feet in front of Kennedy when he spoke. We were standing right close to the steps that led up to the Oval Office. Tim [Timmons] and I were standing side by side. When they announced, "Would all the corpsmen and all the university officials who are here representing Texas Western and Cal come in to meet and shake hands with the president," Tim and I just busted up the steps. We were first or second.

The president meanwhile had gone in and was standing by the desk. As I recall it, he told me that they appreciated our contribution. I have tried many times to recall what I said in response, and I can't recall a word. I stood and talked with him possibly thirty seconds to a minute, and then an assistant told me and Tim, "Go out that door there." As we moved over, I grabbed Tim's arm and said, "We don't have to leave. Let's stand over here and watch him meet our kids." We just stood there. Hatcher saw us stop and didn't make anything of it at all. We wanted to see the proceedings. The president was standing in front of his desk and talking with each one of them briefly, and then they would cut in front of us and go on out the door where we should have gone.

We didn't recruit national championship players; we recruited good players. [Many of] the real good ones were from New York City, where our coach, [Don] Haskins*, was a warm friend of the black man who was the director of athletics for the New York City Public Schools. He got Bobby Joe Hill from Detroit, Orsten Artis from Gary, Indiana, and David Lattin from Houston. The rest of the boys, nearly all of them, came from New York City. They were good players. We didn't recruit to win the national championship; we just got a team under the leadership of the spark plug, Bobby Joe Hill. It really worked. We had a schedule of twenty-six games, and we won every one but the last one. We lost the one in Seattle, the last game of the season.

I haven't seen a team anywhere that meshed their actions and their abilities any better than our team did in the national championship [at College Park, Maryland, in 1966]. The basketball players and the buffs that were along were all staying in the same motel. As we drove back to the motel on the bus the night before the game, Bobby Joe was in the seat behind me. He tapped me on the shoulder and says, "Well, we won all the games for you, Dr. Ray. And we're going to win the one here." That was the first time it really soaked into me that, by God, we were going to do it, and the boys just flat did it. [They were] a superbly knit basketball team.

178

No more than three black boys were playing in any school, anywhere. Kentucky had no black [athletes] at all. That was our opponent in the final. They were dumbfounded that we would field a team of all black boys. I told George McCarty, the director of athletics, to tell Don Haskins that we couldn't play more than three black boys. Haskins came to see me and said, "Dr. Ray, George told me what you said. The way our boys line up now, my six best boys are black. If I leave two or three of them out because they're black, they'll know it. They'll know it; the white boys will know it. They all know who the best basketball players are, just as I do." I said, "Well, Don, you let me study about this overnight." I called him the next morning, and I told him, "Don, you coach the basketball [team], and I'll try to do the rest of my job myself." We were the only one who played five blacks.

Winning the NCAA championship was the biggest thing that ever happened to unify this school with the community. It was really an electric thing. We had captured the imagination of the basketball world all the way across the country. I think the funniest letter I got, after the victory and we were back home, was from an industrialist in Cincinnati, Ohio. He wrote on his engineering firm stationery, "I am pleased with your victory in the NCAA finals. I have always been in favor of integration. I've always been opposed to segregation. And it satisfies me to see the national championship won by a small Negro college."

Sports Illustrated came in to interview some of us [in 1968]. Tom Brookshier interviewed me, and he did a fair job. He wasn't pushy; he wasn't grabbing for some theme to hang on to. The only inkling I got that they were after any kind of special, sensational purpose was [when] he asked me, "Do you feel any guilt about the way the university exploits these black players?" I said, "We don't exploit them. We exchange benefits. They are doing us a good turn, and we're doing them a good turn. There's not a boy on any one of our teams that feels enslaved. He's not a slave. He came here by choice." I think the reason we were panned [in the magazine] was that they were looking for a school that would exemplify integration of black athletes, and who better than us. They were looking for a whipping boy, and they picked us.

I'm not a big planner or dreamer. I'm a man who likes to keep his nose to the grindstone and continue to play it out along well-proven lines. I won't say I was the best, because I doubtless wasn't, but I was the most effective president UTEP ever had. We got things done. One of my colleagues later worked in my office as a vice president. I asked him one time, "Why did you accept a job at Texas Western with all the chances you had elsewhere?" He said, "I came primarily because you were president. I had heard it said that things happen where Joe Ray was in charge." I think that's the nub of it. We didn't stand back and wait for somebody else to do it.

Interviewed by Oscar J. Martinez and Sarah E. John, April-November, 1981, El Paso.

I think I completed the first eleven passes I threw.
I think I could have thrown [the football] between my
legs or over my shoulder and somebody would have
caught it from our team!

William S. Stevens

Student, 1964-1968, 1969-1970
Assistant Coach, 1971-1973

Coming out here, in August of 1964, [was] a drastic change from
what I was used to in Galveston. I don't think any person who's ever come
to El Paso thought it was a great place to live in the first six months.
It was hot; it was dry. Coming out here was going to the other end of
the world — 850 miles from home. I was lonesome; I was homesick. Of
course the architecture was Bhutanese, and it was a drastic change. Everything was a drastic change for me.

I don't think student life today is probably any different than it was
back in '64, in that we do not have a very active campus socially. Back
then, on Friday at twelve noon, the campus was dead. I remember one
of the big arguments we had [over closing] the Student Union Building
on weekends, because nobody ever was around. We argued that they ought
to have it open. Most of us didn't have a whole lot of money, so it was
nice to be able to go over there and do something fairly inexpensive. I
don't think the campus has changed a whole lot in that respect. It's still
a commuter school.

[For social activities] there was the old KPT — the Kern Place Tavern. That was one of the places to go. We use to go up to the Campus Queen. Back then you could get a bean burrito for fifteen cents or something like that. At night that was the place to go. And everybody had beer blasts down [at] the river.

I had gotten married midsemester of my freshmen year, so my campus activity was going home. It was not out running with the boys. I really did not get that involved in any of the campus activities for the most part, because of being married. Every opportunity I had that was free was [spent] trying to find a job to make a buck. The first month [we were married] we lived in this dinky, little apartment on Yandell Street that they should have condemned. There was a fairly long waiting list to get into the campus apartments, because of the inexpensive rent. It took us a semester and half to get in; then we lived there the rest of the time. [Apartment] G-4 still sits there.

My senior year, out of the twenty-two starters on the football team, I would venture to say fifteen of them were married. We all hung around together. A lot of us lived over there in the campus apartments. In the off season, on Friday or Saturday night, we all got together and played cards. None of us could afford to go anywhere, so we did things together that were inexpensive. We loved living over there. We were all struggling through school and didn't have an extra dime. We were all miserable together and had a great time at it.

I planned on being a football coach; that's all I ever wanted to be. I found out you did not have to be a physical education major in order to be a coach, so I changed my major to business. I was going to be an accountant. After taking accounting for one semester, I said, "There's just no way in the world I can be sitting behind a desk, playing accountant, for the rest of my life." I decided I still wanted to be a football coach, so I majored in secondary education with math and history as teaching fields. And then I ended up in banking. How those two come together, I'm not sure.

There were several [individuals] that stuck out in my mind as being good professors. I just loved the excitement Mrs. [Jean H.] Miculka in the Speech Department had about the way she taught. I felt I learned a great deal from her. In the History Department, Dr. [Eugene O.] Porter* was just tops in my book. He always walked in when the bell rang. He was never there early; he was never there late. I think he stood outside and waited until the bell rang, just to walk in at that point. He would pick up his lecture in the middle of the sentence [where] he stopped at the last class. When the bell rang, he stopped right then and there, picked up his little roll book, and walked out the door.

He did an outstanding job of keeping our attention. His tests were tough. They were always written; there was never any multiple choice. He would let you make up the test. You'd throw out something like: 'I think maybe we [should] discuss the Russian Revolution." [Porter would say,] "Well, that's an awfully good question but awfully broad. Don't you think we ought to confine. . . ." He got the exact question he wanted [eventually]. But you felt like you were making up the test. It was great. I've taught several courses in banking, and I've used a lot of those techniques that I learned from him.

A lot of people don't realize the amount of time and effort that goes into athletics. Everybody thinks you've gotten this scholarship for free. But I guarantee that's not the case. It's like any job that you do. If you do it correctly, you're going to put time and effort into it. I would say we spent a good six to seven hours a day in preparation — the workout time, the study time, the conditioning time. I put in a little more as a quarterback, watching film and trying to read defenses. It was like I had a full-time job [while] going to school. During football season I only took twelve hours a semester. During the off season I would take fifteen to eighteen hours. [My] final two semesters I had to take twenty-one hours in order to graduate. I carried about a 3.8 in those two semesters, whereas the other semesters I didn't work as hard because I didn't have to.

Ron Harper was the head coach my freshmen year. Then that staff was let go at the end of the first semester. Bobby Dobbs came in at midyear, and he was here the whole time that I played. The players that people would remember were: Chuck Hughes, Bob Wallace, Freddie Carr, who was All-Pro linebacker, Charlie West, who was an All-American defensive back and also played baseball, and George Daney. My senior year, six of us were all drafted in the top three rounds. Back then, freshmen were not allowed to play varsity. You had to play freshman football. The year Harper's staff was let go, they were 0-8 and 2. We went back home, and everybody said, "How'd the football team do?" Well, they were 0-8-2, [but] the way you said it, it was like they were, oh, 8 and 2, not 0-8 and

2. The following year we came back and were 7 and 3. Then we played against TCU in the Sun Bowl and beat them 14-13.

We started throwing the football bigtime. We ran a draw occasionally, just to let the other team know we had some running backs, but we would throw almost every down. Back then, college football was not as much of a passing [game] as it is today. We were independent at the time, but we still played all the Western Athletic Conference teams. It was not a passing conference; therefore, we were far ahead of the defense. We were able to sneak up on them a little bit that first year.

[My first varsity game] was against North Texas. We ended up beating them 61 to 15, and we threw as a team for almost 600 yards that night. I think I completed the first eleven passes I threw. I think I could have thrown it between my legs or over my shoulder and somebody would have caught it from our team! It was quite an exciting beginning to a football career. We were 6 and 4 the next year [1966]. The defense caught up with us a little bit, and we were not as successful in throwing the football because of that. We had a couple of close games that just didn't work in our favor, whereas they did the year before. There's not a whole lot of difference between a 6-4 season and a 7-3 season.

I think the ball bounced our way a little bit more [in 1967]. The record was 7-2 and 1. We got beat in the last few minutes of the [big] game. Wyoming was going to the Sugar Bowl if they won. We were going to the Sugar Bowl if we won. The loser got to go to the Sun Bowl. We tried a field goal with two seconds remaining, and it was close to being good. I honestly think the referee could have called it either way and felt good about his call. It was just one of those things. We got beat in the final few seconds, or we would have gone to the Sugar Bowl.

We played Ole Miss, the University of Mississippi, [in the Sun Bowl]. Again it was a very close game. Although we were an exciting offensive team, we were really a defensive team. Both the Sun Bowl games were won by the defense. The final score was 14 to 7, and I was selected as the outstanding player. I was very fortunate that I played on quality football teams. It's very easy for the quarterback to get all the glory when you win. We won more games than we lost, so I got a lot of the credit.

At that time, there weren't any Southwest Conference schools that were throwing the football. My real ability as a football player is as a passer. I am not a runner by any stretch of the imagination. I probably never would have had the opportunity to play professional football had I gone to another school.

Back then there was a lot of discussion about how much the players were getting paid. I can tell you we certainly were not paid by any stretch of the imagination. But my mother-in-law and father-in-law bought me a bicycle, a Schwinn three-speed bicycle, for Christmas. I'd wanted a bicycle so I could ride around campus with it. It was right after the Sun Bowl football game my sophomore year, and the big joke on campus was, "Oh, Stevens got a bicycle!" That was my claim to fame, I guess; I got a bicycle for [winning the Sun Bowl].

We had a very unusual situation [concerning race relations]. It was something that I feel very good about, the atmosphere amongst the players. My senior year we were to play [San Jose State] in California. That game was called because of racial problems out at that campus. They were afraid to have the football game. But there were never any real racial problems [here at Texas Western], certainly not within the football team. Several of the black players were married; several of the white players were married. And we socialized together. We were all in the same boat. We didn't have any money to go out, so it drew us all together. We were friends as well as teammates.

I guess I'll always remember something that happened with Freddie Carr. We all got called together at the end of practice. Dobbs made the comment that we had a decision to make about something. He says, "Now, everybody here is free, white, and twenty-one, make a decision." And Freddy Carr just started laughing. Now, he's blacker than the ace of spades. He just starts dying laughing, rolls down on the floor, and Dobbs still has not figured out what he said. We all slowly realize what had been said, and Dobbs was getting mad. Everybody's laughing. Finally, Freddie says, "Coach, I'm not free, white, and twenty-one." And Dobbs just started roaring, after he finally realized what he had said. That was the type of camaraderie that we all had. We could poke fun at each other about things like that.

I don't remember there being a whole lot of [student] protests while I was in school. I think a lot of that has to do with the fact that we were a commuter school. People came in, did their classwork, and headed for work. They didn't hang around in the Student Union and discuss those type of issues. They had other things to do, [such as] supporting their families.

I played professional football with the Green Bay Packers for three years, which was something that I'm quite proud of. I said "played" — I stood on the sidelines and watched. Bart Starr was the quarterback with the Packers [when I came]; he was still the quarterback when I left. It was a great opportunity and certainly financially advantageous. There weren't a lot of kids right out of school that were able to make the kind of money that I was fortunate enough to make. It gave me a great start. Even though I [rarely] played, I'm quite proud of the fact that at least I got to wear a uniform.

I came back and planned on being a football coach. I taught high school here in El Paso for one year, and an opportunity came up to get into the coaching ranks out at the university. I went to work as the receiver coach and quarterback coach. I did that for three years, and I guess I realized I didn't really want to be a football coach all that bad. But my wife and I both dearly loved El Paso and wanted to stay. I got an opportunity to go to work for El Paso National Bank in their marketing and business development area. I very much enjoyed banking and went back to school. I took some of those dreaded accounting courses that I couldn't stand back when I was going to school. I learned what I needed to learn in order to get into the lending side of banking, and I've never regretted it.

As an athlete, certainly two Sun Bowls have to stand out as being a high point within a four-year college career. As a student, certainly getting a degree [was a high point]. As has been mentioned numerous times at different events that I have gone to, so many of the graduates from UTEP are first-time graduates within a family. And that's certainly true with me. I was the first one within my family to get a degree. My mother was quite elated about the idea that I had graduated.

One thing that I would like to throw in [is the argument that] UTEP's not as good a school as some other places. That's definitely not the case; it really isn't. I think we all have learned that you get out of something what you put into it. The quality of education that you can get from UTEP is no better or no worse, in my opinion, than what you can get at 95 percent of the other schools around the country. I'm sure there are some, the Harvards, the Stanfords, that in certain areas might be better than UTEP. But I think you do get out of it what you put into it. And I got as good an education from UTEP as anybody else in the country [got] at the same time.

186

I guess the other thing that gnaws on me is the "dumb jock" syndrome. There are a lot of jocks that probably never should have gone to school, [who] didn't learn anything. But don't include me in that group. That gets rather irritating to me — to stereotype all athletes as "dumb jocks." I think when you do the cross-section of the university, the percentages of those who started and those that finished, that athletics is maybe a little bit higher than the general population of the campus. I do know [that] several of us who played football, basketball, and baseball at the university, despite the fact that we were jocks, turned out to make something out of our lives.

Interviewed by Charles H. Martin, July 31, 1989, El Paso.

Part III:
The University of Texas at El Paso
1967-1991

Texas Western was a small little school at the time,
2,000 students, a glorified high school.

W.H. Timmons

Faculty, 1949-1978

In 1949 I came to UTEP. I completed my degree, a Ph.D. in Latin American history, at the University of Texas, wrapping up a doctorate on the GI Bill after World War II. I had a history professor in college [who] turned me on. So it was history from that point on, with a B.A. from Park College and an M.A. from the University of Chicago, where I had gotten interested in Latin American history. I switched to the University of Texas and started the doctorate there, just before Pearl Harbor. Well, of course, my doctorate was interrupted by World War II, but then I went back on the agenda of the Ph.D.

Jobs were hard to get then in history. This [position] was about the only opening that I came across. It was Dr. [J.L.] Waller*, the chairman of the department here, who hired me. My wife and I decided, "We'll try this school for a year and in the meantime look around for something *decent.*" It wasn't very well known. It had just become Texas Western College after having been the College of Mines for a number of years. But the place took hold.

There were a lot of things about the department that I liked. Dr. Waller was just the epitome of a gentleman and a scholar. The History Department was a fairly strong department at that time. I saw a possibility for

191

teaching Latin American history and Mexican history right here on this border. I didn't move into the Latin American field for quite a while, because back in those days it was the Department of History, Government, and Sociology. So for quite a while I taught, besides the American survey, a survey course in European history and government courses, but eventually I worked into U.S. diplomatic history and then into Mexico.

We liked El Paso, and we liked the college. I decided that there would be a satisfaction in contributing to a school of this size that obviously was going to grow. Texas Western was a small little school at that time, 2,000 students, a glorified high school. There was a small and congenial faculty, but the sororities ran the school. They won all of the school elections, they were the cheerleaders, they did Homecoming, they did it all. And everybody went home at noon. The chairman of the History Department and the president of the school played golf two or three afternoons a week, and there wouldn't be an automobile anywhere on campus after twelve o'clock. It was kind of a country club.

I consider myself a member of what I call the middle generation of faculty. That was because as the school came more and more over into the Liberal Arts, away from engineering and mining, a number of Ph.D.'s were hired in the late 1930s to head up the departments. Some very able, dependable people were hired, and I'll never forget them: Tony Berkman*, [C.A.] Puckett*, Gene Thomas* in engineering, [C.L.] Sonnichsen* in English. You obviously could see that they were trying to build a foundation there of academic quality. Now I came in some years later, in the late '40s, along with Joe Leach, Francis Fugate, [and Olav E.] Eidbo. They were trying to hire Ph.D.'s, and they very definitely were trying to improve academic quality. The next generation, the generation of the '60s and '70s, is where you got a tremendous influx of faculty. So I'm that middle generation that can see both back and forward.

I'm not so sure whether [the students] have changed a great deal. I think we have a better institution now academically than the one that I came to. To be sure, the student body was smaller, the faculty and the classes were smaller, and there was a closer relationship with students, very definitely a much closer relationship then. But academically, intellectually, I think students are about the same and have been just pretty much the same all along. I went back after my retirement and taught a freshman course, and I didn't think that they'd improved that much. Maybe, by virtue of TV, I think they're perhaps somewhat better informed generally about the world they live in, but I can't see any great amount of differences from their academic performance now as opposed to twenty [or] thirty years ago.

I think that there was a much more active social life back in the old days than there is now. The students were proud of what they had, of their student body, and they played an active role in institutional affairs. I can remember chaperoning the dances. You knew all the students, and they knew you. Somehow they'd manage to find funds to bring in big name bands. It was marvelous! Tony Berkman was a dean of men back in those days, and he was a disciplinarian from way back. He was at all the social functions, and there were plenty of them. If he was there at the dance, and usually he was, your job as chaperone, well, you had it made! You could go dance, because he did all the work. He'd take down names; he'd round up all the drunks.

Socially the students were very active. They must have spent a lot more time on social activities then they did on the books! And oh boy, those sororities watched their gals! Boy! I can remember the gal in charge of Zeta Tau Alpha, when I flunked one of her gals. Boy, she was on me. But it was good, though, because they did teach girls the social graces, and they did watch over their studies, too.

One memorable event comes to mind — the 1963 *Flowsheet*. It was dedicated [to me]. That was quite an honor, and I deeply appreciated it. Another one that comes to mind — in 1977 I won the AMOCO teaching award. That recognition was wonderful, and I was proud of [it]. Another highlight was that we had one of the first Peace Corps projects anywhere in the country in 1961. You remember how John F. Kennedy turned professors and students on. It was a project to train surveyors and engineers who were going to go to Tanganyika and build roads. We had about forty of the Peace Corpsmen. Of course, the geologists here were heavily involved. Clyde Kelsey was director of the whole project, and I was associate director. They were a fun bunch. They were so dedicated, and they wanted so much to do a job for the country. There was a spirit that I don't think I've ever seen before or since.

At the end of the project, President Joseph Ray* and Kelsey were invited to the White House for a reception. All the Peace Corps members were invited, too, the whole bunch. Well, Kelsey couldn't go! No, he had to oversee a project he had going in Colombia. So President Joe Ray and I went to the White House to the reception. And this is the hand that shook the hand of JFK! I remember he came out of his office with his entourage, and we had a little get-together in the Rose Garden at the White House. He made a little speech, and he used some of the same language that he used in his inaugural. We had a wonderful time. That was obviously a highlight.

I'm going to mention one more that I'll never forget. I taught that course on Mexico for a number of years, but more and more we began to get students from Juarez. And it made an impression on them. Here was a "maldito gringo" teaching these Mexican students about the history of their country. It made an impression upon me, and I just tried that much harder. I tried to get the story through to them. They were wonderful to work with. But their [prior] knowledge just didn't amount to very much. They'd heard of Miguel Hidalgo and Benito Juarez, but that's about the extent of it. I hope they learned a lot.

One anecdote that comes to mind concerns [C.A.] Puckett*, who was dean of arts and sciences. Dean Puckett was a "one and only." [His] middle name was "catalog" — right to the letter, *always* right to the letter. So I was teaching an advanced course, and I had this very fine student, straight A's in college so far, but the requirements for an advanced course back in those days were junior standing plus six hours of history and six hours of other social science. This particular student was a little older than most and very conscientious, [but] she was short of junior standing. I wasn't going to let that stand in [the way] because she could do the work. This comes up before Puckett, and I explained my position. I was absolutely certain that she was an excellent student, just top notch, and I had no doubt in my mind that she would have no problems in the course. Puckett finally looks up, looks me straight in the eye, and says, "I agree with everything you say, but the answer is no."

I remember teaching a course in European history, and we were on the background of World War I. I was dealing with the diplomatic crisis of 1914. I was going along — oh, I was eloquent! — that's right, building tension, building tension, building tension all the time. And just then some [airplane] broke the sound barrier, and the class just about gave a bark. I think I had said that an explosion could take the place at any time, and then we got this [sonic boom] up in the sky! I'm left speechless! The only thing I can say is, "Well, back in my graduate school days a professor told me that you always have to have a sense of the dramatic, so this is it!" Those are the things, obviously, that you don't ever forget.

I became chairman in 1962 of the Department of History, Government, and Sociology. Right away, they took two-thirds of it away. Nobody was happier about that than I was. Government was set up as Political Science on its own; Sociology the same thing. I welcomed the change because I could focus on History, and we had some hiring to do. Then, after about three years, I simply decided, "Well, we've cleaned up most of the problems, and somebody else can do this thing. I've got other things to do." So from that time it's been a rotational arrangement, which I think is [good]. I think it's worked reasonably well, because one guy doesn't get bogged down with the paper[work] for the rest of his life.

I've never had too many disappointments. I can remember back in the 1950s, though, when money was tight. If you got a two hundred dollar increase, boy! But those were awfully hard days, and there were a lot of people my age getting a two hundred dollar a year raise, and families are coming along, and the oldest one is going to be hitting college. . . . So these were things of rather deep concern.

This institution has been very good to me. Now I'm going to tell you what I think was my major contribution to this institution. [It] is the microfilm program in the Library*. We had a committee of community people called Mission '73 to look over the institution to make recommendations. I was impressed by the language in Mission '73. They put out a little booklet, and quite naturally [it concluded], as many committees have said, "Take advantage of your geographical locations. Do those things to exploit your geographical location here on the border." I took this to heart. So I went to Joe Ray, and I told him that I would put up a thousand dollars if he would come up with four thousand dollars, to get a program started in which we would start microfilming some of the basic printed documentary collections at U.T. Austin, [from] that marvelous Latin American library. We focused first on printed materials, particularly the source materials. He went along with it, and we went to work. After two years, we had five thousand dollars' worth of microfilm of printed source materials from the Latin American collection in Austin.

Well, I said to Joe Ray, "I just consider this Phase One. Let's move it forward. I'll put up another thousand, and you put up whatever you can to go along with my one, and we'll start work in Chihuahua." We already had the records of the ayuntamiento of Ciudad Juarez. That had already been done. That was the beginning. We picked up right there, and we bought the Parral [Archive]. We did one in Janos; we did a major job in Chihuahua City — 700 reels. We did the *Periódico Oficial* of Chihuahua, Chihuahua's leading newspaper. And we did that pretty well, working with Francisco Almada, Chihuahua's distinguished historian. Everything we microfilmed, we left a copy in Mexico. Mexico always got a copy of everything we did. Then we started working in Durango. It turned out, for my two thousand dollars, I guess I must have gotten ten or fifteen thousand dollars' worth of [microfilmed materials]. Scholars around the country know about it, and it's brought them here to El Paso. So I have to say I consider that to be my major contribution.

This school has been very good to me. The decision to retire in 1978 is one that I shall never regret, simply because it's a brand new life for me. I'm doing things that I had to put off through the years. You're born again. You can travel. You can do things you want to do when you want to do them. You can get some writing done. You can help with the historical organizations here locally. This school's been very good to me. This city's been very good to me. And I'm glad to have been a part of it.

Interviewed by Vicki L. Ruiz, October 19, 1983, El Paso.

The University of Texas System was not integrated at the faculty level. . . . I had no idea that there were no blacks.

Marjorie P. Lawson
[1938-1984]
Faculty, 1966-1984

They were still testing the waters in a sense, because I would imagine I was the first black administrator of an academic unit in the U.T. System.

Juan O. Lawson
Faculty, 1967-Present

Marjorie: I went to Howard University in Washington, D.C., and really finished growing up there. I took my master's immediately after my undergraduate degree, and so by that time I had matured, and I had become just about a fixture at Howard. When I started working on my master's, I became a graduate assistant, and I got a chance to [teach freshman English] for very little money. When I got my master's, I got a chance to do the same thing as an instructor for very little money.

Juan: I was in the army. I was a reserve officer, so I had a two-year

197

active duty requirement. They sent me here because I was air defense artillery. I had no idea really of where El Paso was. Well, I had a general idea by looking at the map, but all I knew about it was cowboy pictures. We came out here to serve in the military and stayed. That was 1965 through 1967.

Marjorie: Dear Fort Bliss brought us to El Paso. I was an army wife with no job for the first time in my adult life. It just felt marvelous at first, and then it felt unnatural. I went to Texas Western and applied [for a teaching job], not having any idea what the situation was. Dr. John West, [the chair of the English Department], the bravest man I know, took a chance and hired me in 1966. I didn't fully realize what daring he was displaying. The University of Texas System was not integrated at the faculty level, instructor and above. I had no idea that there were no blacks. I hadn't thought about it; I just needed a job.

I can't remember any unpleasantness because of race. By the time I came here, I was a veteran in the classroom. So although I'm very shy socially, in the classroom I take charge, and there was never any problem. The students did mistake me for a Mexican-American. I'm not obviously black. My eyes aren't dark, and at that time many Mexican-Americans were about my complexion. I've gotten much browner [since then]. It's been seventeen years of Texas sun! I got many strange looks when I said, "I don't speak Spanish."

Juan: I know a little bit more about the behind-the-scenes business when my wife was hired. When Marjorie applied, initially she was rejected, but nicely. Dr. John West indicated to her that he really wanted to hire her, but he was having a little bit of a problem, and that if he were to take that bold step, he wanted a Ph.D. [rather than someone with an M.A.]. Then he tested the waters, and a month or so later he called back.

[In the meantime] he had approached the then dean [of the College of Liberal Arts], Ray Small. Dean Small was a man of forward thinking in race relations. He didn't seem to have any problems in that regard. He took it to the president, then Joe Ray*, and Dr. Ray didn't seem to have any problem. They were all worried about the immediate supervisor, their administrative supervisor. Then Dr. Ray told me what happened. He said that he wanted to do it [hire Marjorie], but he had a problem with the Board of Regents, and he didn't know what to do. He called one of his friends on the Board, who happened to be a little forward on

198

the matter, and asked him how to handle the situation. His instructions from the man were: "Hire, but don't send any pictures."

I started a year later [in 1967]. The climate had changed a bit more. I think the U.T. System was beginning to open up. And since my wife had been hired, then they hired me. At that time the College of Liberal Arts had been split. The College of Science had been completed, and a new dean had been hired, Dr. Lewis Hatch. His first year was my first year. He saw me walking around with my uniform on, and he had gotten wind that I was applying for a job. He saw me going down to the Physics office, and when I came back he was waiting for me.

He asked [if] the chairman had hired me. I told him no; there was some problem that they were discussing. The problem wasn't with the chairman. The chairman was worried about what his superiors would say. Dr. Hatch, being brand new, picked up the phone, called the chairman, used a number of choice words, slammed the phone down, and told me to go back down there. So I went back down there, and I was hired. When I came back, Dr. Hatch asked if I got the job. I said, "Yes." He said, "Fine." That's how I was hired — as not the first but the second [black faculty member]. But at least I was the first black male with a Ph.D.

[As for reactions], in my case, some of the faculty members were from different parts of the country, and they were curious. I'm obviously black, so they didn't have any problems identifying me, and they were curious. Naturally they wanted to know where I was from. They wanted to know about my first name; it was an anomaly. Of course it is, because [there is] no cultural basis for me to have a Spanish first name. They would engage me in conversations. I guess they were really trying to find out if I were real, if I were reasonably intelligent.

Then they would appoint me to committees. I was on too many committees, because they wanted to have a black on the committee. Sometimes as an assistant professor they put me on committees with full professors. I really didn't belong there because I didn't have the experience, but they put me there anyway. They would give me assignments, and without really meaning to, they would often express a little surprise if I could do a job well. Of course, they weren't intending to be mean or insensitive. It was just their first reaction, and they seemingly were surprised if I did certain things well. As time went on, I was generally accepted, and they saw me as an individual without regard to my complexion.

199

During those early years I did make some lasting friendships with several faculty members. Ken Beasley I think of as one very sensitive man with regard to racial issues. He and I met one time when we were serving on a presidential committee. He took me under his wing, so to speak, not in a condescending fashion, but he seemingly just liked me for some reason or another. When he became dean of the Graduate School, he brought me with him and made me the assistant dean. I enjoyed the job with him, and of course that gave me an opportunity to meet all of the other administrators.

I recognized that I needed to do a little bit more academically, so that I could be legitimate in whatever I was doing. I did discuss that matter with Dr. Beasley, because I knew about a number of minorities getting into various positions by virtue of tokenism, or whatever you want to call it, in the university systems across the country, but not really pursuing those things which they should if they wished to be academicians. I went back to my department with the understanding that I'd do my work, publish a number of papers, which I did, and become more academically qualified for my promotions. Dr. Hatch was behind this, too. Both of those men — Ken Beasley and Lewis Hatch — were very influential in my academic career here.

In time I had enough stuff behind me to be promoted up the line until I was full professor. A year later, Dr. Beasley had been made academic vice president, and somehow he fixed it so that I would apply for the dean's job — dean of science. They decided they didn't want an outside candidate. I was a local candidate, and my name appeared on the list. Once my name appeared on the list, that was it. I don't know whether the search committee knew that, but once my name was on the final list, that was it.

In '75 I took over as dean ad interim. Dr. [Arleigh B.] Templeton used that terminology. They were still testing the waters in a sense, because I would imagine I was the first black administrator of an academic unit in the U.T. System. They wouldn't call me acting dean. So they said dean ad interim, and they watched. They wanted to see what the faculty of the College of Science would think, how they would react. The faculty seemed to be very enlightened and open. During those years before I was promoted to full professor, I was on committees with various faculty members, and I made a number of friends. All of the science people had begun to accept me just as an individual, and race didn't play any part.

But the president and the VP didn't know what my relationship was with the faculty. So they tested me for about three or four months, and after they found out that the faculty would work with me and accept me as a supervisor, then they finally changed my designation to dean. That was in March of 1976.

I think that El Paso is a good place because of the multicultural atmosphere. Newcomers are somewhat forced to be reasonable with regard to intercultural and interracial relationships. I think that was a big factor in the way we were accepted here. What was necessary for me, though, was to prove myself. Most black people find this to be the case. Now, everyone has to prove himself, but as I perceive it, a black person has to make sure that he proves his capabilities. That was a personal goal I had in mind all during that time, because of my daddy's influence. [He would say,] "Always prove, son, that you are as good as or better than." So I would not allow myself to get caught up in those things which I knew weren't really important for whatever goals I was trying to achieve. My daddy made that clear to me as I was growing up.

Here I've had a little difficulty with my children. In the earlier years they didn't really understand that they were black, going to the schools that they had been going to. They didn't realize that there was any difference. Then when [a] very few people would insult them racially, they would come home, and they just couldn't understand that. I think they're understanding through my explanations, but still their experiences are far different from mine. I've explained to both of them the way my dad explained it to me, that they must achieve, [that] they must put forth effort to always prove themselves. They don't feel that pressure the way I felt it, [but] a few incidents have occurred to let them know that maybe there is some truth to what Dad is saying. They are learning to cope with the situation. Although attitudes seem to have been changing for the better, we see a little fluctuation. But on the average things have moved forward, as far as we're concerned, since we first became working adults.

Interviewed by Rebecca Craver, February 27, 1984, El Paso.

We would put our blue jeans on, roll them up to our knees . . . and wear these [full circle] skirts over them to come on campus.

Mimi Reisel Gladstein

Student, 1954-1956; 1958-1966
Faculty, 1966-1969; 1971-Present

I've been at UTEP almost continuously since 1954, either as a student or as a professor. I came to Texas Western College in the summer of 1954, straight out of El Paso High. Then I went away to the University of Oklahoma [for two years, but in the summers I attended Texas Western]. I moved to Germany for about a year and a half, and came back and got my bachelor's degree from Texas Western in '59. In 1960 I began my master's degree, which I completed in '66, the first year it was The University of Texas at El Paso.

Those were the halcyon days of academe, when student populations were just soaring, so I decided that I ought to go get my Ph.D. if I wanted to teach at a university. I was going to take a few courses here before I went to enroll in the Ph.D. program at the University of New Mexico. I was at registration, and John West [of the English Department] walked up to me and said, "Can you teach a freshman course for us?" I didn't have better sense than to say, "Yes." So I started that way. I went away in 1970 to work on my degree, and in 1971 I came back to UTEP as a full-time faculty member.

When I was a student here in the summer, I was a part of the College Players, which meant I went to class in the morning and my soul belonged to the Drama Department until midnight after that. Milton Leech* was the chair of the department, and for what he called summer stock we did five productions in six weeks. We started with a musical comedy and ended with Shakespeare, and usually in between we had some kind of mystery or melodrama. In those days there were only two faculty members [in the Drama Department], and they managed to put on this extraordinary program.

One of the [advantages] that the department had at that time was the draft. Fort Bliss was very active, and a lot of young men and women who were just beginning their professional careers had to take time out to be in the service for two years. We benefited from that because Milton had open casting, and we had people who were stationed down here who have since gone on to make quite big names for themselves in theater. We acted with them. Milton also brought in visiting professors from different places who would direct shows or do the costuming.

If you were a College Player in summer stock, you were expected to be involved in all of these five productions in some way. If you were starring in one, then you handled props in another and were building sets for a third. I was here all day long, and then rehearsal would be in the evening. After rehearsal everyone would go to the Hacienda [Restaurant] for something and save very little time to do your homework for your eight o'clock class the next morning.

One amusing [incident about clothing] illustrates how our mind-sets change. When I was in the Drama Department, we had to be building sets and painting them and dragging stuff around. Naturally the best uniform for that was jeans. But there was a rule: A young woman or a girl could not come on campus in pants. If you were seen on campus in pants, you were reported to the dean of women. What we would do is: we had these big peasant skirts in those days, full circle skirts. We would put our blue jeans on, roll them up to our knees, and wear these skirts over them to come on campus. Once we got on the stage in Magoffin [Auditorium], which is where the productions were held, then we'd take our skirts off, and we could go to work.

When I began teaching, about 1968, the first time a female student showed up in my class in pants I was shocked. I remember looking at

204

her and thinking, "She doesn't have the proper respect for this class."
When I was here [as a student] at UTEP, all of my professors — 99 percent of them were male — came to class in coats and ties. Women came
in heels and hose. One of the ways we knew we were in college is that
our professors addressed us Miss or Mister. We were now adult young
people, and we would be addressed properly. And, of course, we were
all dressed very properly also.

I then went for my graduate work to the University of New Mexico,
which was considerably more liberal than UTEP. My professors there wore
sandals and jeans and T-shirts and beads. Some of them took one look
at me and my little heels and hose and bouffant hairdo and thought, "God,
there's a refugee from the supermarket." It was a classic instance of reverse
discrimination. I had to really fight to convince them I had any mind at
all. When I returned from UNM, having been considerably radicalized
by the experience, I was the first female professor to wear pants on this
campus. And I love to tell the story that I thought that I was going to
frizzle a lot of the gray hairs around here, but the second female professor to wear pants was Roberta Walker, who had a beautiful head of white
hair. Here I had thought that wearing pants to my class was an insult
in 1968, [but a few years later] wearing pants was an act of freedom.

We forget that the sixties [as a social movement] didn't begin until about
'66 and really lasted until about '73. In the sixties there was a sensitivity
to issues; there were students that were concerned about the political
situation or [individual] rights. It meant something to them. I think now
when you talk about rights in a class, the students get this glazed look
on their faces. If I could make a generalization, and I think generaliza-
tions are dangerous, it seems to me that the eighties were more like the
fifties. In the fifties we weren't very concerned with political ideas, and
I think our students now don't pay much attention either. The students
in the late sixties and early seventies were serious and concerned about
the world, but that seems to have passed.

I was looking at the whole thing [the Chicano demonstration in December, 1971] from the fourth floor of the Liberal Arts Building. I was teaching in that corner room, which overlooks the Administration Building.
The whole thing looked about as dangerous to me as . . . I mean, if there
was an emergency I didn't see it. Of course, I had been at UNM where
eleven people had been bayoneted. I'd been at UNM where I wouldn't

teach in the Naval Arts Building because there were threats to blow it up. I had seen real riots, and what was going on here was nothing compared to what I had seen in those other places. I think in this riot there couldn't have been more than a hundred people. I saw the police out here, but [the demonstrators that] they were armed against didn't seem to be nearly as threatening. It was like bringing out your cannons to battle flies. The response seemed all out of proportion to the danger.

I remember outside groups coming to campus, like the Fourth World Coalition or something like that, brought here by MEChA [Movimiento Estudiantil Chicano de Aztlán] and by the Black Student Union. I remember a particularly amusing sequence where they were showing a vehemently anti-American, anti-Israeli film called "We Are the Palestinians." They came here because they wanted to mobilize people on behalf of the PLO [Palestine Liberation Organization]. At this meeting one of the students from here got up and said, "How do you feel about Aztlán?" These were outside agitators from Los Angeles, and they said, "Aztlán? What's Aztlán?" And this guy said, "What are you doing, coming over here and asking us to worry about something that's half a world apart, if you're not willing to fight for Aztlán, which is our country which the gringos have taken away from us!" That was the only instance where I had first-hand knowledge of somebody from outside coming in and trying to arouse students. [Our students] said, "No way."

I never did feel that our campus was one of the hotbeds of activity. Even our streaking, which was one of those expressions of the time, was so unimaginative. They would announce that there were going to be streakers at such and such a place, which defeats the whole purpose of streaking. The whole purpose of streaking is shock. In the most unlikely place at the most unlikely time, somebody streaks through. Well, here we'd have this announcement that there're going to be streakers coming down University Avenue in front of the Liberal Arts Building. People would line up on both sides of the streets, and then a truck would drive through with about four or five naked people. I thought, "This is not exactly the zenith of social awareness here." So that's the kind of radical activity [we had] on campus in those days.

Interviewed by Rebecca Craver, March 6, 1984, El Paso.

I would go a whole day without seeing another brown face, and that was traumatic for me.

Jose F. Avila

Student, 1960; 1964-1967; 1970-1974
Dean of Students, 1974-Present

I was born in Newark Maternity Hospital on the south side of El Paso. My mother and father were first-generation Americans from El Paso. Their parents, my grandparents, were all from Chihuahua. I graduated from high school in 1960 and came to Texas Western College that same year. I chose the school because — well, I think I can speak for a lot of Chicanos of my generation — you didn't think about going away. I don't believe that's changed much. Some of it is finances; some of it is family ties; some of it is ties to the culture. You go where you are, and that was Texas Western College. I didn't want to go initially, but my mother was one of those pushers, one of those "My son is going be the best" type of people. So part of the reason I failed was that I didn't want to go. I wasn't motivated to go; I didn't care. It took me three months to realize I didn't belong, so I dropped out and joined the service.

I remember one of the reasons I left in 1960 was because I would go a whole day without seeing another brown face, and that was traumatic for me. The high school I went to was Jefferson High School. It was 97 percent Chicano and 3 percent black; there were no Anglos whatsoever.

207

So when the shoe's on the other foot, and [I was] the minority *minority*, I felt awkward. To a person that had never been out of the barrio very much, to a person that had lived in the Mexican neighborhood where everything is Spanish and where Anglos don't go unless they're there to arrest somebody or to collect bills, it was traumatic [to come to TWC], and I felt out of place.

A lot of it wasn't the fault of the place; a lot of it was my own cultural adjustment. It's easy to go to a university when your parents have [already] gone and there's a foundation for you to build on. Well, I was the first in my family to ever finish high school, much less go to college. In fact, if left up to me, I never would have gone. In those days Chicanos in high school didn't talk about going to college; they talked about which branch of the service to go into. If my mother hadn't pushed me, I might have missed a great opportunity, and I'd be out there digging ditches or painting houses. So I'm grateful to her.

Another part of it was [that] high school was easy for me. I made A's, I never had to hustle, and when I did screw up, the teacher was there to remind me. [But] at the university nobody was going to remind me. I was on my own. If I missed a lecture or something like that, my pride wouldn't allow me to ask for help from an Anglo, and I didn't see another brown face. So I screwed myself up from the beginning.

When I came back in '64, it was better. By then I had gotten over a lot of my cultural hangups. The Air Force helped me to mature and to recognize my abilities. Most important of all, it helped me to fit into American society. I ended up in an intelligence squadron where most of the guys were college graduates. I was one of the few who didn't have a college degree. And they turned me on to the idea that it was possible for me to go to college. I gained some confidence. I could do the job as well as they, so I knew I could make it in college, whereas before I wasn't sure. I came back with the idea that I was going to make it. The major difference was that before, my mother had signed me up to be an engineer. When I did it on my own, I knew I wanted to be a teacher, so I majored in education. I was more motivated to be a teacher than an engineer.

I was here [as an undergraduate] from '64 to '67. The Greek system was still big, [but] I was a typical commuter student. I had a wife and two kids, so my motivation was to get a degree to get a job to support my family. And the sooner I got that done, the better. I really didn't have time to spend on campus, and a lot of it was my ignorance in not knowing what went on. It would have made me a better, well-rounded person if I had participated in activities. But the typical commuter [attitude is]: Get off the campus, go to your job, go home, study, go back to school.

I remember specifically that freshmen were required to do two things: paint the "M" and wear an orange-and-white beanie. I guess I was one of those that helped to end traditions like that, because I refused to paint the "M" and wear a beanie. When this upperclassman threatened to do something, I said, "What are you going to do?" And he couldn't think of an answer. So I imagine that guys like me who were coming back from the service, who were more mature than somebody just coming out of high school, helped to destroy what I now consider good traditions.

I have a Bachelor of Science [degree] in Secondary Education, with teaching fields in biology and history. For four years I was a history teacher at Ysleta High School. Public schools provide horrible counseling. The high school counselors are paid to shuffle paper. And a lot of these students would come in and tell me horror stories when they needed counseling. 'I'm pregnant: what do I do?" "My mother beats me up." "My father molests me." I didn't know how to deal with that; I had no training. I'm sure of my common sense about such things, but I wasn't a counselor.

So I decided that I would kill two birds with one stone. I could go get my graduate degree in counseling, and I would be able to help these students, and at the same time [I could] draw on the GI Bill rather than work part-time. I went to night school [for] my graduate [work] and was never on campus during the day. Interestingly enough, I never got a chance to go back and counsel those high school kids, because as I was doing my last course, my practicum supervisor [told me] the vice president for student affairs was looking for bilingual counselors. Based on [an] interview, I got the job. In the mornings I was a bilingual counselor, and in the afternoons I was an administrative "go-for."

I didn't ask for the job; I fell right into it. I like to think that it was because of my brown skin that I got the job but because of my abilities, regardless of skin, that I kept it. When I came to work, we were probably 20 percent Hispanic. The black population was basically the same as it is now, not many. You've got to remember that from 1971 to now, the enrollment doubled. In those days it was seven or eight thousand students; now it's fifteen [thousand]. A lot of that growth was Hispanics.

In fact, the growth in the last ten years has been in Hispanics, has been in women, and the decline has been in male Anglos. The Anglo population stood still, and the Hispanic population grew.

I got in on the best part of the Chicano movement. I was brand new on campus. I thought of myself as the messiah that was going to bridge the gap in communication, because I knew Anglo society and could exist in it, and I knew the Chicano problems and concerns. Most of the students didn't support the Chicano movement; they just went along with it. In fact, taking over the Administration Building in 1971 was accomplished by about twenty students, period. All the rest joined in [as] merely a reaction against the police, not in support of the movement. As far as the staff, they stayed out of it. The faculty — there were some who got into it, basically because of ACLU [American Civil Liberties Union] support [for] the movement at that time, but it was a small group. As far as my participation in it, I was the only Chicano who stood against the activists. And I stood against them not because I disagreed with them, but because I didn't like their tactics. I feel that violence is always the last resort.

It was my belief at the time that [the Chicano activists] weren't trying to communicate. In 1971 they posed five or six demands. Now one of the demands was illegal according to state law, so there was no way the University would comply. The second demand had already [been met]. The administration gave in on the others. I thought that was a great victory. The vice president for student affairs, whose title is now dean of students, went over there to tell them in writing, "Okay, you've won. We're giving in on these three. We can't give you this one, and this one you already have." He went to the Administration Building, because they had occupied it. Just as he started to give it to them, they tore the stack of papers out of his hands, tore them up, and threw them up in the air. Then they wouldn't leave the building. So what else could they do? They called the police, and it got to be a big mess.

Later on I spoke to one of the leaders, and I said, "Why did you do this, when you had won?" He said, "You don't understand, stupid. We didn't want to win. We wanted the issue; we wanted the publicity." At that point they became my enemies. If you can settle problems through communication in a nice way, I'm all for it, but I won't deal with people who are out to do violence. It hurt me as a Chicano to have to take a stand against Chicanos. But now we think alike. Now they know that the way to get things is through legalities, through MALDEF [Mexican-American Legal Defense and Education Fund], through communication, by getting people inside the system and changing it from within, rather than trying to attack it from without.

Here at UTEP activism began to subside about 1975, because the popularity of demonstrations went down. It was replaced by the stupidity of streaking, which lasted a week or so. Those times also brought the new generation dean. They got rid of the father-in-absence, mother-in-absence deans, the nice people who wanted to talk. And they brought in people like me, people who are half lawyers, half politicians, half police.

You've got to be a glutton for punishment, you've got to be slightly insane, to want to be a dean of students. There are three really horrible jobs on the campus: One is being the president of the University, the second one is being the athletic director, and third one is being the dean of students. If I knew then what I know now, I wouldn't have accepted the job. My life has been threatened more times than I like to mention. It's taken its toll on me. As staff, we don't have tenure. You screw up once big, and that's it, you're gone. I was kidding around once, and I told Dr. [Arleigh B.] Templeton* I wanted tenure. And Dr. Templeton, who was president before Dr. [Haskell] Monroe*, said, "Joe, the only tenure you have is ten seconds to get the hell off my campus when I tell you to get off." He and I used to talk like that. I really loved the man.

As a student and as a dean, I've been associated with UTEP for twenty years, and more and more I feel it truly represents a bilingual, bicultural community that reflects El Paso. I think that's healthy, because we do serve El Paso. In my opinion, UTEP, in enrolling Hispanics and getting them degrees and professional jobs, has done more for the social and economic advancement of Chicanos than any other thing in El Paso.

I have nothing against high standards. I think UTEP has high standards; I think it should have high standards. But I think those high standards should be in the classroom. What I am against is high standards in the admissions process, because I call that elitism, which denies people an opportunity to try. I think it's a racist notion to keep out people with the admissions process. They may not be aware of it but, realistically, higher standards in admissions, high entrance exam scores, will systematically weed out Chicanos from going to universities, and universities

are the one thing that we need to advance ourselves. I think anybody
— not just Chicanos, but anybody — should have a right to be admitted,
and then put them through hell in the classroom. And if they don't make
it, flunk 'em out. I guarantee you there'll be some who make it. Those
are the ones that should get that opportunity to try.

I love that student body. Nobody knows the students better than I do.
I mean, I was one of them; I grew up with them; I taught them in the
public schools; I've cried with them; I've gotten drunk with them. I know
them. They're El Paso for the most part, and I know El Paso.

Interviewed by Kenneth A. LaPrade, November 28, 1984, El Paso.

They sent me a letter telling me that I should live
in the dorm so I could get the experience of being away
from home. They sent the letter to Vietnam!

Dennis Bixler-Marquez

Student, 1968-1973
Faculty, 1978-Present

I was born in Mexico City in 1945. My father was American; my mother
was Mexican, from Torreon. In 1959 I came to the United States. I started
school in a special English program at Father Yermo School and then
transferred to a regular program. I went to El Paso Technical, a vocational high school. I was very attracted to automobiles, so I took body
repair. Instead of playing sports, I spent most of my time working on cars.
When I graduated from high school I worked in the automotive parts
business for about a year and a half. Then I was drafted.

I spent all of 1966 and 1967 in the army. I volunteered for service in
Vietnam just to see what it was like. Then I got tired of Vietnam, and
I told them I wanted to go back to the States, and they said, "Too bad!"
So I stayed eight months in Vietnam. I was assigned to an infantry unit
as a mechanic. When I was discharged from the army, I decided to attend
UTEP. They sent me a letter telling me that I should live in the dorm
so I could get the experience of being away from home. They sent the
letter to Vietnam!

213

I started attending UTEP in the spring of 1968. I completed a Bachelor of Arts in political science and Spanish in 1971. I just crossed the street from the Liberal Arts [Building] and enrolled in a special master's program in education. I worked when I was in college. Even though I had the GI Bill, I had a part-time job, again as an auto mechanic. When I first came, there were a lot of people who had gone into the service and were using the GI Bill to come back, so the University grew by leaps and bounds. Given the percentage of Mexican-Americans that are veterans, you could see a tremendous increase [in] them coming into school. Most of the male students from my high school finished college after having gone through the service. Few of [us] came straight through after high school.

There was a definite shift in the composition of the University because of the Vietnam War. Certainly the University was polarized like the rest of the nation, in terms of the groups for and against the war. I often compare what I went through with what colleagues of mine went through at Berkeley, where they were highly politicized. [Their experience] reflects very strongly in what and how they teach. Because I came back as a veteran, perhaps with more conservative values, it took me quite a while to accept the movements.

[At UTEP there was] nothing approaching the magnitude of a San Francisco State or Columbia or Berkeley, but you [did] have the ethnic renaissance movement growing tremendously. This was also in the midst of the civil rights movement. The black group was very vocal and active, and so was the Mexican-American group. And we had the beginnings of the feminist movement on campus, which had been very late in blossoming here. While most other institutions established ethnic studies programs in that period of time, Women's Studies was instituted here [in the early 1980s], so that gives you an idea. Certainly there were feminists around, but they didn't have the following in this conservative university, as opposed to West Coast universities.

I was involved with MAPA, the Mexican-American Political Association. I was also involved with other groups, such as the Society for the Advancement of Education, where we were trying to bring about change through educational means. We were identifying kids in high school who wanted to go to college, and we would give them the SAT sample test early. We were hoping to attract these people into college preparatory courses so they could succeed. At the same time, through MAPA I was involved in things like voter registration drives. And at the very first year of my graduate program, we had MEChA [Movimiento Estudiantil Chicano de Aztlán] taking over the Administration Building.

MEChA operated under the concept of the University belonging to the people of the city. If you are a potential college student or an adult and you are not necessarily enrolled in UTEP, that would not preclude you from being in MEChA. What you have to understand is that MEChA and other organizations were also redefining whether bona fide university organizations should be exclusively made up of students or should be broadly based in the community, which was something not palatable to the administration.

What was wanted at the time were changes in the curriculum of the University to reflect the ethnic composition of the area, [especially] the establishment of a Chicano Studies major, just like you have Black Studies or Urban Studies in other universities. Though MEChA took the initiative and certainly paid the price — some members were incarcerated — what the Chicano movement was trying to bring about was the legitimization of our cultural values and traditions by mainstreaming that into the body of knowledge that we transmit. And naturally when you're talking about that, you're rocking the educational establishment.

Along with that, MEChA and other organizations were saying, "We're not servicing students who are linguistically different." One of the things that MEChA brought about which had not been done, and they wanted it not just for Mexican-Americans but for every other group that needed it, was a tutorial center. They wrote up a proposal and obtained some monies to provide things like remedial English, mathematics, [and] tutors. This is something the University had not acted upon, even though most major universities had such programs in operation. The University eventually took over the program, and [now it] is a very important academic service that's provided to all students who need it, regardless of ethnic background.

You can see the changes in many things, for example, the type of music that's in the jukebox. One of the things that MEChA and other organizations said, "Well, we should have [the same] right to decide what kind of records are going to be in the jukebox." Now everybody takes it for granted. Also, the type of food that's served [was an issue]. Now you have

Roman numeral one that says "American Food," and under that you have Swedish meatballs and spaghetti and all the other ethnic foods that are not big enough to merit their own Roman numerals because there are not enough Swedes at UTEP. And then there's this whole other area that says "Mexican Food." You have a great deal of crossover. So the average non-Hispanic at UTEP is very much exposed to various aspects of Hispanic culture, whether it be food, music, or cultural entertainment.

You always tend to remember some of the very good teachers you had. Still teaching here in the Mathematics Department is Jesus Provencio, who went out of his way to develop courses and special seminars for people who had difficulties in mathematics, especially if you had difficulties with the language. He was the advisor of the Society for the Advancement of Education that I was affiliated with, so I got to know him well, and I still very much appreciate his commitment to students. I took a course called "The Education of the Mexican-American" under a very good friend and colleague of mine, Dr. Marie Barker, and that eventually influenced me to go into the field of bilingual education, which was a novelty. And then at the master's level, I had Dr. Tomas Arciniega, who is now the president of Cal State-Bakersfield. He was very influential, [as were] several of the faculty here in the Department of Education.

I went through a very innovative two-year master's program [at UTEP]. We were required to work twenty hours a week in the community. We ran into some [problems with] the school system. We had confrontations over curriculum and so forth, and those had a tremendous impact in the views I developed toward what education should be and who should control it. When I went to Stanford, I was able to get a job over people who had been there a year or two because of the credentials that I acquired in the program at UTEP. So the experiences I had at UTEP very much contributed to my success later on in my doctoral program and also in securing employment, so I could afford to be in a doctoral program.

The University has always been a socioeconomic escalator, but it's become more accessible to a broader percentage of the population, especially people who, because of their sex or ethnic or socioeconomic background, had been tracked away [from] that social escalator almost from the first day they hit the public schools. It's not such an elitist concept anymore. Unfortunately there is a [backlash] at the present to move toward some type of elitist [policy]. But I think that it will never go back to the way it was when it was very much the exclusive domain of the middle class.

That is the thing that impresses me the most, because it means that the University is responding. Perhaps not at the rate which everyone desires, but nevertheless [UTEP] has made some changes to meet some of the needs of the community. The composition of the student body has changed. It's not that anyone has been supplanted. It's not [that] one group came at the expense of another, but rather that we [have added] to the diversity of the school. And that to me was something very healthy and very desirable, because this represents precisely some of the things we were working for in the late sixties and early seventies. When you see them closer to realization fourteen years later, you do get a [strong sense] of satisfaction. You don't feel that it was all done in vain.

Interviewed by Randy Scott Hedrick, November 27, 1984, El Paso.

Everyone was streaking. . . . I remember a very old man riding on top of a car going through the main campus, and on his briefcase, which was shielding his important parts, was a bumper sticker that said "I'm proud to be a grandpa."

Thomas F. Meagher
Student, 1972-1977, 1981-1985

I grew up in Las Cruces and moved to the big city, El Paso, upon graduation from Las Cruces High School in 1972. [Before making a decision] I went for an interview at UNM [the University of New Mexico]. I also went to Tucson or Phoenix. The people there were extremely rude when you asked for the catalog and asked about their program. When I came down to UTEP, it was like — "Please come here." I got so much literature and so much help. It was only forty miles away, so I thought, "You can't pass it up."

At the time we were experiencing a nursing shortage in the country. The tuition for nurses [at UTEP] was fifty dollars a semester. You could get your college education for fifty dollars a semester. That was really great. The other attraction was the band. I got called by the person who was running the band at the time, and he said, "Would you like to come on a scholarship?" I said, "Well, I'm a nursing major." He said, "That's all right. You have to do your first two years [on the main campus]. We'll give you a band scholarship to come on down and play in the band."

I played the tuba. It's worth money to someone to have you carry it around.
I said, "Sure, you bet!" So I came down and went on a scholarship at
UTEP for the first two years, playing the tuba and doing my prenursing
courses.

[I got interested in nursing after] a personal situation where I came
across an individual who needed a lot of medical assistance. She was having
a seizure. No one, including me, knew what to do for this person. I really
got the urge at that time, [which] was my last year of high school, that
I didn't want to be in such a situation ever again, when I didn't know
what to do for someone who needed help. I decided at that time to start
looking into nursing schools. My parents didn't think much of it. My parents wanted you to go into a "manly" profession or go into the army.
They thought it was strange that I wanted to be a nurse. But they learned
to accept it. Now they're very glad they did.

So I started UTEP in September of 1972. It was the first semester that
the dorms went coed. It was just prior to them authorizing you to have
alcohol in the dorms. So a lot of time and energy was spent on how to
get it in and out. [It was] a lot of fun. I remember a keg party we had
in the dorm room one weekend. We snuck the keg up, snuck the ice
in, and had a keg party in the dorm room. It was [daring], because if
you got caught you'd be out of Kelly Hall real quick.

I remember the football team; it wasn't very good at the time. I remember the fans singing "Bye, Bye, Bobby" in the stands, because Bobby
Dobbs was the coach at that time. [The band] went on trips to play [at]
football games. In fact, I met my wife on one of those trips to Tucson.
The band now is much more formal. The band then was a rowdy group.
I remember we used to dance in the stands and carry on. We used to
do picture shows and theme marching shows. We'd go from one picture
on the field, which might be a Mexican hat, to another picture, which
might be a pair of castanets. It seemed to be "helter skelter" between
one picture and another. Organized confusion might be a better way of
describing it. It was just a lot of fun. It got me through my first years
in college.

Of the forty-three who graduated [in my nursing class], there were only
three males. [Male enrollment hasn't] ranged any higher than 10 percent of the program. And that's true in the profession today; it's a 95
percent female profession. We weren't treated any differently as far as

I could see. [I was] just another student in the class who was working hard. It was a difficult program to get through. [There was] a lot of studying, a lot of clinical time, just a lot of work. They didn't recommend that you have a part-time job while going to school, because it could jeopardize your success. It didn't stop me, though. I had two part-time jobs and got married and had a kid, all [while] I was going through nursing school.

Hotel Dieu [Hospital] used to have a three-year diploma program, [which] was run by the Daughters of Charity. It was the Hotel Dieu School of Nursing, a very respected school throughout the country. The sisters ran it. Then the sisters sold the school to The University of Texas System. It became part of the [U.T.] System School of Nursing. There were many campuses of the system school at that time. Then about 1976 the System School of Nursing dissolved into regional campuses. What was then the system school [in El Paso] became The University of Texas at El Paso College of Nursing. A few years ago [in 1980] it became the College of Nursing and Allied Health.

We spent a lot of time in the library, which was then located [downtown] at the College of Nursing. [It] saved you a lot of work but made it really parochial, in that nursing students were down at the college and distant from the UTEP main campus. Now the college [library is] in the main University Library, so all the students have to go up there and are more integrated into [UTEP].

There was a lot of clinical time in various hospitals. [At the college] there's a "Sim" [simulation] lab which has been nationally recognized as one of the best equipped Sim labs for nursing instruction in the country. They have mannequins and a mock hospital setup where you practice your clinical skills. Eileen Jacoby was the dean of the college at that time. She was and is a worldwide nursing leader. The one classic instructor at the college was a lady named [Dorothy] Dee Corona, an excellent nurse and smart educator. Spend one class with her, and you've got a role model for nursing. She was excellent.

During the period when the system was transitioning over to UTEP, there was a lot of fear over whether nursing education would go back [to giving] doctors control. There were marches around the school with placards that said "Save our School!" A delegation went to Austin to fight the dissolving of the system. They [feared] that by being decentralized they would lose the power of a [state-wide] system.

Back in 1971-72 there were the so-called "riots" at UTEP. I don't think anybody who was actually on campus thought they were really riots. There were people who were out there talking about "Viva La Raza" and that kind of thing, but they were mostly very peaceful people who were trying to voice their feelings. However, there were [people] on the roofs snapping pictures, and everyone would come out of the SUB [Student Union Building] and watch, which added to the masses of the people and to the anxiety of the administration. No one was really doing anything except watch a bunch of people speak, but there was a big concern. It was funny to watch the nightly news at the time and hear about the "riots" at UTEP. You'd say, "What riot? Was I there today?" There really wasn't [a riot], but that's what they were talking about.

In '73 or '74 we had a rash of streaking. Everyone was streaking. We had a guy who streaked the band hall. Also I think there was somebody who streaked the Sun Bowl that year, from one end to the other. I remember a very old man riding on top of a car going through the main campus, and on his briefcase, which was shielding his important parts, was a bumper sticker that said "I'm proud to be a grandpa." He was riding down University Avenue on top of the car, right in front of the Liberal Arts Building. I think all the students saw it in perspective, as a big joke, as something that's part of college life — "Hey, what's the big deal?" It was something to laugh at and have fun with. But of course the administration had to assume a more authoritarian role. I believe they were threatening to throw people out of school if they got caught streaking. I don't think they needed to throw them out; the embarrassment alone of being caught [should be sufficient punishment]. But it was all in good fun.

I graduated in '77 and went back in '81 to work on my master's. I got that in '85. Now I'm an assistant administrator here at Thomason [Hospital], and I teach at the graduate level in the College of Nursing. I've spent my whole nursing career in El Paso. Whether it's critical care or pediatrics or geriatrics, when everybody else is gone, when the doctor's at home, it's the nurse who's at the bedside. From birth to death and from wellness to illness, it's the nurse who's the true primary care giver. It's fun to be the angel with the lamp, even as a male.

Interviewed by Charles H. Martin, September 25, 1989, El Paso.

When I got elected there actually was a Prospector *reporter who said, "Do you think you're going to be able to keep order in council, being a woman?" I told him, "Well, . . . I can bang that gavel as loud as anybody."*

Luz Villegas
Student, 1977-82

I was born in Chicago and lived there until I was nine years old. My father came from Mexico, and he had a job working with a carpet factory. On a visit to El Paso he met my mother. They got married and went back to Chicago. We came back here for health reasons. My brother had àsthma, and back then doctors recommended a move to a warm climate. Since my mother was originally from El Paso, we came here.

I went to school at Jefferson High School, which is down on Alameda Street. My two main activities were journalism — I was on the yearbook staff — and debate. My brother and I, who are twins, were a debate team. Neither of my parents had [much] formal education. I was the first one in my family to receive a [college] degree, but if it wasn't for a very concerned sociology teacher in high school, [I might not have gone]. He did his part to try to get a lot of the Hispanic students at Jefferson High School to go to college.

I remember he showed up one day in class [with] a stack of UTEP applications. He came up to me and said, "You've got the grades; you're going to college." He handed me an application and said, "Fill this out and send it in." It's almost embarrassing for me to admit it, but that's how I ended up in college. I really didn't have any plans to go, despite the fact that I had done well in high school. When you come from a family [where no one] has had any kind of college education, and you grow up in an area — South El Paso — where not very many people have a college education, [you don't think about going to college]. I wish I knew where he was now. I'm very grateful to him.

I graduated in 1977 and started at UTEP in the fall. It was a big change. You have to remember I went to Jefferson High School, which is probably 98 percent Hispanic. Having grown up in a predominantly Hispanic neighborhood, coming to UTEP was actually a cultural shock for me. I was very concerned about doing well in college. My first year at UTEP was really very quiet, and I spent many, many hours in the library. It wasn't until my sophomore year that I started to get involved in other things; that's when my brother and I joined the debate team. That took up quite a bit of our time. We enjoyed it, because our tournaments were in other cities, mostly in the Southwest. Back then [our coach] was Professor [William D.] Elkins. Dr. Roy Gentry was the assistant coach.

One of our fellow debaters, Victor Castillo, was forming a ticket to run for the student council. This just happened to be a mostly Chicano ticket. A lot of the members of the ticket were [from] the MEChA [Movimiento Estudiantil Chicano de Aztlán] organization. It was by chance that I ended up on their ticket, [since] at the end he realized that he had no women on the ticket. I was a fellow debater, and he just happened to ask whether I might be interested in running for student council, because he needed a girl's name on his ticket.

I was elected to the student council for the following year, which would have been my junior year. Eddie Forkerway, a football player, was president. The following year we formed a ticket, the ACTION ticket, where Luis Patino was the presidential [candidate], and I was running for internal affairs vice president. We had a very big campaign. We had posters; we had campaign photos. *The Prospector* went as far as putting out a special campaign issue that dealt with nothing but the candidates. We were very successful in that three of our four officer candidates got into office.

I remember that when I got elected there actually was a *Prospector* reporter who said, "Do you think you're going to be able to keep order in council, being a woman?" I told him, "Well, I'm very familiar with parliamentary procedures, and I can bang that gavel as loud as anybody." The very first year that I ran for student council, the ticket was primarily a MEChA ticket. If I'm not mistaken that was the last time we ever saw a purely Chicano ticket involved in student government [elections]. There were a good portion of sorority and fraternity students on the tickets [in subsequent years], but they weren't composed completely of them. We knew that if we could get a diverse ticket it would be easier to get into office. If we got an engineering student on our ticket, he'd be pushing [our group] at the Engineering Building. The liberal arts people would be pushing in the Liberal Arts Building. That was the way to get elected. Most of the tickets were very diverse; it was a marketing strategy.

That year [interest in student government] was big, because that's the time that we had the controversy over the budget cuts that Reagan was implementing, which were going to affect our financial aid. Simultaneously on the state level we were also facing increases in tuition. We saw the financial aid cuts as affecting our student body very significantly, because [a high percentage] of our student body at that time was receiving some sort of financial aid. We fought the tuition increases as hard as we could.

At the end of the year, May of '81, I was graduating and had not quite decided what I was going to do. Having an interest in public administration and law, I decided to hang around an extra year and take some additional classes [and run for student council president]. I believe I was the first [female] internal affairs vice president. People were aware that if I were elected I would be the first female student body president, and it was certainly covered by *The Prospector*. But it never became an issue as far as campaigning. I got elected SA president, and I started in June, 1981. One of my personal goals was to unify the student association again. That was one of the things that I did manage to accomplish; I felt very good about that.

We concentrated a lot on trying to provide services on campus. The File-a-Book program [was one of our accomplishments]. It had been in existence for a long time, but we finally got a full-time person to work all day long. File-a-Book is a program whereby students can take their used books, put them on file at the office, and other students could purchase that book. It was a good alternative to buying books, regardless of whether they were used or new, at the book store. They could usually buy a used book at File-a-Book at an even lower price than they could at the book store. We had a Share-a-Ride program, and this year was the first time that we had a computerized program. During registration we had a table available where the students could fill out information as to when they arrived on campus and when they left. Then we were feeding this into a computer and trying to match them with other students. We had this before, but this was the first year we had computerized it.

The fall semester of 1981 we increased the library hours, because we had heard [complaints] about how you couldn't even study [there] during finals. President [Haskell] Monroe* was supportive; the library staff was supportive; everyone was very supportive. We increased the hours, [which] took effect the week before finals and continued through the [end] of finals. Focusing on our goal of helping commuter students, we decided to sponsor a car maintenance workshop. It was held at Ysleta Vocational High School [and] was free. Everything that we did was free to students, since it was student money that we were using to fund these little activities. We put together an apartment referral [guide]. This was aimed at our older student population, students who were married and no longer living at home. All of these were firsts.

Dr. Monroe came from Texas A&M [University]. We spent the first year that he was here explaining what the student body was like. We are a commuter campus, whereas a significant portion of A&M students live on campus. They were very rich in tradition, whereas we lacked some of that tradition. When Dr. Monroe came, he wanted that tradition, that pride [at UTEP]. He was the one who started the tradition of convocations here at UTEP. We had an ice cream social before the convocation, trying to get [students] to attend. That was also about the time we changed the school colors. Dr. Monroe had set up a special committee to look into changing the colors. I was on the committee. Before they had been orange and white. We added the blue, so that the official colors became Miner orange, Columbia blue, [and white].

One of the controversies that we had with the administration that year was [over scholarships]. The administration decided that students receiving academic scholarships had to complete thirty hours within their first [two] semesters. That was a very big controversy; the entire student association was against it. We said, "We see nothing wrong with giving them a full calendar year," which would mean they would be able to use the summer sessions to fulfill that thirty-hour requirement their first year. We fought that very hard, and the administration won out. We didn't forget that loss.

Towards the end of the year, we had a very unfortunate incident. Phil Holt was a nontraditional student. After high school he had served time in the military, and then he had come back to school. He was a senior engineering student [with] high grades, the ideal student, and he got killed on his way to an engineering convention in an automobile accident. We decided to set up a scholarship in Phil's name. The [main] requirement was that [the recipient] be a nontraditional student, one who after graduating from high school had been out of academics for at least a year. The other requirement was that he fulfill thirty hours in one *calendar* year. That was our little contribution to helping the nontraditional student.

Student demonstrations [were rare]. The one that comes to mind was the Iranian one. The Iranian students' group decided to have a demonstration out at the Student Union courtyard. The veterans' group, which was Chi Gamma Iota, had gotten wind of that, and they didn't like it. They thought [it] was somewhat un-American. You have to recall the Iranian students' position at that time. Their funds had been frozen. They couldn't pay for their tuition; they couldn't pay for their housing; they couldn't pay for anything. The university took special measures to provide for them because of that. But they decided to have their demonstration outside the Union.

I was there just as an observer. There were a few people yelling things at the Iranian students, and it just got worse and worse. When the demonstration ended, people started running after them. They dropped everything and started running for their lives. They ran around the Student Union Building to one of the staff entrances to the cafeteria. They kept going from door to door, and that was the first door that they found open. We got the police out there, [but] the students wouldn't leave. They were angry at those Iranian students. After a while it finally calmed down. As far as actual demonstrations, that was the only [one] that I can think of during the time that I was here. Things had calmed down a lot. We caught the tail end of [streaking]. I think it might have been my freshman year when I saw a streaker. We were having one of the Homecoming parades, and there was a streaker running through it. That's the [only one] I remember.

I have very fond memories of UTEP. They [include] the pride that I felt winning those debate trophies and bringing them back to UTEP. That was a good feeling, because I remember going to debate tournaments where people would say, "What's a UTEP?" [I'm proud of] the university having such a unique student body, being a bicultural and a commuter campus. You meet a lot of interesting people here. It is very different from a lot of universities. It's not going to be like your A&Ms or your Texas Techs. It's very, very unique.

Interviewed by Charles H. Martin, October 22, 1989, El Paso.

Every year that I was here we won the [NCAA] team championship. . . . UTEP was the school to be reckoned with.

Milton Ottey
Student, 1980-1985, 1989-1990

I was born in Jamaica and moved to Toronto, Canada, when I was ten years old. I attended several high schools and graduated in 1979. I've been told that I could have been an athlete [in any sport] I wanted, whether football, basketball, or volleyball, or whatever in track and field. Since I excelled in the high jump, I kept with it. I sent letters off to various universities in the fall of '78. One went off to [the University of] California, Berkeley. John Wedell, who was the assistant coach there, got in touch with me. I chose not to take a scholarship that year [because] I wanted to train for the 1980 Olympics. Unfortunately, [Canada] boycotted. I got back to Wedell and found out that he had moved to El Paso. He quickly got back in touch with me and brought me down for a visit.

The only time I'd ever heard of El Paso was in the westerns. When the plane landed, I couldn't see the city [through the window]. All I saw was desert and tumbleweeds. My image was, "This is in the desert!" After the plane turned around, I started breathing a little easier when I saw the city. It was a bit scary, because you're talking to someone who's used to green: green trees, green grass. It was a big difference. I liked the campus, and I liked the architecture. I think I adapted well to El Paso.

I enjoyed Mexican [food]. I like hot spicy things; that's a Caribbean part of me. Other than the fact that I missed home, I didn't really find El Paso all that bad, although it was boring unless you had a car.

I arrived here in the fall of 1980. I came here because I wanted to be the best. I saw the plaques, the trophies, and the people that were here. There was no doubt in my mind that if I came here I would be the best. I had a good coach [in] John Wedell, who taught me a lot. The first year I took second in the NCAA indoor track and field [championships] and second outdoors. The fall of the second year, I improved tremendously. I won at the end of 1982 about twenty-six straight [meets] and received the number one ranking in the world. The following year in February I broke my leg. That curtailed things. Fortunately for me, less than four or five months afterwards, I was back in stiff competition. I placed ninth at the world championship in Helsinki in August of 1983.

When I came to UTEP, Ted Banks* was the head coach, John Wedell was the assistant, and Collin Thurton was a graduate assistant. John took care of my program. On the other hand, Ted was more concerned with the distance runners. But as head coach, he made the decisions. Ted liked to go foreign because it was a field that was untapped. For instance, we had the Tanzanian connection. Apparently [children] there run from their houses to school, so it's a natural process. El Paso is very much like Tanzania, from what I hear. UTEP was the foreign pipeline.

Now the ironic thing about the whole situation was that schools that were against UTEP, UCLA for instance, when they were tops, they won with numerous foreign athletes also. But because they weren't winning, all of the sudden they became xenophobes. We looked at that as being sour grapes. Ted would get T-shirts made up every time we won a championship. As soon as it was announced that we'd won the title, we'd all put on these T-shirts. It would say, "U.T. El Paso — NCAA Champions" for that year, and on the back it would say, "Don't be a Xenophobe." As I saw it, we're all athletes once you put the shoes on.

I held many track records: UTEP records, Canadian records, Commonwealth records, the NCAA record. But as for my own personal goals, I don't try to set any. I just try to jump as high as I can. At the Olympic Games [in 1984] in Los Angeles, I placed sixth, representing Canada. My best year afterwards was 1986. That year I won the unofficial world high jump championships. I won the Canadian Championships, and in

July I jumped 7'7 3/4", which is my career best. I went on to win the Commonwealth Games. The Commonwealth Games are for the ex-British Colonies and have been around for years. I won in 1982; I won in 1986. [The 1982 Games] were held in Brisbane, Australia. Bert Cameron, myself, Suleiman Nyambui, and all the Africans [from UTEP] were there. If we had totaled the amount of medals that were won by UTEP athletes, we would have won the Games [as a team], on the medal count.

Bert Cameron and I are very good friends. We understand each other, because we are from the same island [Jamaica]. And that to me was a plus for UTEP, because I had somebody I could relate to. Bert is a wild guy. He's like a kid, but he could run like a horse. Bert was very, very successful. He won several NCAA [championships] while at UTEP. [He was] number one in the world in 1982. In 1983, world champion, and 1984 would have been his greatest year. He was the favorite for the gold medal [in the Olympics]. But about 100 meters into the [qualifying] race, he grabbed his hamstring and came to a complete stop. Everybody else was at least fifty yards ahead of him. He got back running and ran so hard to qualify. In a 400 you don't come to a dead stop and then do that. But he qualified. Unfortunately, he hurt his hamstring so badly that he could not even walk the next day [and missed the finals]. I really felt it for Bert, because I knew he had the gold medal.

[Suleiman] Nyambui is a man I respect a great deal. He has many titles, [including] a silver medal in the '80 Olympics. He was down to earth and was still living in the dorms. He spoke to everybody, although half the time you couldn't understand what he was saying. He's a joy to be with. It was a great asset for me to have Nyambui. I still respect him; I wish the man could run forever. Nyambui is a great person away from the track. He helped [many of] his fellow countrymen to better themselves.

UTEP had a unique opportunity. You had so many people in one [location]: the Mexicans, the Canadians, the Caribbeans, the Africans. You see that there is a difference and that your own perspective on things is not necessarily the [only] way. So you learn about different cultures. I've seen these guys, the Africans, cook things. You taste the [food], and it's good. So it opens up your mind to different cultures, to different things.

Every year that I was here we won an [NCAA] team championship. Pontiac, Michigan, 1981, we won it indoors. Outdoors we won it in Baton Rouge. In '82 we won [outdoors] in Provo, Utah, hands down. UTEP was the school to be reckoned with. Once we walked on the turf with our uniforms on, everybody knew who we were. There was a sense of pride with this team. The pride of the team was so great you didn't want to let the team down. You wanted to do your job to the best of your ability, because all we had then was ourselves. We did not feel any support from the University [or] the community. I think they got so used to us winning that they took it for granted.

This might sound a bit bitter, because I did feel bitterness at the time. The basketball team won one championship in 1966, and that's all we heard about. "Texas Western 1966 Champion." Here we are; we've won triple crowns; we won mega NCAA championships. Nobody wanted to say, "Hey, way to go." One thing stood out. We went back to Pontiac, Michigan, in [March], 1982, indoors, and we came back with the NCAA championship. And that's the same year that the Miner basketball team did not get invited to [the NCAA Tournament or] the NIT. And there was such a big ruckus about it that the community threw them a parade down Mesa [Street]. And here we are coming in that evening with an NCAA [championship] trophy, and what we're hearing about is a parade that's been thrown for the basketball team because they did not make [a postseason tournament]!

Many people say you can do both [sports and academics, but] it is a hard job. I was an elite athlete. Many of the athletes here were [among the] elite. I'd be on the track from two o'clock until six-thirty working. Then I had to go back to the dorms, eat, study, catch a good night's sleep, and then get up and go to class the next morning. When you're traveling, you leave here Friday. If you have a doubleheader, which can range from Los Angeles to New York to El Paso, [you still] have to get up for class Monday morning. It takes its toll.

Track became my number one focus. I should have concentrated on the classes that I was taking to insure that I graduated. A lot of the kids out there think that just because you're an athlete on scholarship you get special privileges. What they don't understand is that the classes I missed, I had to get the notes for them. I had to make up the test that I missed. So my job is twice as hard. It's two full-time jobs carried out at the same time. It can be done, but sacrifices have to be made. You've got to know what you want.

Now we have a good coach here, a good staff, and we have an interest in building the program and in doing the best job we possibly can with the athletes we have. I think right now we have a very good team. Most of them are here from El Paso, and they're very talented kids, and they all want to work hard. I feel they know that the coaches are now interested in [them as] a person as well as an athlete and a student. That's the image we're trying to project, because we want them to graduate. I personally don't want anyone to be like me. I wish I had finished my education years ago, but unfortunately track had taken a presence in my life where I could make a living out of it. I got to see half of the world without paying for it. Not everybody is capable of doing that. If you can, all the more power to you, but please I hope everybody gets their education.

Interviewed by Charles H. Martin, October 3, 1989, El Paso.

I'm awfully glad they talked me into going, because [receiving the first doctoral degree granted by UTEP] is a milestone that I would not have missed. The feeling was fantastic.

Gary Massingill
Student, 1975-1979

My father was a farmer in Snyder, Texas, and had an eighth grade education. In our family there weren't many people that had an educational background beyond high school, so there wasn't a great push to put me into college. I graduated from Snyder High School in 1964. I had fairly good grades, but I didn't have great study habits.

When I got to college I didn't do so well. I started at Howard County Junior College in Big Spring. I partied a bit, which didn't make my father any more impressed with the idea that I should continue to go to school. They asked for a major, and I went ahead and [selected] geology. There was a professor by the name of Thackery. He had worked for Texaco, and he really developed a desire on my part to continue [with geology]. My grades weren't all that good, except for geology and a few other subjects. I almost had to fight my father to continue in school.

I went to West Texas State in Canyon, which is about fifteen miles south of Amarillo. My grades still [weren't] great. I had a desire to go to college, but that was not the only thing on my mind. I graduated with my bachelor's degree in May, 1969. In December I went into officer training school in San Antonio. I spent three and a half years in the Air Force and got out at the rank of captain.

When I got out, I decided I wanted to go back to school for two reasons. One is I had the GI Bill, and I felt that was a good opportunity. The second reason was that my undergraduate grades were bad. [I] decided that I would try to improve them, and that's the reason why I elected to go back to the same school — West Texas State — in 1972. I spent three years [there] and graduated in 1975 with my master's degree in geology. I had a [straight A] grade average. In terms of rounding me out as a geologist, I really feel like that those years were good. It was a small enough school that they really gave their students extra attention. It was a very enjoyable time for me.

[In the 1970s] things began to look better for geologists, [since] the energy problem had arisen. I had thought about going on for a [Ph.D.]. I had developed a good relationship with Exxon. The year I graduated [the company] was really pushing me hard to go work for them. [They] said, "We want you. You don't need a doctorate." But I was telling them I did want one. Frank Daugherty, who was a professor at West Texas State, was my mentor. He was also a good friend of mine, and he knew [W.N.] McAnulty* of The University of Texas at El Paso. One of the better schools in geology was The University of Texas at Austin, but I never really had a great desire to go there. I liked smaller schools. [UTEP had] a new Ph.D. program, and I thought it would be a good place to get more personalized attention. I wanted that, rather than just being one of hundreds. When I found out that Frank [Daugherty] knew McAnulty and highly recommended [him], I said, "I think I'll give this a try."

McAnulty was more or less the old man of the university at that time. He wasn't the director, but he carried a lot of clout. I think McAnulty's name would be right at the front of the list [of people] who were instrumental in getting that [doctoral] program going. I allotted myself a three-year program, [but] for some reason everyone else allotted me more like a four- or five-year program. I pushed real hard, saying, "Let's get this thing done." On the other hand, they would say, "What's your hurry?" There were five doctoral students while I was there. K.C. Evans was [one] of them; she was working in uranium. Michael Shayphest was a paleontologist. There were no foreign students at that time in the doctoral program.

It seemed like they changed the rules on us every once in a while. We'd be going along, and they would have some kind of meeting and say, "Maybe we need to require this instead [of another course]" and end up deciding to change the requirements. All in all, I feel like it was really a gain for me, [because] I got a really strong background. That background is because of all the tough requirements that they laid on us while we were there.

School was just great, in most cases. [The program] was growing. They didn't always know what they really wanted everyone to do; they were still trying to figure out [a new program]. I think McAnulty was able to smooth over some of the problems. We took a written exam for a whole day [after finishing our coursework], and then you ended up with a half-day oral examination on anything and everything they wanted to ask us. There were only two of us taking both tests the first time, myself and K.C. Evans. The field of geology is quite diverse, but they could ask you anything they wanted to. [It] ended up being quite strenuous. But somehow we managed to struggle through it.

I managed to get funding for my dissertation through the New Mexico Bureau of Mines and Mineral Resources in Socorro. As a matter of fact, the university decided that since I was getting my funding there and actually doing a lot of my work there, [I needed] an off-campus advisor. [So they chose] Chuck Chapin at the New Mexico Bureau. Both McAnulty and Chapin reviewed my dissertation. That got to be pretty interesting, because they had different styles of writing. Before it was over with, my [awkward passages] had long since been corrected, so they were [mostly] changing each other's changes. This was pre-word processor days. There was a woman at the bureau that was assigned to me for typing, and she typed the [manuscript] a *number* of times. Finally I went to McAnulty and said, "Something's got to give here." So he relented.

[The dissertation] was about 300 pages long. It was a fairly detailed geologic map and structural interpretation of the earth around Magdalena, New Mexico, which is about forty miles west of Socorro. This was an area that is structurally very interesting. There is a fissure that runs right through the center of New Mexico — the Rio Grande Rift. It's a position where the Continental Plate is being ripped apart and is spreading. It's also on the southeastern [edge] of the Colorado Plateau. It had some uranium, coal, and oil potential, so there was some good mapping that needed to be done there.

I finished almost everything there was to do with the dissertation before I left the bureau. I took a job in Corpus Christi in January, 1979, but the degree was not conferred until the following semester. I went through the graduation, [but] I would have been willing to skip [it]. I have never been a very ceremonious person; I even missed my high school prom. But [my professors] more or less told me, "You ought to be there." I'm awfully glad they talked me into going, because [receiving the first doctoral degree granted by UTEP] is a milestone that I would not have missed. The feeling was fantastic; it really was.

My father and my mother came. My dad had not been very supportive of me going to school. When I graduated with my master's and started for my doctorate, he asked, "Do you really think you need this? Is this really necessary?" At graduation, he changed totally. Even up until the [degree] was conferred, he was really [skeptical]. But all of a sudden, when he got back home, he was talking about his son the doctor. From that point on, he's never even suggested that I did the wrong thing. So I think that he was quite proud.

Interviewed via telephone by Charles H. Martin, October 30, 1989, El Paso and Reno, Nevada.

*When I first arrived, I wanted to taste the burgers
over here. I wanted to compare them with McDonald's
and Kentucky [Fried Chicken] in Malaysia.*

Charles V. Balang
Student, 1987-1990

I grew up in Sarawak, which was formerly called Borneo, in the eastern part of Malaysia. It's around a one-and-a-half-hour airplane flight from there [to the mainland]. The language of my school was English. I was among the last to have English as the language of instruction. After that it [became] Bahasa Malaysia or Malay, which is the national language now.

[In Malaysia] the government usually sends students overseas after they finish high school, but in order to save money they ask some students to study for two years in Malaysia and take the basic courses before they go to the United States. That's why I went to the TIEC [Texas International Education Consortium*] program in Shah Alam, Kuala Lumpur. I enrolled in January, 1985, in the TOEFL* program, and I did my TOEFL and SAT [preparation] for six months and then went into the TIEC. I was in the TIEC for three years and them came here.

In Sarawak [the schools] use the British system, where the teacher talks a lot and the student just listens. There are no group discussions. [In] the American style, the professor gets more involved with the students. They ask more questions, and they get involved with students in other kinds of activities. After class in Malaysia, there is usually not much contact

239

between the students and the teachers. [At the TIEC] I had classes with three professors from UTEP, Dr. [Carl T.] Jackson, Dr. [Kenton J.] Clymer, and Dr. [H.S.] Oey. When I came over here, I didn't have any more classes with them, because I had finished all my basic courses.

I think it would be better for Malaysian students to be sent straight to the United States, even though it costs more. I think for the students themselves it's much better. Even if they want to make a transition, it doesn't need to take that long. Six months is enough for them to adjust to student life in the United States. When you are in the TIEC, the rigid rules that apply to other universities in Malaysia still apply, even though it is a transition program. The only thing that makes it [different] is that the professors are from the United States. But the rigid rules still apply. You have to wear your hair short; you have to wear a uniform to class; you have to use [socks], this kind of thing.

My major is mechanical engineering. We were given three choices by the Malaysian government before we went overseas. My first choice was quantity survey, because I wanted to go to New Zealand or Australia. My second choice was architecture, because I thought I'd make a lot of money. But I didn't know how to draw. My third choice was mechanical engineering, so they gave me the third choice.

People watch a lot of American television [in Malaysia], so I wanted to see whether the lives that are portrayed on television are true or not. When [told] I was going to go to UTEP, I thought it was a desert and had only one season. At first I was [disappointed], because I wanted to see snow. I came during January, 1987. It was very cold. When I felt the cold, I preferred El Paso [to other places that were even colder].

The first thing that really struck me most was that I thought I would see a lot of Caucasians in El Paso. But after I'd been in El Paso for a few days I saw a lot of Hispanics, who look like Malaysians, so I felt right at home. [People sometimes speak to me in Spanish and mistake me for a Mexican.] When they ask me for directions, I just say, "No comprendo. No hablo español." They are surprised to see a guy who answers back in Spanish but who can't speak Spanish.

When I first arrived, I wanted to taste the burgers over here. I wanted to compare them with McDonald's and Kentucky [Fried Chicken] in Malaysia. I went to a Whataburger, and on the menu they had milkshakes. I wanted to order a Mexican type of flavor. So when the attendant asked,

"What kind of flavor do you want?" I said "chico" several times, and my friend was laughing. At last I really looked carefully at the menu. Then I saw that "chico" means small, so I made a fool of myself there. I miss the open-air food stores [in Malaysia], because over here you eat indoors almost all the time, [except for] picnics. The food here is expensive. There's not as much variety as in Malaysia. Even the Chinese food here, to me it's tasteless. I consider it to be junk food, compared to Chinese food in Malaysia.

The students are more conservative in Malaysia than here [at UTEP]. Students are expected to be respectful to teachers [there]. American students are not as conservative as Malaysian students, because they are allowed more freedom. Malaysia is a Muslim country, so the rules are more rigid. In Malaysia we don't have any kinds of [student] gatherings and big games, like football games. You're not allowed to demonstrate at Malaysian universities. If you do, you get expelled.

[When Malaysian students come to the U.S.], they feel more liberal; they feel more freedom. That's a cultural shock. It's up to them to control their newly-found freedom. When they come here they find out that not everyone is as rich as they portray on the TV. There are Americans who are not middle class; there are people who beg; there are people who don't have homes. That's the thing that surprises them the most.

I found that [UTEP students] are very serious about their classes, especially if they work. If they come back to school, they're very serious about their classes, and they tend to ask more, because they want to feel that they are getting their money's worth. For me, that's what is outstanding about American students. I think history classes are my favorite ones, because for me history teaches people's cultural ways, where they come from, why they act like that, why they have certain kinds of characteristics. So classes taught by both Dr. Jackson [and] Dr. Clymer were very interesting to me.

When you are in Malaysia you are not aware of Mexico. But when I came here, I found that Mexico is interesting. [Right] by the border there's so much difference in standards of living, culture, and language. I found that though Mexicans are poor, they still retain their ethnicity very strongly, just like every other people who emigrate or who are close to a very rich country.

I go to UTEP football and basketball games. At first football was boring to me, because I'd never seen so many people play for one team. It looked as if 100 people were on the field playing [at one time]. To me it was stupid, but then I found out the beauty of the game. Then I came to appreciate it. Basketball was a new experience to me, because I'd never seen people slam dunk. I don't have time for [many student organizations]. I help the Malaysian Student Association, but most of the time I'm involved with the UTEP Soccer Club, because we are trying to make UTEP soccer into an NCAA [sport] by next year. We're getting better at the moment, because we have beaten almost everybody, even the University of Chihuahua, which is known for its good soccer.

I intend to go back to Malaysia, because I miss my country. I've read in the papers that the economy is recovering and that there are a lot of job openings, so for sure I'll be going back. I will remember [UTEP] for its unique architecture. Most of the buildings are Bhutanese. To me that's very unique. It fits perfectly with the surroundings, with the mountains. I will remember the mix of people, just like in Malaysia. I will remember [UTEP's] proximity to Mexico and the opportunity to be near the border and see different cultures.

Interviewed by Charles H. Martin, October 17, 1989, El Paso.

I have always set goals for myself. First I wanted to graduate from high school. Then later on I wanted be an engineer. . . . Now I want to be the president of Bell Helicopter!

Jose I. Oaxaca
Student, 1982-1986

I was born in Juarez, Mexico, and my parents got divorced when I was six years old. My mother wanted a better life for us. She sold the house we had over there when I was eleven, and she used all the money so we could move over here. The first two years we lived with my grandmother in Ysleta. I had Anglo teachers, so it was hard; I couldn't talk to anybody.

[I completed] the third grade [in Juarez], so when we moved to Ysleta I [should have been placed] in the fourth. [But] they wanted to put me in the third grade because I didn't know any English. I told them, "You put me in the third grade, and I'm not going to go to school." The first day, they had a math contest at my classroom. It was real funny. They would have two lines and two people, and then they would give us a problem, and whoever finished first got a piece of candy. In the third grade over there in Juarez I had [learned] division and a little bit of fractions. Here [in the fourth grade] they [were doing] multiplication, so they gave me a multiplication problem. I finished right away, and the poor guy next to me, he took about five minutes to finish.

Then we moved to the Second Ward, South El Paso. That helped; I could talk to people; I could communicate. Probably I didn't learn English as fast, but it made it a lot easier for me. My mom tried [to learn English], but it was so hard that she gave up. [At home] it was Spanish all the time, even television. If you tried to put [on] an English channel, she would get mad at you because she wouldn't understand it. Home was Spanish and school was Spanish. Only with the teachers did we speak English. As I remember, I couldn't carry on a regular conversation in English until I was fourteen or fifteen years old.

At Hart School in the Second Ward you go at your own pace. You don't go with the rest of the class. They'll give you a test, and if you're advanced, they'll give you advanced work. In my math I finished everything they could give me, so I started working with decimals in the fourth grade. Then I started liking getting good grades. I would get A's and B's, and people would notice me more and say, "That's good, that's good." When I started junior high school, I noticed how things were, and I [decided] that I didn't want to live in [government housing] projects all my life and do nothing. So I started liking school more and started learning more. I want to be world famous, hopefully, sometime.

I don't know what made me decide to go to college. I have two older brothers and an older sister, and none of them graduated from high school. They're pretty bright, but they never liked school. Numbers — those were the easiest things for me. When I was six years old, over there in Juarez, my brothers would write on the wall something like "$1+1=2$." They would teach me. Then when my sister was in the first grade, she didn't like school. She would always cry, so I would go with her and stay with her so she wouldn't cry. But I ended up doing the work, and she ended up still crying.

I started working when I was a freshman [in high school]. I took a job as a construction worker. It was hard. Then when I was a sophomore, I was a member of the Boys' Club. We had a Boy of the Year campaign, and I was running for [it], so they offered me a job at Sun Drugs. I worked there for three years. In the summer I would work something like five or six hours a day, and then during school I would work on Saturdays only, like eight or nine hours.

When I was a freshman, I also was in the Summer Engineering Institute* at UTEP. They advertised it in the high schools, but one of the prerequisites was that you had to be a U.S. citizen. I wasn't, so I told the teacher.

They talked to somebody, and they let me. The coordinator was Dr. [Juan] Herrera, and Dr. [Stephen W.] Stafford would help. They introduced us to all kinds of engineering — mechanical, industrial, electrical, metallurgical. We worked with computers, and I liked computers. That's how I started.

I went to Bowie High School from 1978 to 1982, and I graduated in May of 1982. [While] I was going to high school, I started going to UTEP. They had a new program called Junior Scholars. You were allowed to take college courses while in high school. My junior year in high school, I took Calculus I at UTEP; I got an A in that class. My senior year I took Calculus II; I got a B in that class.

I wanted to go to MIT. I had two girlfriends from Bowie. One of them went to MIT, and the other went to Columbia University in New York. So I wanted to go to MIT or Columbia, and I started applying. I also applied to UTEP. The Boys' Club encouraged me the whole time. The counselor's name was Richard Flores. He graduated from [UTEP]. He would tell me, "Go to UTEP. Don't go out of town. It's a cultural shock, and you're going to be alone, and it's a lot of money. Just go to UTEP, and then after that you can go to graduate school out of town." And then he would tell me, "Apply for a scholarship. You'll get it. You'll get some money."

I put a lot of time into my application. I typed everything. I didn't send it by mail. [I thought] maybe it wouldn't get there. I came over and gave it personally to a scholarship officer. So then I got a letter saying that I got the Stevens Scholarship, which is for $1,000 [per year], but it said, "You're still being considered for the Presidential [Scholarship]." And then in March, I was going to a tennis tournament in Deming. I was on the tennis team. We were going to leave, and they came into the office and told me, "Jose, Jose, you got a Presidential Scholarship." I was so surprised. We were invited to a press conference and all this. My mother was proud, and my photo came out in the newspaper and everything.

MIT [offered me] a good financial-aid package, but I would have to borrow about $3,000 every semester — and then work. And since I'm the youngest, I would have [to leave] my mother alone, and I didn't know if I wanted to do that. So after I got the Presidential Scholarship for $1,500 per year, I said, "I'm going to stay here."

[UTEP] was very different from Bowie High School, where probably 99 percent [of the students] are Mexicans. Then you go to college, and it's the opposite — there are Anglos and Mexicans and people from all over the world. That was a big difference right there. I think the biggest shock was that I wasn't disciplined enough. High school was easy, so I wasn't used to doing much homework and studying. Then I got to college, and I started getting into trouble when I had a lot of homework. It took me a couple of semesters, [but] I learned my lesson.

When I started attending UTEP I took a work-study job. Obviously I would have preferred not to work, but that was impossible. It wasn't that easy, but it's "do-able." When I was a senior I took this co-op job in Juarez. I would work nineteen hours a week and go full-time to school. It was with Packard Electric, a subdivision of General Motors. It was good, because I got a lot of experience. So when I got my first real job [after graduation], I knew what to expect.

When I started UTEP, I had to ride the bus all year long. Then my sophomore year my mom loaned me her car. When I was a junior I finally had enough money to buy my first used car. It was a big '76 Plymouth, and it lasted me about a year. After that my mom lent me her car again. I wanted to be a computer programmer more than an electrical engineer, but programming was so easy for me that it was [not] challenging. I [preferred] something more challenging, so I went into "Double E" [Electrical Engineering], and it was a challenge, believe me. It's the hardest, [but] it's exciting.

I was a member of the Mexican-American Engineering Society. We went to high schools like Bowie and Jeff[erson] and Ysleta, where there are Mexican-Americans that might not be motivated to go to college, and we would talk to them. It's called the PACE program, Promotion and Awareness of Careers in Engineering. We tried to get students interested in college that might not [otherwise] be interested because maybe they think it's too hard. I joined "I Triple E" [IEEE], the Institute of Electrical [and Electronics] Engineers. Then I got accepted into the electrical engineers' honor society, Eta Kappa Nu. I also got accepted into the senior honor society, Mortar Board.

I went through the St. Pat's Day initiation when I was a freshman. All the students try to recruit you, so they can paint you green. There were about six of us who said if we do it all together it won't be that bad. You have to get here at eight in the morning, and they'll paint your face with lipstick, crayons, and markers. They'll paint your shirt and your pants,

246

but they tell you to wear something that you can throw away after you finish. The only thing I didn't like is [that] they gave you chewing tobacco. I hated it. I almost threw up. But the good thing is that all the professors are there also, and some of them have to get initiated.

We started in the Union Building, and we'd go all around campus singing two songs. One of them is the Mickey Mouse song: "Who's the leader of the band? M-i-c-k-e-y M-o-u-s-e." And the symbol of that is: To engineers, all the other classes are Mickey Mouse courses. Then we'd leave campus and go over [near] Sun Bowl Drive. They have a cave there which they call the Miner Cave. You stay there and pay respects to it by being silent three minutes. Then they take us over to the back of that company that sells cars, by the University Theater, on some hills. They blindfold you, and then they pour everything on top of you! I mean eggs, food that's been there for days, honey, flour — everything! Then after that, they'll get little groups of about four or five, and they'll take you walking around on the hills to the holy stone, [the Blarney Stone]. They'll pour a bucket of green paint on top of your head, and you have to kiss [the stone]. It's fun; it's part of college life. And man, it gets engineers together.

I'd been wanting to become a U.S. citizen since I was eighteen. When I was a sophomore, I turned in my application. It took a year for them to call me to take the test. And the day they called me back, I had a test on electromagnetic fields at UTEP. I went to talk to the professor, and he told me, "They can wait." Seriously, he wouldn't let me [out of class], so I had to call back and tell them I can't make it. They called me back again, and I had another test that day, but it was [a different] professor. He was nice and told me, "Go ahead. I can always give you a makeup." So I went and took the test, and two months later I became a citizen. The day was January 18, 1985.

I graduated in May, 1986, with a bachelor's [degree] in electrical engineering. My brother was in the navy at that time in Virginia, and he came over for my graduation. My grandparents and my mom [also came]. I was the first one [in my family] to graduate from high school or college. [My mom] was very proud. If it had been up to her, all of us would have graduated from high school and college. She always told us that school was more important [than work], because once you have the education you can do more for yourself.

My first three months I still worked for Packard Electric. They couldn't make me an offer because they had a hiring freeze, so I told them I wasn't going to work for them anymore. I was unemployed for three months. I wrote letters to eight companies, like Rockwell International, McDonnell-Douglas, and Bell Helicopter. I had some interviews at UTEP, too. Bell Helicopter called me. It was funny. They couldn't get in touch with me, and they couldn't leave a message, because my mom didn't know any English. My mom would tell me, "Somebody called you, but I don't know who it was. They didn't know any Spanish, and I don't know any English." Finally they [reached] me, and they flew me over there for an interview. I started working for Bell in February, 1987.

I have always set goals for myself. First I wanted to graduate from high school. Then later on I wanted to be an engineer, and now I am. I wanted to be able to have a better life, the American dream: have a house, two cars. Now I want to be the president of Bell Helicopter!

Interviewed by Rebecca Craver, August 3, 1985, El Paso; interviewed via telephone by Charles H. Martin, September 20, 1989, El Paso and Bedford, Texas.

The real measure of a university is the quality of its graduates. . . . I think the value that we add between admission and graduation of our students is far greater than at most institutions.

Diana Natalicio

Faculty, 1970-1979
Dean of Liberal Arts, 1979-1984
Vice President, 1984-1988
President, 1988-Present

I was the first in my family to go to college, so I feel very sympathetic towards our students, because I was very much like them. I attended St. Louis University as a commuter student, living at home and working part-time as a secretary. In my senior year I applied for a Fulbright scholarship and ended up getting one to Brazil. For the first time in my life I left home, and I went on my first plane ride to Rio de Janeiro. I got down there and did a year as a Fulbright student.

From Rio de Janeiro I went to U.T. Austin and became a [teaching assistant] while working on a master's degree in Portuguese. I completed my degree in 1964 and received a scholarship from the Gulbenkian Foundation in Lisbon and spent the next eighteen months living in Portugal, studying literature. I came back to Texas and was recruited by the graduate program in linguistics at U.T. Austin. I got my doctorate in 1969, worked a year as a research associate in the Center for Communication

Research, and then was offered a faculty appointment as a visiting associate professor at U.T. El Paso.

I came out here and fell in love with the place. I had never been in the desert before, but I found the dry climate to be just exactly right for me. I especially liked being on the border, because my background had been in romance languages and linguistics. When I was offered a [permanent] appointment the following year, I said, "Yes, I'd love to." I've been here ever since. It's been a very good place for me.

I became department chairman of the Modern Languages Department almost by default, because the previous chairman went to Rumania on a Fulbright! I found that I liked the job. After a couple of years I was asked to be associate dean and then dean of the College of Liberal Arts. Following that, Dr. [Joseph D.] Olander left the university, and the vice president's position was open. I decided that I'd like to try that and applied and was selected for that position. And, of course, Dr. [Haskell] Monroe* eventually left. I agreed to be interim president, then subsequently I became a candidate for the position. In February of '88 I was named president by the regents.

Dr. [Joseph R.] Smiley* was president when I arrived. In 1972 Dr. Smiley resigned, and the regents appointed Dr. [Arleigh B.] Templeton* to be our president. What I remember best about Dr. Templeton's tenure was his effectiveness as a spokesman in Austin for U.T. El Paso. He was very good at that. He was very close to a number of people in Austin and therefore could get their attention and could make our case. He was also very effective in getting building projects under way out here, and we certainly needed those. He built a number of buildings that are important to us today: the Special Events Center, for example, where Don Haskins'* basketball team does its thing, the East Union, which is a very fine facility, the Administration Annex, and the Engineering Complex. All of these facilities Dr. Templeton was very much involved in.

Another very important event [in the 1970s] was approval of our doctoral program in geological sciences. That degree was extremely important symbolically. I think we needed the recognition of a doctoral program to be taken more seriously. Geology was a good [choice], because it represented continuity in terms of our institutional history, and it also represented a strength in terms of faculty research and activity.

Under Dr. Monroe's leadership we certainly made progress in expanding our campus facilities. The new building for the College of Business Administration was an important [milestone] for a program that was growing very rapidly. I think the most striking [development] on campus during Dr. Monroe's tenure as president was the construction of the library building, which will be five years old [in 1989]. It's hard to believe that it's already five years old. It is a building that has very high visibility. It is a building that is very impressive in terms of its Bhutanese style, and our students are proud of it.

The 1980s were a little bit uneven in terms of budgetary support. We've had a lot of ups and downs in the state's economy, so we spent more of our time than we would have liked to trying to balance the budget and trying to cope with the constraints imposed upon us. A growing enrollment and a constrained budget made it very difficult to manage. Another major event that occurred was that tuition was increased rather substantially during this period. The steady growth in our enrollment was abruptly truncated by the tuition increase. This had a particularly devastating effect on students from Mexico. Our enrollment went down from over 600 Mexican students to 235. That was very bad in terms of our regional emphasis. I think we have probably seen the worst of the economic problems, but areas like the library are having great difficulty recovering. Problems such as the skyrocketing costs of journal subscriptions make it very difficult for us to keep pace, even if our budget were not constrained. Fiscal constraints were certainly a theme of the '80s; I hope we're getting out of that.

There have been several [milestones since I've been president] that I think are important. One certainly is the authorization that we've just received for a second doctoral program, in electrical engineering. After we succeeded in getting the doctoral degree in geological sciences we were categorized as a single doctoral granting institution by the Coordinating Board*. The designation was extremely frustrating. I don't think that you do anybody very much good by truncating their aspirations, and that's what that category did for us. Achieving authorization for a second doctoral degree really says a good deal about the quality of our faculty over in electrical engineering, but it also says that UTEP is an important institution in the state and that its role is changing. That is extremely important. The degree is important for the people who will be served by it, but [it] is even more important for what it represents for the community and for the institution.

Another major accomplishment was the accreditation of the College of Business [Administration], again because it validates what we do. It says to the world, not just to the community, that we are a quality program, that our graduates have met the highest standards. This is important in terms of our visibility statewide and nationally — that people know we are an institution to be taken seriously. All of our programs are accredited by the Southern Association of Colleges and Schools, and we have specific accreditations in engineering, nursing, and education. But we were conspicuously absent from the roster of institutions that are accredited with business. For several years our programs had been of a quality sufficient to be accredited, but we had to go through the [formal] procedures to earn it. Accreditation really is a stamp of approval for programs in particular disciplines, by people in those disciplines. It says you have met the highest standards.

A major accomplishment [during 1988-89] was that we were able to bring in nearly twenty million dollars in new contract and grant awards for research. This is important because it represents an increase of fifteen million dollars over the previous year's total, [which] was the highest we'd ever had before. We have really made a quantum leap in terms of our research funding. Again this is a major accomplishment, not just because we bring resources to the community and create jobs for students, but also because it again says to the outside world that we are an institution to be reckoned with. Suddenly we are a hot property as an institution. People want to be associated with us; now we don't have to ask to be associated with them. We still have to write proposals, we still have to [produce] quality, but it's very nice to have people call us.

The Diamond Jubilee celebration was an important one in many ways. We divided it into three phases. One was to commemorate the past, a second was to celebrate the present, and a third was to challenge the future. The way we attempted to approach it was to identify historical events that we think deserved commemoration. For example, we commemorated the regents' establishment of [the School of Mines] with a plaque out on the corner of Hawthorne and University avenues. We commemorated service by [members of] the U.T. El Paso community in the

Vietnam conflict by rededicating the memorial triangle to include them. We also attempted to focus on our Bhutanese architecture.

Celebrating the present was primarily an effort to get the word out about us, to let people know who we are and what we're doing, to celebrate our excellence and our quality. Part of [those activities] were TV spots, radio spots, billboards, a music video, and newspaper ads. With respect to the future, we have a project underway which has been named "U.T. El Paso 2001." Its major focus is an attempt to involve members of the El Paso community in evaluating their sense of what El Paso-Juarez will be like at the turn of the century and what its needs will be. The final report will make recommendations to the university about the role that we should play in assisting that development.

Eighty-five percent of our students are drawn from El Paso County. For many students, we are the only option that they have for a four-year degree. In saying that, I think I can say with pride that if you only had one option this would be a very good one. About three-fourths or more of our students are the first in their families to attend college. It's very important to create conditions for success, and we have a strong sensitivity towards the needs of students. We feel that those students who come to us with aspirations for a four-year degree deserve a real chance, and that doesn't mean a revolving door. I also think we can be very proud of our faculty. We have outstanding people who are very committed. Unlike a lot of very large research universities, faculty here have direct contact with undergraduate students, even freshmen. We use [teaching assistants] sparingly. We don't have the kind of distance between faculty and students that you find in many institutions.

We also have a number of support services that help students find their way as first generation college students through this rather large institutional process, [such as] Study Skills and Tutorial Services and the Advising Center. These kinds of support mechanisms are particularly important for first generation students. We're very committed to a quality experience. The real measure of a university is the quality of its graduates. We are not judged by who enters, but by who exits with a degree.

I think the value that we add between admission and graduation of our students is far greater than at most institutions, because many times our students are initially unsure of themselves and don't have the kind of self-confidence that they need. Our students don't normally finish a degree in four years. The average is about six years, because they're employed and have family obligations and simply can't hurry their way through. They're not in a dormitory next door to the campus. They're living at home, just as I did. We need very much to be sensitive to their needs. I think overall we offer a very nice balance between research and teaching. We have a good deal more compassion for students than you find at a strictly research institution. So maybe we have the best of both worlds. We'd like to think so.

Interviewed by Charles H. Martin, November 22, 1989, El Paso, Texas.

GLOSSARY

ALPHA PHI OMEGA, the first social fraternity on campus, was organized in 1919. Until it was disbanded in 1972, the group took its members from the engineering and geology disciplines. It was never affiliated with a national organization.

RUTH AUGUR served as registrar from 1917 until about 1927. She designed the school seal showing the burro with pack, shovel, and the letters "TSM."

FREDERICK W. BACHMANN was professor of modern languages, serving on the faculty more than thirty years, starting in 1933. He died in 1967.

MYRTLE BALL taught drama and speech from 1929 until 1958 and was named professor emerita in 1981. Her husband, William H. Ball, was also a long-time faculty member, teaching chemistry. Mrs. Ball died in 1989.

TED BANKS headed the track program from 1973 to 1982, during which time the Miners won seventeen NCAA and twenty-seven Western Athletic Conference titles.

JOHN G. BARRY was the first president of the College of Mines when it was no longer headed by a dean who reported to The University of Texas in Austin. A mining engineer, he had gained professional experience and taught at the Massachusetts Institute of Technology and the University of Nebraska before serving as president of the College of Mines from 1931 to 1934.

ANTON H. BERKMAN, professor of biological sciences, also served as dean and in 1960 was acting president. He taught from 1927 until 1960 and was named professor emeritus at his retirement. He died in 1973.

COORDINATING BOARD, Texas College and University System, was created by law in 1965, with eighteen members appointed by the governor. It represents the highest authority in public higher education in the state. The board's approval is required for major construction projects, new course offerings and degree programs, and similar major steps taken by universities and colleges of Texas.

EMMET A. DRAKE became associate professor of English and economics at the College of Mines in 1919. He had previously taught at mining schools in Missouri and New Mexico. He remained in El Paso until 1933.

TOMMY DWYER, a civil engineering graduate of Texas A&M, became instructor in engineering in 1914 and also served as the Miners' first football coach. He left Mines in 1920.

NORMA EGG taught English and served as dean of women during her years at the College, 1929 to 1954.

WILSON H. ELKINS was the third president of the College, serving from 1949 to 1954. A star athlete during his student days at The University of Texas, he was also a Rhodes Scholar. He left Texas Western to head the University of Maryland.

GLADYS GREGORY, a faculty member from 1928 to 1962, taught government courses. In 1952 Dr. Gregory became the first female to attain the rank of professor at the college. She died in 1977.

BERTE R. HAIGH, after serving in France during World War I, attended the College of Mines and completed his degree in 1925. After working for an oil company, he returned to teach geology from 1928 to 1934, then became associated with the University Lands Office. He was ultimately geologist-in-charge of the University of Texas' vast land holdings whose income made possible the construction of numerous buildings. Named Outstanding Ex in 1955, he retired in 1976. He died in 1986.

DON HASKINS became basketball coach in 1961, starting his career with a winning season and in 1966 taking the Miners to the national championship. He was twice named Western Athletic Conference Coach of the Year.

VIRGIL HICKS founded the program in radio/television broadcasting and served on the faculty from 1944 to 1971, when he retired as professor emeritus. He died in 1987.

ROBERT HOLLIDAY, an El Paso attorney, served on The University of Texas Board of Regents from 1927 to 1933, the period during which the College of Mines absorbed the former local junior college and greatly increased its course offerings, faculty, and enrollment. Holliday Hall was named in his honor.

HOLLIDAY HALL was built in 1933 as a basketball gymnasium. It also has served as an assembly hall, ballroom, and office building. In recent years it has been used for gymnastics.

ALLEN H. HUGHEY came to El Paso to practice law in 1910 and taught part-time at El Paso High School. His fascination for education led him to the principalship of that school in 1913 and his service as superintendent of El Paso Public Schools from 1919 until 1951.

BURT FRANKLIN JENNESS became a lieutenant commander in the Navy where he served in the Medical Corps for twelve years before joining the Mines faculty in 1918 as lecturer. He was assistant professor of biological sciences and health officer at the time of his retirement in 1957. His hobby was writing poetry, and he wrote a song for the College of Mines. He died in 1972.

KENO HALL was the nickname given by students to the original Burges (now Graham) Hall, built in 1917 as a dormitory. Keno was a popular gambling game in the 1920s.

JOHN W. "CAP" KIDD was a member of the School of Mines' original faculty in 1914 and served as the chief administrative officer (dean) from 1923 to 1927. He was later dean of engineering and superintendent of buildings and grounds. Kidd Field and the Kidd Memorial Seismic Observatory bear his name. He died in 1941.

R. MILTON LEECH headed the Department of Drama and Speech for many years, was vice president (1966-68), and served as acting president in 1968-69. Leech Grove at Wiggins and University is named for him. He joined the faculty in 1949, and upon his retirement in 1984 he was named professor emeritus.

LIBRARY was located on the top floor of Kelly (now Vowell) Hall from 1921 until 1938, when it moved to the top floor of the Administration/Library Building. Upon completion of a separate Administration Building in 1956, the Library expanded to use all of the building it occupied. It was replaced in 1984 by the six-story University Library.

257

WILLIAM N. MCANULTY was a geology professor from 1964 to 1979, named emeritus upon his retirement. He was instrumental in starting the University's first doctoral program. He died in 1980.

HASKELL MONROE served as president from 1980 to 1987, leaving to become chancellor of the University of Missouri at Columbia.

ROSS MOORE, a 1939 graduate, was associated with the institution for forty-one years as student, coach, teacher, and trainer. He was Outstanding Ex-Student of 1975. The Ross Moore Building was named for him in 1985.

MORTAR BOARD, originally as an honor society for senior women, opened its membership to men in 1975.

LLOYD A. NELSON, a member of the first graduating class at the School of Mines in 1916, returned in 1920 to teach geology, staying until his retirement in 1964. An endowed professorship was established in his honor after his death in 1964.

H.D. PALLISTER was professor of geology and mining from 1915 to 1920. A man with wide professional experience, he taught at the Pennsylvania State School of Mines before coming to El Paso.

PEEDOGGIE was a term coined by Cap Kidd from "pedagogue" to describe nonengineers. It is still in use, especially during the annual St. Patrick's Day observance.

EUGENE O. PORTER, professor of history, was a faculty member from 1940 until he retired in 1969 as professor emeritus. He died in 1979.

C.A. PUCKETT served as dean of the college from 1927 to 1931, when the chief administrative position was changed to president. A professor of education, he also was acting president in 1934-35. He retired in 1960 and died ten years later.

HOWARD QUINN taught geology from 1924 to 1965, retiring as professor emeritus. He died in 1976.

JOSEPH M. RAY was president from 1960 to 1968 and continued as professor of political science until his retirement in 1975, when he was named president emeritus and professor emeritus. He died in 1991.

FRANKLIN H. SEAMON taught chemistry and assaying from 1915 to 1941.

WILLIAM H. SEAMON, brother of F.H. Seamon, was professor of mining and geology from 1918 to 1928.

JOSEPH R. SMILEY served two terms as president, 1958-60 and 1969-72. A professor of modern languages, he remained on the faculty until 1980, when he retired as professor emeritus. He died in 1990.

CHARLES LELAND SONNICHSEN taught English from 1930 to 1972 and was dean of the Graduate School. He retired as professor emeritus and moved to Tucson, where he continued to write books until his death in 1991.

CHARLES STEEN, a 1943 graduate, was named Outstanding Ex-Student in 1958. He was celebrated as the United States' foremost uranium developer.

SUMMER ENGINEERING INSTITUTE was started in 1976 by W. Lionel Craver, Jr., and Leland Blank, professors in the Mechanical and Industrial Engineering Department, in an effort to introduce Mexican-Americans and other minorities to engineering and to recruit these students for UTEP. The program was originally funded with a $240,000 grant from the Alfred P. Sloan Foundation of New York and is still active today.

ARLEIGH B. TEMPLETON was president from 1972 until 1980, a period of significant growth in enrollment and construction.

TEST OF ENGLISH AS A FOREIGN LANGUAGE (TOEFL) is the means by which foreign students demonstrate their English proficiency in order to qualify for admission to American universities.

TEXAS EMPLOYMENT RULE under the 1945 appropriations bill prohibited payment to husband and wife teaching at the same state-financed institution. The 1947 appropriations bill did not carry that provision, so Mrs. Mary Kelly Quinn, wife of Professor Howard Quinn, was able to resume her faculty position. William H. Ball and his wife, Myrtle, also on the Mines faculty, were similarly affected by the bill; she taught at Loretto Academy during the two-year period.

TEXAS INTERNATIONAL EDUCATION CONSORTIUM was a program involving UTEP and nearly a dozen other Texas universities from 1985 to 1989. Faculty members spent periods in Malaysia preparing students there to enter the Texas universities they represented.

EUGENE M. THOMAS, a 1926 graduate, served on the faculty from 1930 to 1966, much of that time as dean of engineering. He also was ad interim president in 1948. He was 1964 Outstanding Ex-Student and professor emeritus. He died in 1980.

E.A. THORMODSGAARD was professor of music from 1949 to 1978, when he retired as professor emeritus. He died in 1989.

SALVADOR F. TREVINO, a 1941 graduate, had a distinguished career as a mining engineer in Mexico and in 1961 was honored as Outstanding Ex-Student.

JOHN L. WALLER, history professor and chair of the department for many years, served on the faculty form 1931 to 1958 and was then named professor emeritus. He died in 1978.

DOSSIE M. WIGGINS, second president of Mines, served from 1935 until 1948, when he left to become president of Texas Tech. He died in 1978.

JUDSON F. WILLIAMS was dean of student life and a member of the journalism faculty from 1940 to 1956. He became a prominent El Paso businessman and served as mayor. He chaired the Mission '73 Committee, which pointed the way toward university status for the college.

VERA WISE was a faculty member from 1939 to 1962 and chaired the Art Department, the first woman department head. She died in 1978.

STEVEN H. WORRELL was the first head (dean) of the College, serving from 1914 to 1923. He left to pursue his engineering career in Mexico and Hawaii, where he died in 1938.

ZETA TAU ALPHA LODGE was built in 1941 and acquired by the University in 1969 as the Administration Annex. It is now the Alumni and Development Building. Three other contemporary sorority lodges were razed for construction of the Education Building.

Rude Praks

Censrel & Pissiggrs Just

In
America   322   Kiddy
          2100   2 Vid85

1-800
9 2 7   Rocket

4774   4890

Knives